"*The Secret Gospel of Mark* is a portrait of the artist, narrated by a priest and a poet and a gay man with tenderness and searing honesty. Spencer Reece weaves the poetry he loves into how he has lived, the poetry as solace and relief, as confirmation and rescue, as redemption."

—COLM TÓIBÍN

"Spencer Reece brings into sharp focus a life of authentic despair and ultimate redemption. His descriptions are bracing, honest, often lyrical, and sometimes violent, and they are also deeply psychologically penetrating, characterized by hard-won insight and profound revelation. This is a bildungsroman of gay self-acceptance as the acceptance of others has inflected it; it is a book about poetry that is itself a compilation of prose poems; it is a tender but unforgivingly clear-sighted exposition of Christian faith."

—ANDREW SOLOMON,
National Book Award–winning author
of *Far from the Tree*

"Spencer Reece's *The Secret Gospel of Mark* is 'a memoir-breviary, a poetry devotional' for our time, in the company of Thomas Merton's *The Seven Storey Mountain*. With extraordinary candor, Reece discloses the whole of his life, body and soul, as poet and priest, brother and son. It is an extraordinary journey of sexual and spiritual awakening, in the company of poets from beginning to end. A profound and necessary work, luminous and full of grace."

—CAROLYN FORCHÉ,
poet and author of *What You Have Heard Is True:
A Memoir of Witness and Resistance*

The
Secret Gospel
of Mark

A POET'S MEMOIR

Spencer Reece

Seven Stories Press
New York • Oakland • London

A SEVEN STORIES PRESS FIRST EDITION

Seven Stories Press
140 Watts Street
New York, NY 10013
sevenstories.com

College professors and high school and middle school teachers may order free examination copies of Seven Stories Press books. To order, visit www.sevenstories.com, or fax request on school letterhead to (212) 226-1411.

Library of Congress Cataloging-in-Publication Data

Names: Reece, Spencer, author.
Title: The secret gospel of Mark : a poet's memoir / by Spencer Reece.
Description: New York, NY : Seven Stories Press, [2020]
Identifiers: LCCN 2020043137 (print) | LCCN 2020043138 (ebook) | ISBN 9781644210420 (hardcover) | ISBN 9781644210437 (ebook)
Subjects: LCSH: Reece, Spencer. | Poets, American--Biography. | Gay clergy--United States--Biography. | Poetry--History and criticism.
Classification: LCC PS3618.E4354 Z46 2020 (print) | LCC PS3618.E4354 (ebook) | DDC 811/.6 [B]--dc23
LC record available at https://lccn.loc.gov/2020043137
LC ebook record available at https://lccn.loc.gov/2020043138

Printed in the United States of America

9 8 7 6 5 4 3 2 1

For
John Crowley, John DesLauriers, Hugo García García
believers

The healed wound is not the disappeared wound.
—JEANETTE WINTERSON

CONTENTS

O Love, How Did You Get Here?

1.

I am myself the matter of my book.

When there is no faith joy is destroyed. At eighteen, I wanted to die. Up there, in Brunswick, Maine, the first state to greet the morning sun, at the far corner of the graveyard was an old tool-shed, a light gray color, painted so often the wood slats had the consistency of frosting. I moved quickly to the small crooked door that was never locked. Inside, the chilly room was the size of a sacristy, just enough room if you spread out your arms to spin around. The place smelled of coffin sawdust, plastic flowers, and metal tools. There was an odd crinkled map with the layout of the graveyard and numbers for each square.

I peered around to make sure no one had followed me. Then I stripped, hungry and desperate. I ripped my clothes off. My underwear landed in a coffin. Nude, steaming, I shook like a bell struck. I took out the stolen *Playgirl* magazine I'd seques-tered in my backpack and slammed it open on the coffin planks. My hands shook. I shook. I straddled the planks atop two saw horses. Slivers caught in my upper inner thighs. I galloped like a cowboy, a giddy-up swirl of saliva, sweat, and chuffing. Then I shuddered, sputtered, spumed, squirted, shot. My face grew taut like Christ's on the cross. A need claimed me and left me gratified. The toolshed stilled. The pines stilled. The graves observed my act and went back to their talk with each other. A dead hive above me stuck there like a dusty cherub. The nude man's limbs on the glossy centerfold stuck together from my semen with the consistency of egg yolks.

What an astonishment! I couldn't stop my body from this hunt and release upon those nude altarpieces. I drank with similar push-pull greed. I said to myself, "I will never do this again." But within a week, I'd be back in that toolshed. My armpits sweat. I wiped myself with a handkerchief left by a mourner. Yet the spice of my act lingered on me and in me and through me. I asked the universe to exterminate me like a rat. I thought God heard me.

2.

Buttoned up, magazine hidden in my backpack, I went back to my dorm room at Bowdoin and held Sylvia Plath's *Ariel* once more, opening and closing the book like a door to a room. I stared at the white spaces around those poems as much as the poems themselves. I looked at the title poem:

> *And I*
> *Am the arrow,*
>
> *The dew that flies*
> *Suicidal, at one with the drive*
> *Into the red*
>
> *Eye, the cauldron of morning.*

I was her "I." I wanted to turn into dew. In the poem Plath recalls riding her horse, which, I'd read in the footnotes from our class anthology, she had named Ariel. The poem's rhythm galloped forward with its crazed logic. The syllables shot off like rockets. I liked saying the end of the poem, the way all the vowels in "suicidal" and "dew" and "cauldron" and "morning" rolled around like marbles in my mouth. I liked the way "I" and "do" showed up as "eye" and "dew," repeating themselves, the way the marriage vow repeats, "I do," and "I do," and the way that echoed the story of her failed marriage to the English poet

Ted Hughes. The promise of the ordinary conventional life was failing me. I wanted to gallop off the page of the poem and out of the world as she had done, even as I hid in the poem from the world. What had she harnessed with language? I'd memorized the piece, for I liked *saying* it as much as reading it: the thing sort of galloped *in my mouth*. It worked on me like a charm.

I'd learned in my Shakespeare class that Ariel was the ephemeral spirit from *The Tempest* who at the play's end was set free from the island by Prospero. Ariel had been instrumental in the matchmaking of Miranda and Ferdinand and so freedom was granted for Ariel. I could see the irony in Plath picking a character connected to matchmaking when her own matchmaking had been a disaster. Furthermore, in poem after poem, Plath's suicide plans were setting her free from *her* British island. The poet played Russian roulette on the page. The poems married freedom to death. Her anger, her freedom—the poems reached deep into my guts.

I had stopped going to my economics, Greek, and ethology classes. My absence did not disturb. My notebooks went blank. I tried my hand at a few poems from my manual typewriter. I mainly echoed Plath. As the snowy weeks went on I started disappearing. I wasn't in the lunch room, then wasn't at parties or theater rehearsals, then struggled to appear anywhere. I was wearing a sweatshirt from my prep school—a dull blue, tattered at the neck, the school's golden name faded over my heart. I'd worn the same sweatshirt for over a month. I gave off a musty scent. My hair had gone greasy. I was erasing and erasing myself. I was a palimpsest. What lay beneath down to the bone was hate and shame. If you scraped the bone the marrow revealed zero love for me.

3.

By nine p.m. the Friday night before Christmas break I was drinking Southern Comfort alone in my room. My roommates were out. They'd mainly kept to themselves as a catatonia overtook me that first term. A letter to my grandmother in Connecticut remained unfinished on my desk. My mind jittered. One bottle drunk I chugged a second. I exited Moore Hall, my flat-roofed Georgian four-story brick dorm with many white-trimmed paned windows. I moved away. I heard behind me the laughter of my classmates hooting in the zoo of rooms. Many of the panes of glass had fogged up from human heat. I looked back at the dorm where they had laughed at me—the faggot.

The beautiful black Maine night propelled me; it pushed me like a deep cold river—dragging with it the reflections of the cold stars; the same stars dragged behind me like the tin cans attached to a car after a wedding. Stars announced my marriage to the night. Silence pitched me further forward. Alcohol tickled the back of my throat, electrified my nerves, accelerated my walk. Christmas was coming.

My L. L. Bean boots, the laces not tied, crunched the snow as I stepped into the wood across the street, slipping into the dark, as if moving behind a stage curtain. Christmas trees were lit in some of the windows of the old Colonials, looking like those distant lights of a shore town when you move out into the sea. Behind me I could hear the laughter weaken—all of them pumped up with their promise and plans, mating and grooming. I could see the white steeple of the Congregation-alist church rising above the white pines, scolding the town.

I went into the woods and back to the graveyard. I knew the path well. A hockey puck thwacked against the hockey rink boards near the dorm, each puck-thwack sounded like a nail driven in—*thwack, thwack, thwack*. I made tracks on the white white snow.

The trees whispered to me—"Do it! Do it!" Under the marble moonglow, "Fever 103°" and "Edge" and "Balloons" on the tip of my tongue—slugging Southern Comfort and swallowing sleeping pills I'd stored up for this night—I leaned against the tombstone, my back pressed against someone's dates, and slipped under the beautiful white cover of *Ariel*.

4.

I was born on August 27, 1963, in Hartford, Connecticut. Martin Luther King Jr. gave his "I Have a Dream" speech that day. Bravery shook the air and my parents shook with the joy of me and I shook with the joy of their welcome.

That hot Hartford afternoon, after the delivery, my grandmother asked her daughter: "Loretta, did you have the baby yet?" I was enormous—ten pounds, the size of a car engine—and had made my mother enormous. My religious grandmother, upon seeing me, prophesied my girth would lead me to a religious vocation. "Something about his size," my grandmother said with awe. My much-less-religious mother rolled her exhausted eyes. *From every mountainside let freedom ring...*

Although I had been named Mark Spencer Reece, Mark being the most popular boy name at the time, within two years my parents had dropped the "Mark." They felt it didn't suit me. The Mark that is me became a ghost, a vague or hidden or forgotten version of me. Could it be then that I split down the middle by age two? A part of me was seen and named, and a part was unseen and barely recognizable. The part that was named and called was literary or theatrical—Edmund Spenser or Spencer Tracy. The unnamed part summoned up the most staccato, rapid-fire, shaky accounts of all the gospels.

5.

Before I knew it I was five. We'd moved to the Midwest for my father's job, departing the cramped East Coast for the expansive horizons that matched equally expansive wheat fields.

We lived in a basement apartment on Franklin Avenue in Minneapolis, Minnesota. Our living room was also the kitchen and our two windows looked out on window wells. There was a beige sectional couch with giant buttons like on a winter coat. There was a telephone my mother was often on, talking to her mother back in Connecticut, giving her reports of how different life was in the Midwest: "Ma, they wear face masks in winter with holes *only* for your eyes and mouth. I saw a blind man who put a scarf *over* the eyeholes! Sometimes it gets to be thirty-two below here!"

Next to his side of the bed, my father had set up many piles of books and papers. He left a typewriter out on the kitchen table. Although my father went to the hospital all day, he especially liked to come home and read and write. He did this when he and my mother were not arguing. He screwed his lips up when he thought, as if he was about to kiss something, and then wrote things out in longhand. He did not have a proper desk. He always wrote under haphazard circumstances. The act said: *Discount what you love.* The act said to me: *Don't discount what you love.*

The busy street was close. Cars went by like a river. Many Sioux and Ojibowe inhabited that neighborhood, ripped up by the roots from the land that was once theirs. Mixed with the traffic their grievances rumbled: thuds, shopping carts unmanned, silences. My tiny child heart could barely understand these injustices from our window wells.

My father and I were walking away from the apartment down to the Mississippi River, his giant, size-thirteen feet followed by my itsy-bitsy ones. Twigs snapped underfoot. I was always following him. Tall, agile, wearing horn-rimmed glasses, my father was always making fun of his baldness. He had a slow circumspection that often defines men from the South. The reading and the writing shone on him, through his glasses, and he emanated intelligence and kindness. A watcher of basketball games and football games and baseball games and golf and tennis: he often spent time directing men in sporting events through the television, while I watched him.

My father never said much about my wetting my pants, or my inability to tie my shoes or tell time. My grandmother back in Connecticut had often looked at me silently with disapproval, but my dad never did. I already seemed to be living in a parallel reality, my fantasy world expanding and growing, as big as an ocean liner on wheels that I was pulling with a rope behind me. I was king and mayor of several countries and the brother to many made-up families and the friend of friends not seen and the speaker of secret languages and the narrator of stories. I thought to tell my father more of my elaborate extraordinary embroidered life, but I resisted. I kept quiet. He needed quiet. He and I relied on telepathy. He had much on his mind: work, being a pathologist, doing autopsies, reading slides with their purple smears through that microscope, a wife, a son, and money—how much he had, how much more he needed. Worries over money grinded away inside his core. Beneath his gentle manner there was rage.

Why was his wife never pleased with what he made? Many nights the poor woman slid down the wall in tears as I placed all my books on my twin bed like ships in a harbor, where I would moor myself to sleep despite the crashing sound of their marital strife. Her needs pushed and roared as the Mississippi pushed, her demands relentless, and an unnameable misery inside her matched the sounds of the river, a churning argument no one could win. My mother and father argued every night. I did not understand it. I desired to make her pleased. I desired for him to be at peace. There she was, sliding down the kitchen wall, in tears, like a religious saint. There he was picking up a beer and watching the football game or turning to his papers to try and write something. He would sigh in the most disparaging way.

Loretta Witkins Reece, did I have any idea who you were? Do any of us know our parents? In the bulk and pang of her avalanching before my Little Boy Blue self is the foundation on which all my memory is built. I will spend a fair amount of my time on the planet trying to rescue and reassemble and resurrect her. And my father standing near will devote his life to attempts to make her happy. Richard Lee Reece, the middle name in honor of General Lee, how could I know you either? In fact, the chord struck between my father and my mother will amount to devotion but it will take most of my life to truly hear it, let alone appreciate and understand it, and I wonder still if I fully understand it.

My mother was born the same year as Plath. She had about her the can-do energy of a 1950s American housewife. Her brunette hair carefully bobbed and held in place with pins. She wore heels and formfitting knee-length skirts. Her decorous smile accompanied her voluptuous figure: shapely legs, thin waist, and ample breasts. Her brown eyes contained a cello-like autumnal melancholy that called me. She was a New Englander from Connecticut and pronounced her state's name with sharp, crisp consonants. My mother looked like Plath, as seen in the black-and-white photos taken after she'd married Ted Hughes. Drink in hand, charm bracelet dangling, red lipstick applied, my mother seemed to be trying to say from every posed angle, "I am the perfect American wife." My mother, my brown-haired, brown-eyed, brown-freckled, cinnamon-and-clove, apple-eating, fire-crackling, leaf-raking beautiful mother.

6.

After Ted Hughes abandoned Plath, she left with her two small children, Frieda and Nicholas, for London. That cold winter she found all three of them a place on 23 Fitzroy Road, the same place where Yeats had once lived, and she felt that joy of connecting to the tribe of poets now that her own idea of family had been destroyed. That winter a depression overtook her.

Plath was haunted by the early death of her father from diabetes when she was ten. In her poem "Daddy" she seemed to attempt two things simultaneously: lay the subject to rest and tear it open. She'd tried earlier in her title poem "The Colossus," but the material felt more distant there. Here the words she placed and ordered practically boiled:

> *You do not do, you do not do*
> *Any more, black shoe*
> *In which I have lived like a foot*
> *For thirty years, poor and white,*
> *Barely daring to breathe or Achoo.*
>
> *Daddy, I have had to kill you.*
> *You died before I had time——*
> *Marble-heavy, a bag full of God,*
> *Ghastly statue with one gray toe*
> *Big as a Frisco seal*

And a head in the freakish Atlantic
Where it pours bean green over blue
In the waters off beautiful Nauset.
I used to pray to recover you.
Ach, du.

The two sounds of this spooky, childlike rhyming poem, the "oo" coming up against the "k" of "black," reoccur throughout the piece. Words like "gobbledygoo" collide with "Meinkampf look." The poem nearly combusts every time you read it. Through the childlike sing-song maniacal tone she was able to speak a truth that her adult consciousness had trouble accepting. I imagine this sound ticker-taped through her head in those final days as *Ariel* grew in her hands.

Her mother, Aurelia Plath, in a late interview, and in the softest wounded voice, wondered why her daughter could not let go of her past. She couldn't shake it. Her past seemed to possess her. The poem follows her possession to the end, grimly concluding:

I was ten when they buried you.
At twenty I tried to die
And get back, back, back to you.
I thought even the bones would do.

But they pulled me out of the sack,
And they stuck me together with glue.
And then I knew what to do.
I made a model of you,
A man in black with a Meinkampf look

And a love of the rack and the screw.
And I said I do, I do.
So daddy, I'm finally through.
The black telephone's off at the root,
The voices just can't worm through.

If I've killed one man, I've killed two—
The vampire who said he was you
And drank my blood for a year,
Seven years, if you want to know.
Daddy, you can lie back now.

There's a stake in your fat black heart
And the villagers never liked you.
They are dancing and stamping on you.
They always knew it was you.
Daddy, daddy, you bastard, I'm through.

In February, one dawn, she kissed her children good-bye, opened their window a crack, left them each a pitcher of milk with two glasses and cookies, then proceeded to tape their bedroom door shut, cutting the tape in stripes with her scissors. Next she went into her kitchen, opened the oven, turned on the gas, and gently placed her head on a pillow on the oven door. She died. On her desk she left the *Ariel* poems and a second novel and a diary. The novel disappeared. Hughes destroyed the diary. But *Ariel, Ariel* glowed on her desk and took in the light of cold London. *Ariel* glowed wherever Hughes moved it. She'd stamped out the words from the keys of her manual typewriter, the words like tracks in the snow of the white pages, leading somewhere. Stripped of the poems Hughes most feared, *Ariel* orbited the world.

As Plath's voice took hold, filling bookshops and libraries, I was learning the alphabet and nursery rhymes. My mother grew more agitated and distracted beside me, as she hauled me off to one library after the next. She paid close attention to me. She valued literature and books over just about everything else. She too had lost her father young, at twenty, also from diabetes. After one leg was amputated and before they amputated the second, he died in a pool of his own blood on the operating table. My mother never righted herself after his death.

"It leaves a hole," she would say over and again in tears as I grew next to her. "Oh, how I wish that I could talk to him, tell him all that I've done," she'd say in a voice of great despair. "Some things," she'd say, "you never get over." She'd say, "He always kept saying to me, 'I'll never live to be half a man.'" All this was compounded by the tragedy that six weeks later her brother, whom she loved dearly, died in a car crash at the age of twenty-two. As long as I have known her, spanning half a century and more, she has always said, and I mean *always*, before anyone gets in a car, "Be careful out there on the road."

Yet, unlike Plath, my mother did not implode from the early death of a father; rather, she exploded. One minute we'd be planting tulips together and the next minute she was yelling, arguing with someone on the phone. She was no victim. She was not someone to mess with and didn't play fair. I could see, even that young, that most people gave her a wide berth. When she argued she knew who she was. Her heart was a pot left simmering on the stove. She cared little for what others thought of her. My mother persevered. She canvassed for Richard Nixon in our lower-class neighborhood full of Angela Davis supporters. We went door to door. One door after the other was slammed in our face. We never stopped. She never declared, "I'm through."

Shortly after that presidential election, we left our basement apartment surrounded by the poor on Franklin Avenue for a home in a wealthy white suburb of Minneapolis called Edina. A driving wave of energy encompassed my parents as they got caught up in acquisition and accomplishment, rising up in the affable wealth of provincial Midwestern society. All seemed bountiful: country clubs and tennis matches. Why would we think there was anything treacherous about it? And yet. Where had my Black and Latino friends all gone? Cybil and Antonito? I missed them. When I told Cybil and her mom that we were moving, her mother looked out at cold Minneapolis in the saddest way. There was some resignation to her expression. I didn't understand it, but I knew I couldn't fix it. For a long time I couldn't understand why they never came to our house in the suburbs. I began to adapt to absences.

7.

My new front teeth were big and strong. In 1970, my mother, unable to bear more children, after failed attempts with fertility medications, decided along with my father to adopt my baby brother. I was excited about the prospect of family expansion. My parents had to try several times and to meet with several groups and social workers. They had gone to the Minneapolis airport and watched Korean babies come off a plane with name tags on them. Finally, news reached us that we would have my brother from a small hospital in Iowa. We wended our way down in our station wagon to collect him. We three were like the three kings out to find the baby in the barn. He was as small and delicate as a book of poems. My parents named him Carter Straight Reece. Suddenly in naming him he became ours. The name was concrete-sounding and yet what was this mystery now beside me? The adoption was private. The exact story of what happened is unclear. One story involved a young woman having a child out of wedlock. Another story involved a father dying in Vietnam. We left the hospital with our bundle. I've often thought of the anonymous woman who must have been in that same building who released and gave away what she had nourished in her body. I wanted to honor her and do her justice. I vowed to be the best brother ever. I said this to the shiny linoleum hospital walls.

I started watching over my brother, my worried face moving over the crib like the Hindenburg. At night when my parents pulled back the beer can tops, and the little metal tabs collected on the coffee table like commas as their conversations sprawled into messy paragraphs, my heart sank. Dad sipped another drink. I would need to double my efforts as a father stand-in. Although I was just seven my face looked wizened as a school principal when it came to my brother.

"You have had enough," said my mother with venom. My little brother gurgled in his crib. I held on to his impossibly tiny hand that grasped mine. I squeezed my eyes shut to make the arguing disappear, but it intensified.

"I know, I know," Dad said, with food on his face. An argument ensued about money. Something about my father buying my mother the same gift for Christmas as he did for her birthday. My mother insisted on something. They roared at one another.

"You're chicken shit," said my mother.

"God dammit!" my father said, like a hammer.

"You've got no balls!" hissed Mom.

"If people knew," she continued. "If people knew what I had to put up with half the time. If they only knew . . ."

"Jesus Christ! For God's sake, can you for once in your life just shut up!" my father said.

"You've got to ask for more money," she commanded.

Silence grew in me. I wet the bed. I loved my parents like gods. They were animals backed into corners. Money drove them to distraction and weighed us down with sadness.

8.

The TV sets had all gone to color. *The Ed Sullivan Show* introduced Diana Ross, who sang with the Supremes. How Diana Ross glowed and shimmered with her sequins for the American public as she demanded that we stop in the name of love. She shimmied right at me. I shimmied right back at her. I assumed she knew something I knew. My parents laughed now as if there had been no arguing in the other room. A wild feminine energy bubbled inside me as my brother threw his rattle at me, looking like a tiny judge in his high chair. Something might be wrong with me. I would need to be punished severely. What could my grandmother say to her Catholic priest about this, behind a screen in a confessional booth in Hartford? I swiveled my hips. I wagged my finger back at her. We were both being hurled forward, catapulted by difference. It was important my parents not witness my dance. Diana and I both began dancing faster and faster and faster and faster. We wanted to prevent elimination. We understood each other.

9.

I was ten. Intent on losing his Southern accent, Dad tried to shape his words in a Northern way: pronouncing "dammit" as two chopped syllables, not as a syrupy drawn-out tune, changing his name to "Dick" instead of "*Riiiii*-chard," and saying "How are you?" with three chopped syllables, not "How are yoo-*uuu*?" He smoked cigarettes, held back.

Dad spoke in his new way with my mother that hot summer we drove down in the pale-vanilla station wagon to Tennessee to visit Dad's people for the first time. My mother had never visited the South and seemed hesitant about it. Cornfields turned into hills with hickory trees. *Everyone* spoke slower, as we pulled into gas stations.

The Kennedys and Martin Luther King Jr. and Malcolm X had all been shot, and my father and mother were left speechless. A policeman in a gas station looked suspiciously at a group of Black men entering the restaurant. As they left, the policeman spit on the ground and said, "Goddamn niggers." My parents looked away. They had never used this word. My child body felt the force of hate with the word, and I felt safe in a car with two adults who didn't use it. My father was from this place but had abandoned certain aspects of it. The Vietnam War was growing louder as boys kept coming off planes without their legs. My babysitters wore bell-bottoms with floral patterns and the boys kept growing their hair down to their shoulders. And Walter Cronkite kept saying good-night in the most decorous way, which somehow made us feel safe.

In the hot car, the vinyl sticking to our sweating skin, I rolled down my window with the hand crank and rubbed my blanket against my nose. I'd carried this blanket with me everywhere until it had diminished to the size of a postage stamp, rubbed it back and forth under my nose, like a charm, a talisman to instinctively keep the danger and hatred and confusion of the world away from me.

In Tennessee, with its soft brown hills and trash-colored oak trees, I roughhoused with my two cousins, Kathy and John, in a small house down there in Oak Ridge, a town once called "the Secret City." My father's family moved to Oak Ridge to help build the atomic bombs that blew up Hiroshima and Nagasaki. My grandfather was a chemical engineer down on his luck and so he left the soap factory and the family packed up and came over those muddy Tennessee hills.

My father's family was made up of old Americans of Welsh and English ancestry. Some said a little Spanish and Cherokee had been introduced along the way. They'd come over in the 1600s from England as indentured servants. Old white folks, ponderous, tall, myopic, with eyes like pebbles behind often filmy lenses, giraffe-necked, knobby-kneed, long-fingered, soft chucklers, large flat feet, some bald, some bristle-headed, people eager to leave the room, often moving across the land-scape alone. Reeces were introverts, hiders, first persons to leave a party. Then one day as the generations passed, they would lie down quietly and die, passing the family Bible to the next tall quiet one. They settled into the anonymous Midwest for over a century and took to towns like Bedford, Iowa, which Walmart has eliminated. They were readers, voracious readers, as far as I can tell. I hear them still turning pages by lamplight surrounded by Iowa cornfields. Outside the bedroom window, the corns' silky stalks murmuring like a mob, reminding them of work ahead, while throughout the nights, my dead relatives, whose names have slipped from my mind, read and read— paperbacks by Michener, biographies, books of physics, comic books, sports pages, Bibles. Maybe, and probably, *not* poetry, but everything else.

That day in Tennessee, as we four tumbled out of our hot station wagon, which was playing a song by the 5th Dimension about letting the sun shine in, Grandpa Reece asked me, "Have you ever read the dictionary? I read the whole thing every year." And he meant *read it like a novel.* By thirty I will closely resemble this man in height and feature and receding hairline.

John and I hid under our grandmother's bed. Small humble shoe box of a house. My mother began to argue with my grandfather. A distant din. I hated arguing. The Southerners didn't take to my mother, the Yankee wife, and some had rumored "Jew wife," a subject my mother swatted away with a wave of her hand and a quick subject change. My grandfather was suspicious of everything from the North. My mother's relatives were all Lithuanian immigrants from places that sounded Martian, Vilnius and Kaunas. Her father, she once said, didn't know how to write in English. She was raised Catholic yet constantly speculated about her father being Jewish. "We just didn't talk about who we were," she said. ("I may be a bit of a Jew," Plath wrote.) I rubbed the blanket swatch under my nose faster and with fury.

"Your brother was the smart one," said Grandpa Reece to my father.

"I want you to stop insulting my husband," said my mother to my grandfather. "You are jealous of him."

The Southerners were not used to a forthright and direct

woman. While she might be judicious in responses to politics or religion, or be mute on the topic of Jews, or save herself for harping behind closed doors with my father, if you backed her up against a wall and said something about her husband or me or my brother, she dropped all sense of circumspection and came out swinging. Brave she was.

An awkward silence followed: the ice cubes melted in the cocktail glasses and spread like cancer cells under a microscope. My baby brother clung to my mother's knees. Weirdly, my brother and I looked much alike: blond, sturdy, with bright teeth and dirty fingernails. My mother doted on my brother and I looked on as a separate older child does. The strongest emotion I felt about my new sibling was worry. Something close to forlorn, the way Frieda must have felt about Nicholas.

"You think we will know each other for a long time?" John asked me, under the bed.

"Yeah," I said. "Why not?" I rubbed the cotton under my nose like a pom-pom.

"Why do you do that with your nose?" he asked.

"I don't know," I said.

"You are my kin," said John.

"What's kin?" I said.

"My blood, my skin, it rhymes with kin, we are blood brothers, you and me," said John.

"Kin and skin, kin and skin, kin and skin," Kathy repeated endlessly. Kathy put her head under the bed and made her eyes cross upside down.

The next day we packed a lunch and visited an aunt who lived in a mental hospital. This fascinated me. Even then I had an intense curiosity about people left in the world without consolation. Did she just never go home? We played hide-and-seek on the grounds with this strange lady on a day pass. She had that look on her face you frequently see on the Madonna when Christ is a small child, somewhat detached yet not unaware of something dire looming, as if she knows what's coming and she will brace herself for it.

After I'd read a few of Plath's biographies, I imagined Plath as my aunt. When she was writing the *Ariel* poems on her Smith memorandum paper, as Nicholas and Frieda played on the rug before her, she must have had the strangest look in her eye.

We kids darted in and out of the roadside ditch among the mugwort, elephant grass, rescue grass, and the plumeless thistle, all scratches and giggles, the sharp ugly leaves scissoring our thighs. My mother was rocking my brother in a white bassinet in the far distance, I could barely see them, they looked like a faint dab of white paint. Yet once my brother was in the world I always tracked him as best I could. The strange lady yammered about Christ and no one paid attention. She was pathetically overdressed in the heat and held a patent-leather pocketbook as determinedly as I hung on to my little blanket swatch.

"They're all crazy," my mother said, in the car on our way back to Minnesota. She looked irritated and said, "You could have at least told me half of them were nuts!" She reserved "schizophrenic" for a more clinical conversation later with my father that I might have eavesdropped on. My mother had been a nurse who graduated from Mass General in a beautiful prim white uniform with a cap on her head. I loved that picture of her. She looked like a movie star. I loved even more in my teen years when she told us of the late-night shifts she did at McLean, the world-famous mental hospital. She told stories about a woman named Edwina who wore a wastepaper basket on her head. She told us stories about a psychopath who had killed his wife. They were scary stories. I liked scary stories. Later I learned she had been there when Plath and Lowell were sent to McLean. She described Plath as "that sad girl."

Her tone in the station wagon told Dad and me we wouldn't go back to Tennessee soon. I *did* want to visit my cousins again. I didn't understand my mother's tone. The crazy woman fascinated me. What was her room like? She was exotic as Jesus. How could I understand that possibly my mother's severity was connected to a fierce protection? My father grew silent. I rubbed that cloth under my nose.

My mother looked over her shoulder at us two boys in the back seat. My brother was in a car seat, and soft as a mushroom. I held his little hand. Our mother looked at us for a moment with a nervous love, the way Sylvia must have looked at Frieda and Nicholas, managing a marriage and children, a woman coming of age after World War II and with the Vietnam War creeping into every conversation, a woman in a world of men. I looked back at her with devotion as Frieda and Nicholas must have looked at Sylvia. My pants were wet. I smelled pungent and feral, like a muskrat.

10.

Some acts change a life. Some acts leave a scar. When I was twelve and my brother was five we were playing in a cornfield. The blue sky was enormous over Minnesota. Our parents argued in a nearby farmhouse they had just purchased, a place for them to get away on the weekends. They were packing up our station wagon to go back. They were making plans to build a tennis court. My brother must have been about twenty feet from me. Beneath us was the deep rich black earth and the cornstalks came up to my neck. We had spent hours running after one another, up and down the aisles as if we were crazed shoppers in God's department store. My brother was calling my name. I picked up a piece of wood, part of a branch, thick as a hammer, which had been cut at angles at either end. I threw the wood at my brother with all my force thinking it would land near him. I watched the plank sail through the air like a bird. The plank landed half an inch beneath his eye and gouged into his cheek. Blood shot from his face like water from a broken water balloon, right beneath the jelly of his eye. My brother yelled and ran to the house. I was tempted to run into the woods. Then I too ran towards my screaming parents. My parents dropped whatever they were doing when they saw my brother's face covered in blood and snot. "We've got to get him to the hospital now!" my mother yelled. My father fumbled for his keys. "Who did this?" my mother screamed. "What happened?" That day began my hate for myself. I wanted to be removed. For half an hour my brother screamed in the car. My mother looked at me as if I was a monster. Blood was all over the place. A doctor stitched the wound and a nurse held his beautiful head. I told him how sorry I was. "It was an accident," I said. I began to get a hint of how awful humans could be. How awful I could be. The less of me the better.

11.

I saw insults and spittle and disfiguring and bruising.

—JULIAN OF NORWICH

I was sixteen. Breck School, the Episcopal prep school, sat on a relatively small parcel of two or three acres overlooking the Mississippi River. My parents sent me there because they wanted the best education possible, not out of any religious conviction. Instead of churchgoing my parents preferred on Sunday to bury themselves under the steeples of the opened *New York Times.*

The Mississippi deepens and widens there. On either side were high treacherous bluffs. At the bottom, the river moved thick and dark and primordial: once, dinosaurs had lapped at its shores. Our school stood over that grand crossroads on a bluff overlooking the river, set back from the road. There was a beautiful green lawn where I had been sent to sit in my early years to let my urine-stained gray trousers dry in the sun until my mother could arrive. The school was two stories, flat-roofed, and yellow. The structure in essence was a long set of boxes like a freight train. Inside the rooms were green and beige linoleum throughout with cinder-block walls, and additional prefab walls put up over the years to create new spaces. The place was drenched with the rich blue scent of mimeograph paper and always in the background was that sound of some diligent teacher turning the hand crank to the machine, which sounded like a meat slicer. The entire effect was like that of a factory. Towards one far end was the chapel that rose up majestically, made of wood and limestone. It was like an upside-down ark, and *it* was beautiful, with huge plate-glass windows that overlooked the oak trees and the river.

We sang hymns every morning. Next to me often stood Daryl, who was seventeen. I was one grade behind. He had brown hair and brown eyes. He was from Chicago. He was in the school plays. He was theatrical: every few seconds he flipped his big brown lock of hair out of his left eye, a nervous tick, for the thick hair completely covered the side of his face like Veronica Lake's. Once he sported a boa to school over his uniform. The boa astonished me. How bold. I both admired and was distant from him. I ignored overtures of friendship. I did not want to be what he was.

Not far from the school grounds, we were on the orange school bus when the boys started in. The bus followed the Mississippi, swerving to the left and swerving to the right, and the younger kids squealed. Two Black kids on that bus route, Heidi and Stanley, were dropped off early in the route. Then we zoomed into white suburbia, where the world was organized into a well-trimmed existence. We lived on a chessboard.

"Faggot!" came the first volley, and then I turned and saw what I saw. One of the boys had taken Daryl's head and slammed it against the window of the bus. The bus driver grimaced and chuckled. Time dilated. Another boy kicked Daryl and yelled, "Faggot!" again louder. They were on him in a pack. Daryl didn't fight back. Why didn't he fight back? Why didn't I defend him? Why didn't anyone defend him? Why did we all sit there?

I turned again to see blood coming out in a long string from the corner of Daryl's mouth, thick, congealed, like an umbilical cord. Kids squealed like pigs seconds from slaughter. Midwestern stuccoed bungalows and Pennsylvania Dutch houses went by—chain link fences, mowed lawns, everything ordered, a mother in her apron waving. Daryl got off the bus. The boys rested back into their seats, smug.

The next day we entered the chapel in rows by grade. The headmaster stepped out onto the dark wooden parquet stage. He asked us to be quiet. He looked somber. He said Daryl hanged himself from the rafter in the basement of his parents' house. Daryl had slipped the rope around his theatrical neck. He swung in the Minnesota afternoon back and forth, back and forth, the way a crucifix hangs and swings around a priest's neck.

I'd returned home on the school bus once more. Some were quieter than before, but those same boys kept laughing and jeering, readying for new prospects. My turn would come. One day I would be just like Stephen in the Book of Acts. I would be kicked and spit upon. My brother was silent as a cat and slept next to me in his snowmobile suit. The scar next to his eye was now small but present enough to remind me how quickly beauty could be ruined. I would lay down my life before I let those boys attack my brother. They might go after me, and they did, but if they touched my brother I would attack. They knew that. There lingered my obligation to the anonymous woman who had given us my brother, as much a ghost as my first name.

I told my mother what had happened to Daryl.

"That's terrible," she said. "Did the boys tease him?" I shrugged my shoulders in an ambiguous manner and mentioned nothing of the bus. Silence was becoming my mode of being. I think my mother began to know what I knew, and I knew what she knew. Neither one of us was going to say it.

That night my parents had a cocktail party. The cleaning lady was pulling large long-stemmed glasses from a cupboard making the clattering chime sound of an expert bell ringer. My father came home late and exhausted from work and needed his drink. The desk where he used to write was piled up with bills now.

That evening many doctors and their wives came to the house, plus one female doctor and her doctor husband. Many of them were from Eastern Europe and had last names like Tamasek, Kellen, and Shliecher, sounds that matched the k sound in Plath's "Daddy." They mainly emphasized how wonderful America was and yet underneath the convivial melody of success rumbled hints of past atrocities and losses. These immigrants were drawn to my mother, for she had a way of listening to them and understanding their desire that the humdrum conventional Midwest rarely did.

The moment came for me to play the piano. My mother beckoned me. The doctors quieted. I played Schumann's "Träumerei." It had taken years for me to get it right. I'd been taking lessons from one Barbara Smith, a Quaker. Mrs. Smith was circumspect and dutiful, and her silence steeped in the spiritual incense of Quakerism must have aided her, for at lesson time she needed patience. I had a hard time with the music and sought an invented harmony rather than the written notes. As I fingered the final chords and lifted my foot from the pedal and the doctors began to talk once more and clink their glasses, Daryl's corpse swung in my mind back and forth.

"Love your enemies," I'd heard that Jesus had said, in one of our morning chapels at Breck School. But how on earth to do that? How to love the boys that killed Daryl?

12.

My senior year in high school. The bell rang. I did not go to the school prom that year. Something ominous built in me, a retreat. Jack Wyrtzen, a prominent evangelist, wrote in *Newsweek*: "Homosexuality is a sin so rotten, so low, even cats and dogs don't practice it." Later, scientists would discover lesbian seagulls. But not yet.

In AP English class, I opened the Norton anthology and read Sylvia Plath's "Lady Lazarus." "I have done it again," she began, "One year in every ten." The bravado cut through the silence filling me. A precision to her words. "Perfection is terrible," she wrote in "The Munich Mannequins," "it cannot have children." Plath's incantatory tone combined with her tragedy caught my attention: Plath dead at thirty, her all-American virtuosity, her scholarships, her perfect academic record, her Marilyn Monroe-like trajectory—I fell for it. I did not know who I was but I identified with her—or I wanted to somehow *be* her.

I went back to "Lady Lazarus."

> *Ash, ash—*
> *You poke and stir.*
> *Flesh, bone, there is nothing there——*
>
> *A cake of soap,*
> *A wedding ring,*
> *A gold filling.*

Herr God, Herr Lucifer
Beware
Beware.

Out of the ash
I rise with my red hair
And I eat men like air.

The poem was a Byzantine icon, a portal into anger—"organized violence," Henri Cole called poetry, and this was. Plath's presence in "Lady Lazarus" opened up a way to make sense of rage, depression, shame, layers of repressed, inarticulate complex emotions.

Ms. Young taught us. In the 1970s "Ms." had just started to be used as a proper address. People used "Ms." with a certain thrill, drawing out the "z" sound like hornets. Women were exalted in a new way that was in the air and on our tongues. Dear Ms. Young *was* young, beautiful, a Norwegian Minnesotan, blonde, and smart. She received a full scholarship for an MA from William and Mary. This impressed us. She kept the cleanest classroom ever. She was Plathian in her blond perfection. All the students were in love with Ms. Young. It was impossible not to be. Especially I was in love with her.

The class was small, just ten. We incubated in her immaculate aura. I felt love. Names and voices were coming to me like proteins building a placenta: J. D. Salinger and Seymour Glass and the banana fish, F. Scott Fitzgerald and his parties, Ernest Hemingway and those masculine sentences, Dylan Thomas and his words cobbled together so they sprung kisses, Virginia Woolf and her circuitous magnetic mind, William Shakespeare and all those sonnets like music boxes, Truman Capote and the

Clutter family, Philip Larkin and his meter and humor and his use of the word "fuck," James Baldwin and Giovanni's room, Toni Morrison and Sula and that girl in *The Bluest Eye*. Literature was an Advent calendar where I kept opening doors. No end to the names. Under the glow lamp of my pimpled teenage face, the poems and the words on the page hatched, cracked the shells of emotions—at my Midwestern desk I was a frenzy of feathers and wings and poems and would have done anything to fly and fly over the troubled suburbs and the bullies. At times I did.

I was in love with Ms. Young. I loved that she loved literature and I felt inexplicably attracted to her physically, which perplexed me.

Maybe I wasn't a faggot? I prayed every night for this to be true. Yet an interest in *Architectural Digest* won out over even understanding the rules of the Super Bowl. An erotic pull to naked men teamed my brain. And why did my hands flutter as if I was Italian? Boys hissed at me like vipers. Girls hung in the shadows. I corked myself. What happened beneath my gray trousers was all volcanoes and earthquakes. At night I shot geysers. I was close to insane. When my Connecticut grandmother or my Southern grandfather asked about girlfriends I became shy. I crossed and crossed my legs as if my body was a set of scissors trying to edit me right out of life.

In that AP English class, I sat there. Out the window lay the future—the whole lives of us students. Where would we go? Our thoughts about poems rolled out of that classroom across the great wild clean empty plains of Minnesota. Especially Sylvia Plath.

Plath's broken spirit called to me and I barely understood why. She became my gospel. Dying was her art and she did it exceptionally well, so well it cast a spell on me. She did it so it felt real, so real I felt myself becoming more real. She had a call and her call called me. I bought all her biographies, I read them all. I read *The Bell Jar*. I bought *Ariel* with the beautiful paperback white cover and the large letters and the blurb from Robert Lowell in purple ink. I bought the short story collection *Johnny Panic and the Bible of Dreams*. I bought *Colossus*, with the tan-and-blue-striped cover, then all the rest of them: *Winter Trees*, the collected, the selected, the letters, the journals. I found her on cassette tapes and observed how her accent had become British; she'd changed her accent as my father had—a loss crossed with ambition there. Out of her hurts, she constructed poems made from her reversals. Rupture made the poems. "Fever 103°" closed:

> *I think I am going up,*
> *I think I may rise——*
> *The beads of hot metal fly, and I love, I*
>
> *Am a pure acetylene*
> *Virgin*
> *Attended by roses,*
>
> *By kisses, by cherubim,*
> *By whatever these pink things mean!*
> *Not you, nor him*
>
> *Nor him, nor him*
> *(My selves dissolving, old whore petticoats)——*
> *To Paradise.*

That lone "I," lemming-like, on the cliff's edge of the first stanza I recognized. She bypassed the cherubim we sang about in chapel and rocketed to oblivion with poetry and fashioned herself something remarkable, casting off her petticoats. I clung to her lines as a promise: outside my cerebral, spiritual love for Ms. Young (I did my homework with an intense desire to please her), I was a horror to myself. I thought maybe these feelings I had for her could graft to physical attractions to other girls, that I might unscramble my dreams about beautiful men.

I sat at my desk in my room after my homework was done. I picked my nose. My brother had gone to sleep. My parents had gone to sleep. My Connecticut grandmother was smoking or going to church. My Southern grandfather was reading the dictionary and not speaking to my mother. I began to bargain with the universe. No. I began to beg the universe. More like an animal than a human. The way Plath must have bargained in those final hours in that grim cold London apartment, with the zoo across the street and the wolves howling, trying at times to reason with Ted Hughes to come back and be with her, though a part of her must have known he never would. There is the saddest story of her going out at night after the children were asleep to the pay phone at the end of the snowy street to call Hughes who must have been deep in one of his numerous affairs. She'd married a man who was never going to be faithful, and perhaps she was too young to understand what she'd chosen. She wanted to think it might be different. So did I. Maybe I *could* be different. But I was too young to know much: I believed in absolutes. I was begging to be changed or eliminated. I don't think I would have called that prayer but in intensity and supplication it might have looked like prayer. I beseeched the stars to change me. Nothing happened.

13.

The summer before college, in that empty hot Midwestern August, a month heavy with waiting, when the macadam streets were quiet as museums and everyone was off at a camp or in a cabin up north, I lolled on my bed with the AC window unit going. In Edina, our suburb, the giant elms brushed against the house like erasers. I was tall with glasses and people said I looked like my father. I'd been accepted to Bowdoin College and had graduated in the top 10 percent of my class. I'd worked for that spot. Only AP English I'd floated through with ease. Every other class was memorization and flash cards and charts, whereas the poetry I metabolized. I'd been on the track team and the basketball team, acted in school plays and edited the newspaper and yearbook. I'd even been nominated for homecoming king, which felt like a lie and a success. The SATs had been difficult for me, as I was thinking like a poet and every multiple-choice answer seemed possible. Despite several tutors I struggled with those pencils and those dots.

I rarely heard from my Southern cousins. We never visited. They never visited. Maybe a Christmas call. John's voice deepened and grew distant. He'd gotten in trouble with his drinking. He wasn't going to college.

My brother grew in the next bedroom and we built towns in the sandbox from my maps up until I left for college. I was always the mayor and he was always renting the worst land and I was always raising the rent. By this time in our brotherly bond we dealt in secrets and silence, and when our parents yelled about money we played together all the harder and I drew more maps. I was happier to play with my brother than with kids my own age, who might have a greater awareness of a growing effeminacy in me. With my brother the bubble of fantasy held firm even as pubic hair multiplied on my crotch.

When the days at the end of August grew too hot, I was in my bedroom, absorbed reading Edward Butscher's *Sylvia Plath: Method and Madness*, a trashy biography of Plath. I read every word slowly and underlined passages.

Plath left Devon, leaving the bee boxes and the phone pulled out of the wall. She packed the children into the back seat. She headed to London. Winter pressed down. It would be the coldest winter London had in nearly one hundred years. Her pipes froze, the children couldn't be bathed properly. The cold temperatures clarified her vision.

The BBC interviewed her and she was smoking, something she took up at the end. She was just thirty. The country, whose accent she'd faithfully adopted, had a man in it who had betrayed her. What must that have felt like to have his British accent in her mouth? I'd gone to the library that summer and heard her interviewed on a record. There was something sad *and* comical about hearing her speak in her faux-British accent. I wondered if she felt that particular loneliness of someone who does not belong to the place she was in.

She wrote to her mother that she was writing the poems that would make her name. She had stopped washing herself. Al Alvarez, a friend, a lover, a poetry critic, commented on her animal stench when he saw her in those final days. She did not tell her mother about this. Ted Hughes was busy bedding another woman, who would soon be pregnant and produce a third child for him. Later that woman committed suicide. She asphyxiated herself and their child.

I went back to *Ariel*. I reread her poem to her infant son "Nick and the Candlestick," which concludes:

> *O love, how did you get here?*
> *O embryo*
>
> *Remembering, even in sleep,*
> *Your crossed position.*
> *The blood blooms clean*
>
> *In you, ruby.*
> *The pain*
> *You wake to is not yours.*
>
> *Love, love,*
> *I have hung our cave with roses,*
> *With soft rugs—*
>
> *The last of Victoriana.*
> *Let the stars*
> *Plummet to their dark address,*
>
> *Let the mercuric*
> *Atoms that cripple drip*
> *Into the terrible well,*
>
> *You are the one*
> *Solid the spaces lean on, envious.*
> *You are the baby in the barn.*

How wild. Reading it brought Ms. Young back to my mind and that was comforting. The shock and charm and charge of Plath's voice, intelligent, sharp, leaping in a bold set of associations. The ragged line edges emphasized the rapid jump and pace, the o's hurling the poem forward: "embryo" and "yellows" and "ruby" and "you." "Embryo" and "pain" remained lonely on their ledges. Religion was ancillary. What Plath believed in was her beautiful child. Before she shut the door of the book, before I shut the door on the book that summer, I read again how Plath apologized for the legacy of pain she was about to leave. Nicholas is a baby Christ she's abandoning. Christ appeared as a literary trope for her, not something spiritually useful. That's about as useful as Christ felt to me, a decorative figurine, nothing practical.

The biography and the poems melded in my brain into one. I found her argument for suicide appealing. If the world dealt you what felt like the most unfair card, you had options: you could opt out. In the same breath, her tremendous drive through Smith and on to Cambridge to write poems and be published inspired me. I would start working on poems now too, I thought. I would start sending them out the way she did. At the same time, when sexual thoughts came to me I began to think more and more the solution would be to kill myself, which would help me leave my parents with less disappointment than unraveling my perversion before them.

Ariel convinced me. I'd hoped the biography might reveal more information about her children in present time, for they were roughly my age, but there wasn't much to go on. The suicide had left in its wake a resounding silence in America and in Britain regarding any information about Plath's two children. What did Nicholas think now, I wondered? I wondered about mothers and their sons, the complex and tense bond between them. Maybe silence was the best response to a mother?

14.

The week before I went to college, my mother made attempts to reach out to me. Instead, I fought with her. "You all right, darling?" she said. She asked about girls. Then stopped. We fought over my allowance, what I would wear to college, just about everything. I accused her of being ill-fitted to guide me, having gone, I said, to Barry College, "a two-bit excuse for a college." The minute I said it I regretted it. I was trapped. She was trying to get me out. But what could she do? What could I do? The fighting we did was love, but it had no resolution. I stomped off alone. She did her best not to look worried.

That last week, my tipsy parents disappeared every night down a dark wood corridor. I drew my last maps for imaginary countries and bequeathed them to my brother. "Here," I said. "It's up to you now." I told my brother less and less about myself. I was convinced what possessed me sexually was like a virus and might infect him. I trained him in all things masculine: reprimanding him for having friends that were girls. He looked at me with hurt. I felt justified.

High school friends invited me to our last parties, but I always refused. I didn't like drinking. I didn't like how it numbed my gods, how it robbed me of a calm connection to my parents. Once their drinking started all sense was wiped away, replaced by gibberish and yelling. I vowed not to drink.

In my room, reading the Bowdoin College brochure once more and looking at a photograph of the dormitory I'd soon be living in, I planned to completely reverse my sexuality to be acceptable. Suicide could do that. Dead was better than authentic. My heart chilled. I planned.

My mother had been preoccupied with finances that week, dealing with a new interior decorator, having fired the last one. The zest and zing of money flowed through her commands: *Do this! Move this! Get me this! Clean that!* The house cluttered with bohemian objets d'art: a carved mandolin player, a sconce, a marble bust from Scotland. More than once that summer, she had a dress in her hand with the tag still on it. Her closet filled with shoes in boxes.

Vibrant yet trapped, coaching my father on how to behave in his medical practice and ask his partners for more money, while losing herself, assuming the role of a father, a defender, she was a general. My mother unsexed herself as I prepared to go to college. There was a frenetic sadness to her. She would say, "I could've been a decorator." Or she would say, "I could've gone into business for myself." I was sad to happen upon her oil landscape paintings half-done in a closet.

She called her mother back in Connecticut the day before I left. She told her I was on my way to college and I would be stopping by Hartford to see her on my way up. The relationship was strained between the two now that my grandmother had taken up with the Irishman, who made it plain he did not like my mother. How could I know how isolated my mother felt? As Plath ran up against a separation with Aurelia, my mother separated herself in Minnesota from *her* mother. Mom was alone. I knew not what she faced.

My last night in Minneapolis came. I burrowed into Plath. I readied my suitcases. I called my new roommates. The stars took their place dispassionately. My mother was at the other end of the house, reading. She read like mad when she wasn't making meals, buying real estate, having dresses shipped to the house, or drinking wine with my father. She read so much at times that there were only little pathways to the sides of her bed, waist-high cliffs of books teetering on either side of her. She read everything about the Bloomsbury group, then all Winston Churchill's speeches in one week. She read recipe books and she read biographies. This act seemed to give her the greatest solace. Her skin practically smelled of books. Vita Sackville-West's Sissinghurst was reflected in her irises. When she finished arguing with my father or a bill collector on the phone, there would be the sound of her turning pages. Her fingertips and her nails with their nail polish tapped the pages like moths butting against a lit plate-glass window.

15.

I contemplated rivers, razors, ropes, rifles, and railroad tracks. *If I could die*, I thought on the plane out of Minneapolis, *this could be resolved*. My request to God was some kind of prayer, but I didn't really know *what* prayer was. I hadn't had much practice. But I was talking awfully intently to outer space, to *something*, up there in the clouds that day.

I'd seen my Connecticut grandmother through the crack in her bedroom door solemnly put her hands together with a rosary and a Bible. She called that prayer. This was similar, yet without the salvation I imagined might be contained in her whispers. I was asking for the opposite of saving. I was asking to leapfrog over my grandmother to get to death before she could.

Nana, as I called my grandmother, had a passive strong faith, never asking anyone to attend her church. I doubted her Catholic priest in Hartford even knew who she was in all her decades of attendance. My mother didn't encourage us to go with her when we visited. We didn't seem to find religion that compelling. Nana always went alone. The only time she would get dressed up: heels, black dress, hat, shiny black patent-leather pocketbook.

That late August day, I visited her in the ignored end of Hartford where she sat in her run-down house next to a McDonald's. The whole house had the look of a forgotten grave: the name of the mailbox you couldn't read, and a fine film of highway dust covered everything outside and in. An abandoned baby stroller was discarded on the sidewalk in front of the busy street. The neighborhood was now Jamaican and Puerto Rican, and she remained there, referring to her neighbors as "the coloreds." I thought to tell her we didn't use that word anymore, but I didn't. I was losing interest in corrections besides the one to correct myself out of existence. Or I was a person committed to unawareness. Or I was a person without guts.

She was dressed in a terry-cloth ruby-colored bathrobe she wore daily, monthly, yearly, chain-smoking but oddly never inhaling. She was scrupulously isolated with a drunk Irish husband who broke furniture in rages and worked on the police force. She ignored him as best she could. While I visited he went to the garage. After he died it was discovered the garage had stacks of his pornography. Nana talked about people that were dead more than people that were living. Endlessly puffing, she was a smoke machine. Her face cool and formidable as a marble Mary in the graveyard. Born to Lithuanian immigrants, she hadn't graduated from high school and trusted superstition more than facts. She had worked for decades in collections for the Sage-Allen department store. She knew how to listen.

"What's the name of that college?" she said. My going to a college in the East was a novelty to her. No one in our family, on either side, had done such a thing. She toasted a bagel, slathered butter on it, and gave it to me. Above the kitchen door was a crucifix. Above our heads an ugly fluorescent light with a metal pull chain starkly lit our faces. Out the window a boom box blasted the lyrics from a Frankie Goes to Hollywood song: *Relax, don't do it, when you want to come. Relax don't do it . . .* I felt dread. I needed help. I wanted to yell. I said nothing.

Why Should You Be One Too?

16.

I thirst.

—JOHN 19:28

I was eighteen when the drinking started. It was 1981, and I was heading off into the Maine woods, under the huge deep-green pines, to attend Bowdoin College. In the dark living room in Minneapolis, my parents sat with their wine glasses like a queen and king overseeing a fading empire. I was shy and reserved, a reader, a Reece. I was far from the Southern town of my father's family and the tattered run-down north end of Hartford where my mother's Lithuanian immigrant family had landed. My parents had invested much in me. They had, in my mother's words, "jumped class." They banked now on an even greater success: me.

Pimples grew from my temples. I looked as if I was about to rut and grow antlers. I was turning into a man who loved men, or a man who loved men and women, but men more. But I did not know how to be that person.

At the time no one used the word "gay"—not that I remember—only the clinical "homosexual," which carried undertones of a disease, something electric shock might undo. Later in the decade American states repealed their anti-sodomy laws. Homosexuality would be removed from the American Psychiatric Association's list of mental disorders. But not yet.

Libidinous impulses surged inside me. When I arrived in Brunswick, Maine, the small town that houses Bowdoin College, I found my way into an old independent drugstore with high ceilings, creaking wood floors, and no mirrors. It stocked *Playgirl*. There I discovered the golden buttocks of naked blond farm boys who lolled on haystacks in barns in Louisiana. I couldn't bring myself to buy a copy, because that would be admitting that I was homosexual to another person, the shopkeeper, so instead I shoplifted. I would buy extra tubes of toothpaste to make up for my theft. I wedged the glossy magazine against my midriff and my body throbbed against it with expectation. I would take the magazine like an animal with kill in its teeth, back to a bathroom in the economics building where I masturbated in a cave of shame—my body shaking like a washing machine. Then would come the horror and revulsion that would course through every fiber of my body. I'd throw the magazine away. I would pray to die.

I wanted to be like all the other boys. I wanted to be a part of something. I did not want to be different. I drank. I attended fraternity parties. I drank Cape Codders, gin and tonics, kegs of beer. I chatted with girls. I danced.

My first drink brought me to life. My soul opened in a way I had experienced only with poems and books up to that point. I doubt I would have used the word "soul" then, but that part of me that was not flesh was alert and looking for clues. Booze, like poems, unlatched that. The next drink went down flawlessly. The ice, the charge, created an alchemical click inside. There was another drink and another. Suddenly everything that had been stuck was greased. I wasn't bad. Liquor flowed through me. I had nerve.

17.

I sat hungover in the back row of a course called "Religious Poets." My brain was an aborted fetus pickled in the jar of my skull. The class met in the oldest building on campus, filled with crooked staircases and tiny fireplaces. On the syllabus were three poets: T. S. Eliot, Gerard Manley Hopkins, and Elizabeth Bishop. Much discussion revolved around the fact that Bishop wasn't religious like the other two. So why, our provocative professor slyly queried, had she presented her this way to us? Our professor was a bohemian Jewish intellectual who dressed in tweed skirts and L. L. Bean boots, her wild hair hadn't been combed since Woodstock.

I never gave her an answer then. I mainly stared at the floor in class. But I did like the clarity of the poems. I was doing the reading, and it helped that the font of Bishop's poems had been made larger, which I assumed was done because she had written fewer poems than most. There were religious allusions, but the whole tenor of her work was secular. There were no traces of the homosexuality or the alcoholism that our professor kept gingerly referencing. She told us Bishop had an exotic lover in Brazil named Lota. The class laughed. Homosexuality was cause for a good laugh. Maybe, the professor coaxed us, Bishop had faith *in poetry*, in the clarity and accuracy she strove for there, and could that serve as a religion to her, a way of navigating the world?

We studied "Over 2,000 Illustrations and a Complete Concordance," which ends:

Everything only connected by "and" and "and."
Open the book. (The gilt rubs off the edges
of the pages and pollinates the fingertips.)
Open the heavy book. Why couldn't we have seen
this old Nativity while we were at it?
—the dark ajar, the rocks breaking with light,
an undisturbed, unbreathing flame,
colorless, sparkless, freely fed on straw,
and, lulled within, a family with pets,
—and looked and looked our infant sight away.

Bishop came at faith sideways, acknowledging it out of the corner of her eye, the Nativity manger scene reduced to "a family with pets," which I loved. This felt perfectly natural to me.

By concentrating and concentrating with her "famous eye," as Robert Lowell called it, she winds up the poem about reading with a lament: though a book could capture life, an experience might be missed—"Why couldn't we have seen this old Nativity while we were at it?" She missed the opportunity but still had her concordance.

Through the prism of this poem, I recognized my stalled life: I'd read my way through much turmoil. Reading had always been my escape hatch. Now, in college, much of life—the fraternity parties, the dating, my parents' drinking, my drinking—confounded me. So I didn't need to be prompted more than twice to "Open the book" and "pollinate" my fingertips.

I joined the literary magazine staff and began trying to write my own poems. The magazine was called *The Quill.* The editor was Nick Thorndike. He was taller than I was, had a soft voice, and kept talking about James Wright. Behind his tortoiseshell-framed glasses, his eyes delighted in the name of every poet I mentioned to him. He mentioned poets I hadn't heard of yet, with Russian names and Spanish names, like Yevtushenko and Neruda. I couldn't put words to it, but I admired Nick and knew he would be a famous poet. In most matters, men compete with one another. But I did not compete with Nick about poetry. I wanted him to succeed. He would. A pure emotion I felt for him. I had few pure emotions.

Back in my dorm room, I typed poems out on a manual typewriter and then crossed out the lines. It was painting more than writing, I suppose, just mixing colors. Something in the action of saying and erasing, saying and erasing, gave me solace, and perhaps a deeper solace even than reading. This private "useless concentration," as Bishop called it, aided me immensely.

I drank whole bottles of wine now, sometimes a bottle of vodka, the steel clarity of that clear liquid giving me peace as I barricaded myself against my impulses. I didn't view it as problematic. I thought this would now be my new adult self: Spencer, the hard drinker. When I saw Nick at parties and began talking about poems I frequently had trouble getting the words out. He avoided me.

The call of the drink increased. It overtook the poetry. My writing did not peter out completely—but my "infant sight" shrank.

18.

Though my writing dissipated, I kept reading Bishop. The amber and umber leaves fell across the window panes and blew against the Andrew Wyeth houses. Students started dating one another. I dated no one. I remained alone with Bishop. Her poems had a slow, burning effect on me, unlike the immediacy I was used to from reading Sylvia Plath in high school. I was drawn to Bishop's sound and rhythm first, before I captured her meanings.

One element of that sound was something you might call "Yankee." I associated that term with the Northeast where my mother's people came from and where I was now enrolled in college. The Yankee diction meant: keep a distance from your neighbors, recall Robert Frost's stone fences, allow people space, keep your guard up. In her prose poem "Strayed Crab," Bishop uses the voice of that crustacean to amplify all things Yankee: "I believe in the oblique, the indirect approach, and I keep my feelings to myself."

Yankee meant Anglo-Saxon. Yankee meant houses on Cape Cod. Yankee meant Harvard legacies. Yankee meant trust funds. Yankee meant people like Nick Thorndike. My mother wanted to be part of it. She liked the Yankee mentality even though she was Lithuanian, the child of immigrants. She wanted to assimilate. She wanted to pass. My mother would always say, "We are private people, Spencer." My mother repeated this phrase about privacy to me like a chant, and during my weekly calls home, I could imagine her shaking her head like Katharine Hepburn all the way back in Minnesota. Because of my mother, I associated privacy with dignity. Bishop's poems supported this private way of living. My mother's sense of privacy manifested itself in muteness over anything too personal: the screaming inside our living room was never ever to be mentioned outside the home or to her. Certainly I was never to ask her about why, when I was young, she had once slid down a wall in tears. I was taught that people would respect a repression more than a confession.

Bishop said proudly that she believed in closets and more closets. She said that she wished the Confessional poets would keep their revelations to themselves. Her poems build pressure and force through strenuous evasion. Her silences riveted me: she was all about what she wasn't saying, which neatly encapsulated what I knew growing up. And the way I was living now.

I read and reread "Crusoe in England," where Bishop writes of sad lonely Robinson Crusoe and his famous encounter with Friday:

> *Just when I thought I couldn't stand it*
> *another minute longer, Friday came.*
> *(Accounts of that have everything all wrong.)*
> *Friday was nice.*
> *Friday was nice, and we were friends.*
> *If only he had been a woman!*
> *I wanted to propagate my kind,*
> *and so did he, I think, poor boy.*
> *He'd pet the baby goats sometimes,*
> *and race with them, or carry one around.*
> *—Pretty to watch; he had a pretty body.*

There it was—the pretty body, pretty to watch. Out in the open. Was describing gay male attraction a way of keeping some distance from her lesbianism? Coyly she kept it all private and yet she managed to write about it. And even she managed to write in a way that shows how someone might try to hide or minimize their sexuality. As soon as I had what amounted to a sexuality I started throwing my voice like this, forcing my listener to focus on anything but me. When I saw this poem I knew what Bishop was doing. She loved to track the mind in action. Her repetitions of Friday's being nice (has "nice" ever been used better in a poem?) displayed a mind hesitating to say the truth the way my own mind hesitated when I felt attracted to men and said I wasn't. "Pretty to watch; he had a pretty body." I saw that line as a mumble, the way I would have mumbled it to myself as I woke from my bed, having had another wet dream about my muscular, hairy roommate. I lived under a tyranny of watching, of being drawn to pretty bodies that the world told me were the wrong gender.

Bishop became a manual for me as I entered college. The poems had friendly, unobtrusive sounds such as:

> Time to plant tears, says the almanac.
> The grandmother sings to the marvelous stove
> and the child draws another inscrutable house.

I appreciated her plain chant. These words didn't make demands on me. I knew that child drawing inscrutable houses. I was that child. I knew how to plant tears rather than shed them openly.

I went beyond the assigned poems and read more, read what scant biographical information I could. I learned that despite all the prodding from fellow poets May Swenson and Adrienne Rich, Bishop couldn't bring herself to publish about her lesbian self. What she left was a set of poems that held back. That drew me in. Slowly.

In adapting her life to her gay self, Bishop never had to contend with parental disappointment. By the time she was six her father had died and her mother had gone to a mental asylum. Bishop never saw her mother again. In her sixties, she received a prize from a university in Nova Scotia. She sat on the stage. Over the heads of the audience, across the street, was the mental hospital where her mother had died when Bishop was twenty-three. Over the decades since her mother's death, Bishop had tried to find out more about her mother but it proved challenging. No one knows if she managed to find out much. The clinical records state: she threw her clothes out the window, she ate plaster from the walls, she sat unspeaking for days. Whatever Bishop learned she didn't discuss. Bishop said that she didn't dote on the fact she had a classically horrible childhood. She was like my mother that way, not wanting to draw attention to what makes us vulnerable. My mother always said, "Everyone has tragedy, you don't need to go looking for it."

A few years before her death, Bishop said to her former student Millie Nash that maybe she'd been better off without a mother. Her early independence gave her freedom with her sexuality. In the 1950s and 1960s, still a repressive time for homosexuals, she lived her private life as she pleased with many lesbian affairs. She tried to regulate her binge drinking as best she could.

Closeted, alienated, drinking, I found myself aligning with all this in Bishop. But Bishop hadn't dealt with the disappointment of a mother. I was at a sorry crossroads with mine, the bittersweet separation perhaps all mothers and sons have, where I was disappointing her and she was disappointing me, the way we all sooner or later disappoint each other. For me, disappointments churned in my head and stomach every phone call home. I was growing unexplainable to my mother. I gave vague answers to all her questions. There set in a rift and a cliff. She'd ask if I had a girlfriend. Sometimes when she called me her words slurred. I read more.

19.

As the first term closed, we read "In the Waiting Room":

> *But I felt: you are an I,*
> *you are an Elizabeth,*
> *you are one of them.*
> *Why should you be one, too?*
> *I scarcely dared to look*
> *to see what it was I was.*
> *I gave a sidelong glance*
> *—I couldn't look any higher—*
> *at shadowy gray knees,*
> *trousers and skirts and boots*
> *and different pairs of hands*
> *lying under the lamps.*
> *I knew that nothing stranger*
> *had ever happened, that nothing*
> *stranger could ever happen.*

In the poem, a child Elizabeth shyly tries to take in the pendulous breasts of the naked African women in a *National Geographic*. As I read this poem, I knew the shame creeping into the poem, the way it felt to be a child fascinated with the same sex. Now, at eighteen years old, I could scarcely look in a mirror, much less a magazine. If I was what I thought I was, what Bishop thought she was, then I needed to murder me.

The thought kept coming, with the plodding, simple logic of Bishop's three-beat trimeter lines. The more I repressed those naked men, the more they appeared. If I killed the person I could kill the sex.

I looked out through the white-trimmed window in my dorm room. The window had six panes on top and six on the bottom. There was nothing more to say. Pine cones near the window swung like corpses.

20.

The term ended. My suitcases were packed so I could spend Christmas with my family. Up and down the hallways of Moore Hall students planned, exchanged presents, laughed on the phone with their parents, waving plane tickets. It was night. I walked out the front door and to the graveyard. I took a bottle of Southern Comfort with me and a bottle of sleeping pills, and I emptied them both into my mouth. I lingered in the snow with the graves. I passed out. As my cure started to take effect some muscle inside me reacted. Some voice said, "Get up!" I took myself to the infirmary, dizzy, told the nurses I was sick, went into the toilet, and vomited all that I had swallowed.

The next day I went home for Christmas break. I'd rarely changed my clothes the whole first term. I had razor cuts on my wrists, which I kept covered with the torn, stained sleeves of the one sweatshirt I wore. The sweatshirt had the name of my prep school, Breck, in faded letters, and had bleach and food stains on it. A widening chasm had grown up between my mother's emotional world and mine: her attention was divided between a series of real estate interests and the pressing need to buy decorations for the tree. Where once as a small boy I'd been her close confidant, now I struggled. I'd become monosyllabic. She must have felt helpless herself I now think. What could she do? Controlling, strong, she shook and rustled like an old oak.

One night I went out with old high school friends to a movie, and my mother read my diary. She confronted me, sobbing, when I returned, but it wasn't the suicidal thoughts that had brought her to tears.

"Are you a homosexual?" she asked. Her tone was filled with disgust and hatred. Or was it love cloaked in fear? How could I understand that she was one small figure speaking out of an enormous tapestry? How could I see that two thousand years of silence was pressing on her shoulders?

"No," I said. My brother stood in the shadows of that house filled with antiques and witnessed. I was denying who I was. I was denying who I was to save him, them, us, me. I felt dread and self-loathing beyond measure and guilt that my brother observed my hypocritical salvation. My near-constant request to be removed from the planet was met with continual stubborn silence.

"They tie each other up in Greenwich Village and have anal sex," she screamed. She looked as if she was watching a horror film. She didn't know what to do with me. I didn't know what to do with me. My father said nothing. I thought he had pity for me, but I wasn't sure. The animal in me was electrified by clues about sex, all kinds. His silence widened the space between us. I wanted to disappear. I wanted to appear. What book could save me?

In the hopes of fixing me, we as a family agreed I would see a psychologist when I returned to Bowdoin. There was the idea in the air that if I really did think I was homosexual, a psychologist might be able to talk me out of it. I was a puppy. I needed to be trained. There was hope in my mother's voice now. Although I still denied the charge, I was hopeful too. Maybe I could be changed. Maybe I could be like everyone else.

21.

The college psychologist was from Argentina, in his midfifties, and as dashingly handsome as a bullfighter. He had a fairly heavy accent and mispronounced words and forgot others, which, considering our topic of conversation, added a heightened level of comedy to our sessions. I sensed that he wasn't understanding everything I was saying. We sat in a little room in the infirmary, mostly taken up with his bicycle and various bicycle parts.

My heart sank about one minute into our first meeting when I realized I wasn't going to say the word "gay" or "homosexual" and neither was he. There was no book in his office resembling anything that might be helpful. We were going to pretend my homosexuality didn't exist.

Our conversation was laughably leaden. We were like two very bad actors in a college play.

"How you?" he said.

"Fine," I responded, my body language robotic.

"Your mother had spoken to me and said you try to attempt suicide."

"Yes."

"How are you now?"

"Fine."

"Do you want to commit suicide now?"

"No."

"Good."

This was the caveman-like level of our communication. The sessions were useless.

In a year or two everyone would start dying of AIDS. But we didn't know that in his office. What we knew was silence, elaborate and subtle and vast. What I knew was an avalanche of shame. He was married to one of the tenured professors on the psychology faculty. I suspected this job had been given to her handsome husband as a compensation: something to keep him busy between his bicycle races.

Instead of curing my homosexuality our sessions provoked it. I found myself drawn to his dark skin, deep black eyes, and muscular build—especially the lower half of his body, those thighs and buttocks tightly encased in his pants as if with shrink wrap. I had to repress the attraction every time I looked at him. This wasn't how *The Bell Jar* had gone. There, Esther Greenwood, Sylvia Plath's stand-in, had returned to Smith after her dramatic suicide attempt, triumphantly. In her real life Plath resurrected herself nicely, galvanized to embrace a new life in college with her dyed-blond pageboy bob. They wrote her up in the newspapers. My suicide attempt had generated no star treatment. I failed my classes first term. To the college I was an embarrassment. I was going backwards. Drinking called me.

The psychologist kept telling me to enjoy my life. His hands were full of grease and chains. He had started working on his bicycle during our sessions, and as he worked he would hardly look at me. Something Bishop once wrote to her physician, Anny Baumann, began to haunt me: "I feel some sort of cycle settling in." So it was going with me, a cycle of drinking to get through the days. After our sessions I would go back to my room and pour myself a glass of wine to blot out the unspoken homosexuality.

James Merrill said Bishop was always impersonating an ordinary woman. Her years were spent carrying out those impersonations: Vassar girl, a woman smiling with perfectly manicured nails, then wrapped in furs like a Scarsdale matron, later a woman with blue eye shadow in a light-blue pantsuit. I too was eager to be somebody who could pass. I was now doing my best to curb my theatrical gestures. Intellectually I constructed a genuine interest in girls. Sometimes it worked. When it did not, which happened more often, I wanted to disappear.

I told my parents I was better. They believed me. I believed me. I stopped seeing the psychologist soon after we started our sessions, having decided the answer to my problem lay in drink rather than therapy. He zoomed around the campus on his bike. I repressed my fantasies about the two of us naked. I drank more. I found myself unable to make it into the classroom. I was going down some dark tunnel. I tried to make it to the literary magazine meetings, smelling like a brewery. I vaguely wondered if Nick might be gay. Neither of us dared bring that to utterance back then. I fumbled into romances with women where they became nurses instead of lovers.

In a moment of sobriety in the dining hall at Coles Tower, having a coffee with Nick and talking about poems, he said he had heard someone say Wesleyan was the most liberal of the schools in the Northeast. His eyebrows arched and he looked out the window. If I changed schools, I might change.

22.

My junior and senior years were spent at Wesleyan. My grandmother was not far in Hartford. I avoided calling her. I rented a small room in a wooden clapboard house with three other students, across from a liquor store called Sunshine Farms.

Every night I walked through the door of Sunshine Farms and the owner said "Hello" a little too knowingly.

"I will have four bottles of the white wine," I said, with the same guilt I felt when I shoplifted *Playgirl*.

These wine bottles were Italian, had a colorful label on them like lovely Florentine stationery: green and rose squiggles, with some gold strewn throughout. When my housemate Laura moved in at the beginning of the year, her parents had bought her one of these bottles to celebrate. Two or three nights in, I drank everything in the house, including Laura's bottle. The next morning I left her a note: "Dear Laura, I am so sorry for drinking the bottle that your parents gave you. As soon as Sunshine Farms opens I will replace it." And I did.

Laura never drank that bottle. I did. Every night. A month later, I stopped writing her notes and bought a case of bottles. I drank the case. I replaced Laura's bottle over one hundred times.

I had a girlfriend. Maybe I could add to that heterosexuality and leave my parents pleased, or so I hoped. K. and I met at a party in the dark tunnels that connected the dormitories at Wesleyan. She was kind and smart, the two qualities I love. I drank my way through the sex with her. I prayed to something for the power to do this. I enjoyed it. I was attracted to her. I figured the drinking would subdue my brain packed full of gay desire.

K. studied classics and looked like Patti Smith. She translated Catullus until dawn. She was willowy with smudged mascara that gave her a raccoon look. Night after night in her bed we explored, aided by my inebriation. The record needle skipped on a song by the British band The The, singing, "This is the day your life will surely change." In a dirty crumbling student house with the paint coming off the ceiling—*This is the day*—I drank enough to kill an ox.

One morning I woke in K.'s bed blinded. She took me to the hospital. Somehow in my drinking I had ripped my corneas. "Have you been drinking?" the doctor asked. I said, "No, not much," yet I could smell the acrid tang of alcohol pushing through my pores.

After a week of healing, my eyesight restored, I made it to the library. I went to the room where they kept the records and played the voice of Robert Lowell, Bishop's best literary friend. Lowell read "Skunk Hour," which he dedicated to her. I grimaced when he got to the part about the fairy decorator, spoken in his best high-brow Boston Brahmin accent:

> *And now our fairy*
> *decorator brightens his shop for fall;*
> *his fishnet's filled with orange cork,*
> *orange, his cobbler's bench and awl;*
> *there is no money in his work,*
> *he'd rather marry.*

This was all I saw for a future: hairdressers, florists, maybe real estate agents—all court-jester versions of Dom DeLuise. Lowell's no-money pathetic effeminate sales clerk: that, I did *not* want to become.

23.

Most evenings I was carried out of parties and thrown into bushes. I fell down on the dance floor to the tune of the Go-Go's singing brightly or the Smiths singing one of their sarcastic dirges. Then I fell down a set of stairs.

People told me not to call them back. People stopped inviting me to parties. People said: "I saw you." And I wondered what they saw. "I have a red light that goes on and tells me to stop," my mother told me over the telephone, talking about the drinking. Red light. Where was my red light? Never had such a light. Only green. I did not mention anything to my mother about girlfriends or the poems I scribbled. The list of subjects we did not discuss lengthened. What had happened to us?

One night I drank all Laura's wine bottles and suddenly I was in the street in front of Sunshine Farms. My blue terry-cloth bathrobe was half-off, mud on my naked body. I'd dyed my hair white like Billy Idol. Mascara dripped from my eyes. A cigarette in hand, hate of me coursed through every vein. I exploded out in my drunkenness with an aggressive flamboyance, more auto-da-fé than drag queen. I dared anyone to stop me. My tongue grew vicious. I was Lear's fool. I ran pell-mell into the audience.

"We are going to have to take you in. This is the tenth time the neighbors complained about the noise here," said the policeman.

Crapulous thing, I said something unintelligible.

"Listen, the neighbors have called again, we receive three calls a week from them."

A record skipped from the bedroom above—Marianne Faithfull singing, "What are you takin' for beauty's sake?"

The officer gave me a fine and retreated. I'd drunk my way through the dark night. Now dawn tinted every little thing. Silverware shone. Telephones gleamed. Mirrors glinted. Windows flashed. The sun rose. I belonged nowhere. The house in front of me looked forlorn. I trudged up the stairs. My roommates woke to their studies. I recalled the night in pieces: naked, the yellow Sunshine Farms sign, the terrible thought that I would need to apologize to Laura again, replace her bottles, and what on earth was it I'd said? K., who had been keeping pace with my drinking and managing to keep her classics grades high, began to step back into the shadows. I was alone in my bedroom. Lawn mowers revved. Paperboys threw papers onto doorsteps. Birds sang. I had a set of crossed-out poems next to the typewriter. How would I enter this world?

The phone rang. The receiver shook in its cradle and the noise jangled me as if I had launched myself into a circus ride. The sky was full of colors already and I was drained of them. It was my aunt from Tennessee. My aunt who never called me. Her name was Mary Sue and the lilt and tilt of her Southern accent I'd associated with wry humor. She'd said with regard to a distant relative who was a nymphomaniac: "Honey, that girl goes through boyfriends like paper underwear." I held the receiver. She wasn't laughing as she introduced herself. Her tone was cold. In my other hand was the tattered fine I'd been given for disturbing the peace.

"Spencer, how are you?" There was a pause, maybe she was smoking. Her accent expanded the syllables so they dripped like candlewax.

"What is it?" I said.

"John Steven is dead," she said, and perhaps she herself was surprised to hear herself say this news so plainly, so flatly. There are words that change the world. Those four did. John Steven, my cousin, my kin, the same age as me, had been having trouble with his drinking. That much I knew. Someone had wanted to get him into treatment. His story line tumbled through my mind from pieces of telephone conversations I'd had over the years. We hadn't seen each other much.

"What are you saying?" I asked. My bed was wet with last night's urine and vomit. I was sweating. I shook.

"We don't know. Grandpa Reece is very upset as you can imagine. Your Aunt Pattie is beside herself, and your uncle . . . well . . ."

"What happened?" I asked. "What happened to John?"

"He was in a bar, down there in Florida. His sister Kathy said he saw somethin' he wasn't supposed to see. I don't know what. He—well, they—well, some men I guess took him to the river down there in Saint Augustine. He'd started drinking again and his sister has small children and she said he couldn't stay there if he drank and I guess he drank and then, well. He went to this bar I guess and they drowned him. Aunt Pattie is beside herself. Your uncle George had trouble identifying the body. They think the police are involved somehow. They don't know who did it. They don't know."

My aunt's words took dominion over that morning—the seconds, the minutes. In the Connecticut air, the birds flew through car exhaust.

24.

What happened to John that night? Was the bar dark? How did the men grab John? Had he said something? Had he touched someone? Had the men said something? Once I saw what I saw I could not unsee it.

The men yanked John. They ripped out his beautiful hair in patches. They punched him in the stomach. They held him down. They kicked him in the head. They broke his fingers. They broke his ribs. They broke his legs. They broke his teeth. They grunted. They spit. They laughed. They dragged the body, and the body picked up trash and thorns and burs. The laughter of the men mixed with the sound of the wind moving the leaves in the sassafras trees. Dirt was on John. He pleaded. Gravel was shoved into his eyelids. He had sand in his throat. Blood came out of his ears. They held his beautiful head under the mucky water until John screamed no more, until the last mercurial orb of oxygen bubbled out from his lips. The men walked away. The corpse floated. The world went on. The men went on.

Later a relative said John might have been gay and that was why the men did it. If John *was* gay his tough demeanor hid his nature. Or was it a drug deal gone wrong? Or was it—what? The murder went unsolved.

25.

After John's death my drinking worsened. I would drink three or four drinks before I went to parties so it could seem as if I was drinking as much as everyone else at the party. I started drinking after the party too, with a sense of release that I wasn't being watched or monitored. I drank Scotch neat now. I could drink an entire bottle of the stuff. The side effect of this was that my stomach was so full of acid the following morning that I couldn't keep food down. I grew thin. My face bloated. When I was drunk I was dramatic and gleeful, unlike my shy self. This was fun for others to watch, but at other moments I skittered into disasters: I fell down stairs, I picked a fight with a friend over something I couldn't remember afterwards, I babbled incoherently into phones to Nick who would cut the calls short and leave me talking to a dead line. I'd call him the next day to apologize. Bishop said to her psychiatrist, Ruth Foster: "If only I didn't feel I were that dreadful thing an alcoholic." Her dread matched mine.

Sometimes the drinking worked. On those nights it was nuclear energy—all the lights went on. I kept drinking, trying to get back to that magically connecting moment, but it happened less. At the center of my drinking now swirled the bloated body of John. I kept thinking about his drinking, where that had led him. Uncle George said he couldn't recognize him. The body was purple, swollen up. He could recognize him only by his teeth. Aunt Pattie had started seeing him in grocery stores. She said that he was speaking to her through the birds.

Drinks I took led me to hell. Charming phrases and flirty behavior diminished. I ended up ignored.

One night the beautiful white Congregational church stared down at me from the top of the green. Strict prim traditional Yankee New England was all around me. I went to a fraternity party at Chi Psi one night, and I could barely stand. The men in the fraternity were muscular and beautiful in their polo shirts, the place had an animal stench of sweat mixed with sweet colognes, and K. was in the library reading Horace. I smoked a cigarette with a gesture more Bette Davis than Gary Merrill, lingering too long in my leering look at one of the men. The young fraternity brother had biceps like a cougar's haunches, his chest was large, and I could see erect nipples through his tight shirt like nails sticking out from a hunk of wood. I salivated.

"Goddamn faggot," he said when he caught my look. He punched me in the face. He and his cohorts with all their horse muscle threw me out onto the lawn, and my body lay splayed out much as John's must have been. The town spun. I couldn't speak to anyone about what had happened, not even K. Muteness deepened in me. My cheekbone stung from the bruise.

Even if I was attending the most bohemian liberal college in the world, I could not undo the self-hate that mixed in with each neat Scotch I threw back.

26.

The one creative writing class I took at Wesleyan was taught by Annie Dillard. An acclaimed nature writer and modern transcendentalist, pregnant for the first time, close to forty, hair dyed Marilyn Monroe blond, she chain-smoked Merits. I was amazed by this woman. We all were. She'd won the Pulitzer for her Thoreau-like book *Pilgrim at Tinker Creek*. She radiated intelligence like an electrical storm. Gave off wisdom like heat. Her wit whipped around that room like a cyclone. We held our notebooks down.

Between classes, I slyly went to the Olin Library on campus and found her work in the stacks. I read:

> It is a weakening and discoloring idea, that rustic people knew God personally once upon a time—or even knew selflessness or courage or literature—but that it is too late for us. In fact, the absolute is available to everyone in every age. There never was a more holy age than ours, and never a less.

She bowled me over. Her verbs! How she ended that sentence "never a less." The text sparkled in the stacks. The idea, too, of something "holy" whispered to me, although the idea of religion felt remote. Of all the creative writing teachers on the planet, *this one* landed in front of me like a space probe.

At the time creative writing wasn't held up as a major in

undergraduate programs. Not knowing where to place us, the university gave our class a room in the chemistry department. Perched between Bunsen burners, Dillard sat in front of us like a Greek goddess. We brought in poems like offerings.

Her teaching style was unorthodox. Weekly she'd go down the class's list of student names alphabetically. Week one, she started with *A*. "Alice has written the most amazing poem," she'd say. "I had to tell my friends at the *New York Times* about it. It shook me to my foot soles!" she'd say. Alice beamed. The following week Alice would be forgotten and we'd be on to Beatrice or Charles. And so on. Until we reached the end of the list. While the praise was not genuine, my oh my, we lapped up what we could like puppies.

More and more, I longed to be a writer. How to get there? In those classes determination began to stir within me. Where that came from I wasn't sure. An awareness sparked. Dillard believed in me too, although I wasn't sure what that was based on. I sat before a woman who had accomplished what I wanted to accomplish. That was my absolute.

I wanted to communicate something true on paper, something about the way my life swung between buttoned-up repressions and drunken outbursts. I tried valiantly to stay on top of our assignments despite my drinking. Even though the class met in the afternoons I had trouble getting there, and when I did I smelled as rank as a sticky barroom floor. My favorite assignment, which we did weekly, was to type out the poems of the poets we liked, so we could feel the words go through us and onto the paper. If I kept typing Bishop's poems, might some of her brilliance rub off on me?

I read more of Dillard's writing. On Christmas break, her memoir *An American Childhood* came out. The sentences and paragraphs were exquisite. Like Bishop's Yankee sensibility, the memoir steered clear of anything shameful. Keep your guard up, the book said. I followed her example and kept trying to write.

By a miracle I graduated from Wesleyan in 1985. I felt a perfect failure. The night of my graduation I drank to black out. I remember only brief glimpses of things: a set of dark-green trees, a person pulling me out of a ditch, making out with a man or a woman, I can't be sure which, pulling the fire alarm in someone's dormitory, hitting my head on a rock, waking up with a scab and blood caked on my cheek. No, *The Bell Jar* this was not. No *Mademoiselle* scholarship. No Fulbright to Cambridge. No poems in the *New Yorker*. No typing my thesis on Dostoevsky while on the roof of my dorm to improve my tan.

I didn't know what to do next. I had applied to a graduate program in England to study the poems of George Herbert, but there was a fear in me. How long could I bluff my way through classes? The way I drank I was fortunate if my academic work was mediocre. What good was it to study? Would they ever take me? And why was there this persistent urge to want to die?

I applied to the Bread Loaf Writers' Conference. Nick had written me from Bowdoin that he'd gone there and he'd found it helpful. Dillard encouraged me and wrote me a letter of recommendation. I was accepted. Before I left Dillard puffed on her cigarette and said: "Spencer, if you want to write, and I hope you will, study something else." This last Zen koan of hers shot out at my hungover, sullen, sallow face like a party favor. Behind the wink of her blue eye, clouded over by her smoke, the comment seeded in me the confidence that would keep me writing, wherever I went.

27.

When I arrived at Bread Loaf a woman stood in the lobby—blonde, tall, young, smart—a Piero della Francesca angel, attentive, listening, glittering with a golden aura. Most of the writers were older. This girl was mischievous and welcoming. Her eyes said: *Get over here.* I found her irresistible. I introduced myself. She said her name was Katherine Buechner: quickly, I learned she was the daughter of Frederick Buechner, a theologian and writer of religious books I'd heard of rather than read. We were fast friends.

She was twenty-seven and contemplating becoming a minister. A woman considering being a minister in those days was novel and brave. I admired her for it. I wondered for the first time about ministry, about what that word exactly meant. She told me Howard Nemerov, who was her instructor there, had called her "another one of those smartass Bennington girls." Her head titled back as she said this in a Yankee way, deprecatory and convivial. I mimicked the gesture.

Most of Bread Loaf I spent with Katherine. We became inseparable, together through the barn dances and evenings in the old rockers rocking in the twilight breeze and the cocktail hours and conversations with casual references to where Robert Frost did this or that, where Carson McCullers had sat, what Anne Sexton had done. Katherine was not drinking. This struck me. She never said much about it. She just did not do it.

One night I got separated from her, as drinkers often separate themselves out from sober people. I got so drunk that I woke up at a desk where I seemed to be writing a poem, only to find I was not in my room but a stranger's. I don't remember if it was a man or a woman. I don't remember what they said. I had to be escorted back to my room—or did I stumble there myself? When I got up the next morning I was horrified. In the long breakfast room at a long table, with my eyes all puffed up under dark sunglasses I said to Katherine: "Why don't you drink?" My headache was intense. My eyes felt as if they were being unscrewed from my head. I kept glancing up, worried I would run across someone from the night before.

"It was a problem for me," Katherine said. Her tone was casual.

"What do you mean?" I asked. The clock with the painted face and roman numerals clicked behind us. Dust increased on the court cupboard with the inlaid ash and maple wood.

"Just couldn't stop once I started," she said.

We moved to the lobby. The writers had gone off to workshops and we skipped our appointments to poke and prod poems like lab animals. We sat in two tattered armchairs, where hundreds of other writers must have sat, the butterscotch upholstery molted onto the small of our backs. I thought of what Bishop had said about her drinking: it "had to stop" followed by her hopeful statement, "It can be done." Aspiring writers passed us, talking about workshops and agents.

"Now I go to meetings," Katherine told me. It sounded simple. Tall spruce darkened in the distance, hayfields deepened to orange, with bits of brown. Fresh mountain water sluiced through the dolomite and granite rocks. Fall was coming, things were rolling up, things were being put away, vegetables canned, hay bales picked up.

"You really don't drink anymore? And it's okay?" I asked. I was thinking of my parents drinking every night in their living room, how the drinks mounted and mounted and I watched. How necessary it all seemed. I pushed that thought away.

She smiled at me with mysterious welcome. I wasn't ready to stop drinking, but her example held me. Bright news on that Vermont mountaintop had been declared. I noted it.

28.

Later that year I lived in a thirty-three-story high-rise in Minneapolis. My parents were nearby. I visited them regularly. My sexuality remained unspoken. They emptied countless wine glasses and droned on about the Republican Party. In the living room, bottles came and went. I drank with them: we sounded as if we were underwater. We got maudlin, laughed, held our heads up, then dropped them. Would this be my life?

My brother disappeared from the room. He told me he had begun to measure our parents' intake by marking the bottles with his pencil: he didn't believe what they said they were drinking measured up with what they were actually drinking. My father slurred. Five or six drinks in my mother began yelling.

"You're chicken shit!" she said to my father. Her hair was frosted. They both had blown up like wood ticks with drink. What had happened to their earlier enthusiasm? What happened to the woman I knew who laughed like a hyena in her leather pantsuit and turquoise jewelry? I missed her. What happened to their joy in singing along with the Beatles on *The Ed Sullivan Show*? Still they always trundled off to bed together, waking up to work and pick up the phone and go to the hairdresser and then repeat the same evening all over again. My mother never laughed in a carefree manner anymore. My father looked defeated. I tried to unsee it. This erasure of former affability happened fast. I didn't want to connect it with what was happening to me. Meanwhile, they paid my rent.

Miraculously (and that is the right word), I was accepted for the MA on Herbert at the University of York—Herbert was one of Bishop's favorites. I love imagining her getting up from her chair and dancing to samba records in Brazil, tipsy, while in her purse were her lipsticks, cigarettes, a fifth of gin, and her marked-up paperback of Herbert. It was a brand-new MA, so I figured the professors must have mercifully overlooked my spotty college academic records, the grades that looked like a fever chart. It was another chance.

In the year before I went to England, I tried out various jobs. Each one ended a week later: I would call in sick, unable to return, my whole body aching. I'd smell like garbage left out too long in a hot kitchen. I soured with Scotch and beer sweat. I was a telephone answerer, a stage manager, substitute teacher, a volunteer with the mentally disabled.

My apartment was on the top floor. The elevator, the carpeted hall, the freshly painted walls, the modern windows—all this was lost on me. I drank alone every night. I woke up to weird, unexplainable bruises. I canceled appointments. I threw bottles down the long garbage chute before the evening's drinking began as a way to stop myself from drinking too much. I wandered out to the liquor stores and replaced what I'd thrown out. I staggered through the streets.

In modern Minneapolis, with all its clean sidewalks and cool glass buildings, there was a gay bar called the Saloon on Hennepin Avenue. Neon lassoes decorated the walls and the walls were constructed like stables. I would stumble in late at night, once the drinking had started. Annie Lennox and Boy George and Bronski Beat sang through the darkness, "Karma Chameleon" and "Missionary Man" and "Smalltown Boy" all put a bounce in my drunk step. I danced by myself. I hoped to connect with a man. I swerved. The men made space around me. The alcohol altered me, made me presentable, or so I thought. I did incredible dance moves, more seizure than Baryshnikov. I claimed I was alive and available. *Cry boy cry.* Then I fell down. I wet my pants. I burped up vomit the consistency of pudding. I wiped it away with my hand. The bouncers helped me up, and out. I careered home alone.

My revulsion with myself accelerated. I ignored the mirror in the bathroom of the apartment. When I looked into it Lowell's quote about the "fairy decorator" haunted me. Shame ate me. If anyone commented on the possibility of my being gay I flipped into a rabid attack or sunk into a glum stupor that lasted for hours. I navigated socially by ceasing to speak to people that questioned me.

I called Katherine. I didn't know what else to do. My soiled clothes were in the washing machine. My head throbbed. I was ready to try anything. I asked her about AA.

"What do they do at those meetings?"

"Talk," Katherine said.

She made it sound easy. Why then was sobriety elusive to me? I was frightened of going. Bishop had been exposed to AA, but it never took. What if it didn't take for me? Then what?

Katherine encouraged me. I decided, after some time, that I would try. I dressed up, wore a pocket square in my sports jacket—an attempt to pass as affluent and secure. I looked out the apartment window from thirty-three floors up, thinking of days blurred with hangovers, sending half bottles whistling down the metallic garbage chute. Cool, white stone, the Basilica of Saint Mary sat on the Minneapolis cityscape like a sundial. I needed repair.

29.

The meeting was in a skyscraper downtown called the Piper Jaffray building, sixty or so floors of sparkling blue glass. In a boardroom, at lunch hour, I found a group of alcoholics. A woman named Mary appeared. Who was she? A housewife? A businesswoman? I can't recall now. She walked into the meeting as I was sitting down with coffee in a Styrofoam cup. She came to my side and said, "Glad to have you here." Her touch was genuine, soft, unlike what I had grown used to in bars. I raised my hand when they asked if there were any newcomers.

Another man, a stockbroker with red suspenders, turned to me, "Here, you might need this." He handed me a big blue book, a manual about the size of Bishop's *Complete Poems*. On the wall was a large placard made of a shiny material like those maps they rolled down in geography class in high school. The paper crinkled and cracked. Twelve steps were outlined in boldface. God mentioned more than a few times. This did not repel me immediately. My associations with religion were fairly calming: my prep school, although Episcopal, had more Jews in it than Episcopalians, but I had never minded the prayers. My silent grandmother in her kitchen smoking came to mind: if a faith helped her, perhaps it might help me. Nick had written me that he was applying to divinity school and *he was a poet*. My agnostic parents had always encouraged me to investigate. I wondered if this might be a cult. But if the embarrassment would stop, I was willing. My eyes darted. I questioned.

AA was a family, people related to each other through suffering and joy, and I was adopted. People asked for my phone number and took it down. No one had done that in a while. When I could look at people I caught a glint of something close to pure glee mixed with a nonjudgmental love. I couldn't recall the last time I'd seen such a look. They wanted me. When was the last time someone had wanted me?

Church before church, a glimpse of heaven, I stood in AA with my cup of coffee—jobless, jittery, handkerchiefed. In that AA huddle, I thought again of my cousin John. His face surfaced in the fluorescence of that first meeting, as I contemplated stopping, actually stopping. I heard his voice. I saw his bloated corpse floating down the river. I heard the plash and retreat of the men after they'd finished killing him.

A Bishop poem came to me. "Little Exercise."

> *Now the storm goes away again in a series*
> *of small, badly lit battle-scenes,*
> *each in "Another part of the field."*

> *Think of someone sleeping in the bottom of a row-boat*
> *tied to a mangrove root or the pile of a bridge;*
> *think of him as uninjured, barely disturbed.*

I wanted John in that boat, barely disturbed. But it was impossible. He was dead. Now I was in the boat.

30.

I stayed sober. I stopped smoking. The air grew clearer. I woke each morning without headaches. I remembered what had happened the night before. Embarrassment left me. AA members—ex-cons, librarians, cops, secretaries, every color and sexual persuasion—hinted that the awfulness of drinking was going to be replaced by cheerfulness. My world was expanding, moving out from the fixed world of books and drinks. My fingers were now "pollinated" with coffee grinds, and often I had medallions for lengths of sobriety in my palms. Maybe my self-loathing would dissipate. But sober or not, I was indelibly gay. That desire rooted in my groin, heart, and cortex. That still shamed me.

I began wondering about Bishop's apparent ease with the sexuality she kept off stage. She said to Lowell once, "I never met a woman I couldn't make." Maybe it was her orphan status that allowed her to easily live out her desire. Maybe the drink gave her confidence. It hadn't helped me that way. Bishop always said how shy she was, but apparently she wasn't when it came to sex. I, too, was shy. Without booze, I became shier. Without my drinks, sex, there in Minneapolis, with AIDS coming onto the scene, vexed me. How on earth could I approach it without first blacking out? Black out did not lead to sex, it led to passing out, to vomit. A dirty, ignored celibate who pissed on himself, I was attended to by police.

I felt there, in AA, in landlocked Minneapolis, I was in an

incomprehensible sea. The waves of voices, the coffee cups like buoy bells, the strange mystery of it. What would my life be like now that I did not have the ability to immerse myself in drink? I hoped AA might save me. If I couldn't make a go of AA, I felt then that I would need to take myself out of life once and for all. Why sexuality continued to confound me I did not know. I did not know either why sobriety suddenly started burning in me there in Minneapolis. I still don't know. I might never know. Mystery manifested and filled in more edges of everything I knew. I was slightly unmoored by mystery and wanted still in my youth more definitive answers to things, and yet there, peeping out from behind nearly all of Bishop's poems, was a reminder that life is mystery.

31.

Bishop died in 1979 from a cerebral aneurysm. Her young lover Alice Methfessel discovered her in her Lewis Wharf apartment in Boston's North End when she went to pick her up for a dinner party. Alice was thirty-six, Elizabeth sixty-eight. The last poem Bishop published in the *New Yorker* came posthumously. It was entitled "Sonnet":

> *Caught—the bubble*
> *in the spirit-level,*
> *a creature divided;*
> *and the compass needle*
> *wobbling and wavering,*
> *undecided.*
> *Freed—the broken*
> *thermometer's mercury*
> *running away;*
> *and the rainbow-bird*
> *from the narrow bevel*
> *of the empty mirror,*
> *flying wherever*
> *it feels like, gay!*

I read the poem again there in my apartment in Minneapolis as I gathered my belongings, preparing to leave for England. The poem surprised me. Surprise I treasure most in my reaction to poetry.

That narrow poem on a broken thermometer extended its hand to me, welcomed me, just as Katherine had at Bread Loaf, as the AA members had in the skyscraper. She ended on that word "gay" with a "rainbow-bird" above it. The prominence of the word "gay" was creeping into the margins of the world. The year before she wrote the poem, Harvey Milk had been shot and killed by Dan White. While she wrote it San Francisco had adopted the rainbow flags for the gay community. Hard not to imagine some of that seeped into her thoughts. I readied my steamer trunk and the Minneapolis skyscrapers glittered in the afternoon.

The sonnet had only two sentences and each began with a past participle rather than a subject, emphasizing two actions, caught and freed, the way a bird can be, and the way any gay person can be, caught by society's admonishing rules, but freed by the knowledge that they can be loved as they are. To be authentic, a gay person breaks convention the way Bishop broke the sonnet.

I was beginning to feel my way to freedom. I placed Bishop's poems gently into the steamer trunk. I tapped the cover the way one might tap the shoulder of an old friend. How on earth did she manage to balance her drinking with writing such memorable lasting poems? What will, what despair, what exertion did she have to keep at bay and write what she did? The AA meetings had given me a way out of my daily embarrassment, of being a drunk, and maybe, maybe, there would be more to life for me.

Bishop's poetry gave me something that I hadn't found before. A space to breathe. A stance—the art moving through her, rather than being about her—that would give me space to live and figure my way into a sexual life where I could be proud (or "claim," perhaps that is a better word here?) to be "what it was I was," the way I was starting to claim my sobriety.

A Broken Altar

32.

I landed at Heathrow. I took the train six hours north from London. Suddenly York sprung up on the British landscape, between the weeping silver pear trees and the red cedars, with its Gothic minster. The cathedral at the center a paperweight that holds the whole town down. From the center of the minster the town spread out like a messy desk. In one far corner of this desk the modern University of York sat.

The 1960s buildings, built to last only a few decades, rose on a series of islands connected by bridges. The muddy stream and lake the campus encompassed were overpopulated with ducks and their voluminous excrement, their loose anuses going off like firecrackers. The effect, an astonishing English grayness, the paper-thin walls and the slippery duck shit subtly emphasizing a Philip Larkin-like world of post-World War II British desultory cheerfulness. The cleaning ladies waddled with buckets and said, "Ta luv, ta luv . . ." in their Yorkshire accents. In this uninspired architecture, I traveled down linoleum corridors, past porters, over bridges, over lumps of duck shit, and found my way to my dorm room and put down my suitcase.

In the news, Rock Hudson had died. Nancy Reagan refused his pleas for help in Paris, where he'd hoped for a cure. They had been old friends from their Hollywood days, but the lines from the White House went silent when the secret got out that Hudson was gay and infected. Refused treatment in Paris for an experimental drug, Hudson went back home and died. The week after I arrived, Liberace died.

Jumpy, edgy, defensive, itchy, one month sober, jet-lagged, I put my manual typewriter down on my desk in my small graduate school bedroom that had the personality of the inside of a Kleenex box. Fleetingly I thought, I *could* start the drinking up again here. In the same breath I looked at the single monk-like bed and imagined it strewn with urine and vomit.

I thought back over college: all the missed opportunities, all the hangovers that had subtracted me. I ordered a crate of Perrier mineral water from the off-license near the university. The porter in the college laughed at me—an excessive, materialistic American. In a rare moment, I didn't care what someone else thought of me. As I carried the crate to my room, a second chance tickled the back of my throat: the gasp sounded like a door being unlatched.

I was in a seminar with seven other students for this relatively new MA program. One of the students, another American, from New York City, named Eve Rothman, brown Jewfro, pink eyes on and off from all her reading (we loved each other instantly), asked: "Can we type our thesis on a computer?" The group looked at her strangely—as if she'd asked for a castle. I loved her directness.

Meanwhile I felt raw: a jumble of repressions and posing, hoping people assumed I was straight.

Drinking bottle after bottle of water, taking hot bath after hot bath, I sweat the booze out of me: someone at the meeting said it would take six months to get it out. One afternoon one of the MA students, a beautiful Irish girl with blue eyes and fair skin, hinted that I might be gay by alluding to the fact my cologne smelled feminine. I exploded. I raged.

"What are you insinuating? Just what are you insinuating?" I yelled at the woman and she, who had grown up in the Troubles, looked shocked. In following seminars, I refused to speak to her.

Poetry helped block out the fact there was so much wrong inside me. My porridge-colored British days filled with George Herbert. I liked the scale of Herbert—just two books. I'd picked up the paperbacks in a bookshop in York, and they soon had clotted cream and tea stains on them with my handwriting in the margins. One prose, a manual on how to be a priest, *The Country Parson*, and the other, *The Temple*, which held all the poems. In the days after it was published in the seventeenth century, people called the book of poems "The Church." I looked on this spiritual dwelling place where I could make sense of things. A paper-and-ink church where—for a few precious hours between self-hatred, moments in which I approached intimacy with myself, as if I was strapping myself into the electric chair—I could enter, the way others went into the physical building.

His scanty biography intrigued me. He lived with his wife in the country and priested three years down by the River Nadder near some water meadows. This was the 1600s in England, near Salisbury Cathedral. Proud priest, he donned his cassock and trounced through the fields to bless the crops. His favorite adjective was "clean," and indeed the poems had an emotional cleanness about them. Apparently this attitude applied to his living; he liked his house decorating simple, he said, as if the décor reflected the soul. In that minimalist rectory, they say he was happy with a wife we know little about, and happy being a rector in the countryside. He'd left behind opportunities to work in the government. On his days off he'd take his lute and go and practice with others at Salisbury. Parishioners whispered that he came from a wealthy family. Someone whispered he'd been born in a castle. His priestly choice surprised many, maybe even at times himself.

Some of the poems were architectural, as if he was building his own castle, the way I built rock villages with my brother in the backyard of our house in the suburbs under a yew tree. His own temple. A few are shape poems, one looking like a set of wings, and one constructed to look like an altar, a sly form of evangelism, his Anglican word-altar—and if he dared to think he might be published after his death, this altar would reproduce and reproduce: growing poetry readers, yes, and, if they were believers, growing a pop-up church between page and reader:

> A broken ALTAR, Lord, thy servant rears,
> Made of a heart and cemented with tears:
> Whose parts are as thy hand did frame;
> No workman's tool hath touch'd the same.
> A HEART alone
> Is such a stone,
> As nothing but
> Thy pow'r doth cut.
> Wherefore each part
> Of my hard heart
> Meets in this frame,
> To praise thy name:
> That if I chance to hold my peace,
> These stones to praise thee may not cease.
> Oh, let thy blessed SACRIFICE be mine,
> And sanctify this ALTAR to be thine.

The "built-ness" of this poem impressed me, the way he had carpentered it. I began to consider poems as sturdy things. My own life rather closely resembled a broken altar cemented with tears. My altar was made of poetry and glued together now with AA slogans: "Keep it Simple, Stupid" and "Listen and Learn." I was trying to build a frame for my spirit to walk through: if only I could *find* one. I was trying to find a way to survive a growing sense that I was too odd, even sober. "Lord," Herbert would exclaim, and I felt he really meant it, that he had a connection with his God. I wondered if I started plugging in that word what it might light up for me. I kept my face pressed into literature—my open book, the spine's glue cracking on my plain desk, I stared and stared at Herbert's spiritual furniture.

33.

In the evenings I walked the three-mile trek into the medieval town of York to go to AA. Unbeknownst to me, York was the national UK headquarters for AA. They had just started the meetings there—in a Quaker meeting house and in the boardroom of the large mental hospital across the street from the house where W. H. Auden was born. In the Quaker meeting house, we met in the basement. You could still smoke then in AA, the effect being of dry ice during a Broadway production; you'd be lucky if you could identify people across the room. In the boardroom of the mental hospital we met at an officious wooden table surrounded by oil portraits of dignified wax-colored British male doctors, while in the background sometimes patients screamed, which made the crystal chandelier jitter ever so slightly. I'd admired many of Auden's poems and tried to cut my hair in a long flip of a bang the way his looked in the pictures of him and Isherwood. I memorized poems by Auden and Herbert. The meters were subtle and exacting, which I felt inside my mouth and brain once I'd memorized them. Herbert's sound felt clean, Auden's felt convinced.

Sometimes I worked on poems about my love for men I had furtive attractions to, exercising my slippery "you" pronoun. "Looking up at the stars, I know quite well," Auden wrote, "That, for all they care, I can go to hell." Looking up at the British stars every Sunday night, I trudged off to the meeting in the mental asylum, occasionally tripping over hedgehogs, which are prodigious there. Auden's poem continues: "But on earth indifference is the least / We have to dread from man or beast."

Each AA meeting replaced indifference with unconditional love. People gave me cassette tapes of speakers at AA conventions, which I listened to in my little college bedroom, on a tape deck wedged next to my manual typewriter. That room was turning into a Dominican cell: I played those tapes like prayers. The stories of those who had been humiliated and destroyed by drink and were now resurrected gave me hope. I played the tapes multiple times. I memorized what they said. I did not have much to say in the meetings but figured if I said something from the tapes, people might find *that* helpful. They did. I said the words *faith* and *hope* more—words Herbert used.

The atmosphere of those meetings was Quaker-like, hewn plain and clear, people speaking spontaneously if the spirit moved them, wildly liberating for the class-conscious Brits, every accent mingling with the other: we were equals.

I found a kind sponsor named John, who worked at the headquarters of AA. John T. was in his fifties. Old. He had penetrating blue eyes; they sparkled like Christmas tree lights when I would meet him for tea and scones in the city center. Every day around five o'clock, having swigged another Perrier bottle, I called John from the phone booth in Goodricke College, where I lived. He was reserved: intimate topics were broached with more tentativeness than a police squad detonating a bomb.

"If equal affection cannot be," Auden wrote, "Let the more loving one be me." Romantic love felt a long way off. What love I had exchanged with my mother and father felt off balance, not equal, their great investment in my education a giant plus sign in contrast to the minus of me. Neither did my romantic explorations in college feel equal. Either I was dating a girl whom I loved but was not equally attracted to or I'd had a drunken naked fumble with a man who told me after our passion was spent that he was not gay. Auden's petition to be the more loving one was challenging as I didn't love myself much. Self-loathing boxed me, stopped me from considering that anyone might find me attractive: if someone made an overture of interest, I sabotaged it. Where there was *some* level of equanimity was in AA.

"How are you doing?" John T. said on the phone.

"Fine," I said from my phone booth in the college. In the cafeteria, students, scarves wrapped around their necks, sipped their tea and ate Yorkshire pie.

"Did you feel like drinking today?" asked John T.

"No, no. I had this run-in with this girl the other day, though," I mumbled. I felt separated from the British students and their scarves much the way I'd felt separated from the first graders as I wet my pants and was sent to the front lawn.

"What happened?"

"I probably need to do a ninth step on it. Maybe it sounds ridiculous, but she was making fun of my cologne, calling it perfume, and I just . . . well . . . I blew a gasket," I said.

"Well," said John T., "it's not like you are dressing up as Judy Garland for your seminars . . ." A gentle laughter. John smoked. A connection between two men. A nod. A sort of "You're all right, kid." Without him saying it. For a flash, in the phone booth, I felt a smidge of love for me, the gay drunk, although I winced at that descriptor. AA was love. AA spread love. In AA, surrounded by British accents and urns of tea, an old British lady told me, "Luv, now eat plenty of candy if you feel like drinking: booze has a lot of sugar in it, and the candy bars will replace the craving."

The message of Christ's love that Herbert wrote about I liked. Could I transfer the love in AA to Christ? I had trouble separating that message of love from what fundamentalists said or even what conservative Episcopalians alluded to in decorous ways in my early life about gay people. There was a general consensus to hate people like me. Certainly, without the Church saying anything specific, I was beholden to the impression that anything positive about homosexuality was never to come from a pulpit. Digging deeper, it is conceivable that I clung to homophobia as some way of keeping myself *from* daring to imagine what I would look like if I accepted myself. Whatever the case, the Church championed homophobia. I was discouraged from existing. Few things threatened Christians more than two men in love. More than lesbians for some reason. But Herbert I did not feel was homophobic. Nor was Christ, as far as I could tell. With Herbert, I read on.

What faith I mustered, fueled by my sponsor John T. and the months sober spent in the Quaker meeting house, I did not associate with judgment. John said, "You can't keep a good man down." Not being well versed in the Bible, I assumed fundamentalists knew *more*, and that it must be right: Christianity was beautiful except when it came to gay men.

I complicated matters. I wouldn't call myself "out." That word was just being used then. I was not at the forefront of any movement. I bargained with myself and God every night. That was the extent of my prayer. The prayer went: *Maybe I can change myself or hide myself.*

Reading Herbert, in the beige library, looking out on the foggy green lawn footnoted with hedgehogs, as I began to write flashcards for my thesis—then, there, I wondered if I could be a priest like Herbert. I said this to myself in a quiet voice, so quiet I barely heard it. Could this faith business support me as it had for Herbert? Could I declare faith and skip the sexuality?

I fell upon Herbert's poem "Prayer (I)":

> Prayer the church's banquet, angel's age,
> God's breath in man returning to his birth,
> The soul in paraphrase, heart in pilgrimage,
> The Christian plummet sounding heav'n and earth
> Engine against th' Almighty, sinner's tow'r,
> Reversed thunder, Christ-side-piercing spear,
> The six-days world transposing in an hour,
> A kind of tune, which all things hear and fear;
> Softness, and peace, and joy, and love, and bliss,
> Exalted manna, gladness of the best,
> Heaven in ordinary, man well drest,
> The milky way, the bird of Paradise,
> Church-bells beyond the stars heard, the soul's blood,
> The land of spices; something understood.

This verbal rainbow! A list of twenty-seven metaphors. The sound differed from Plath: Herbert opened doors that gave me reasons to live. Although ancient, it felt modern. This run-on fragment of associations excited me. The poem spun around on the page like a spiritual cyclone, though it had its own comforting order, which embodied praying. I'd never considered praying as a cornucopia of possibilities.

Plath and Bishop hardly spoke to God. "Herr God" was a taunt, not a conversation starter. Or Bishop to Lowell: "I believe now that complete agnosticism and straddling the fence on everything is my natural posture—although I wish it weren't." "The soul in paraphrase" caught my attention. That aptly described my turn to share in AA meetings. I was weekly paraphrasing my soul. I was searching for "something understood." Prayer was "a kind of tune." Could I be understood? What kind of tune would that make?

34.

I wrote my not-very-good thesis on the expression of humility in Herbert, comparing it to the work of his mother's admirer, John Donne. I typed and typed, using lots of Wite-Out, all crusted at the tip of the bottle like a mouth with a bad case of herpes blisters.

What I seemed to be writing about him, to him, was a love letter. Or maybe it was a love letter to myself? I had to think through the paragraph before I laid it down; otherwise I had to retype the entire page. Scissors and Scotch tape were employed to move things around. His quiet, soft iambs emanated humility in comparison to Donne with his floods and trumpets and his "Death, be not proud." I typed over one hundred pages in my little box room at Goodricke College. My skin throbbed from a recent bath. The ducks swam outside my window. Clang clang and bang bang went my typewriter. My fingers blackened from rethreading the ink ribbon. What research I'd done didn't amount to profundity or originality. But once I'd bound and finished the thing I did something profound.

Close to the end of my year in England, I took a weekend off and visited Herbert's chapel at Bemerton, where he served as a priest for three years before he died at forty of consumption. The stone chapel was not much bigger than a garage. Though the Anglican Church is not known for pilgrimage sites, the places Herbert moved and walked among began to feel infused with faith for me. As Little Gidding illuminated T. S. Eliot, that little chapel where Herbert, a rich, prominent man, had fled and where he was so happy for a time inspired me. Even though the church was more museum than worship space, I *felt* something religious. The place spoke to me. The place welcomed me. The cold church stones tingled my foot soles. I did something I'd not done before. I knelt at the altar.

35.

Katherine Buechner had gone on to Harvard Divinity School. She wrote fondly of it in her letters to me, encouraging me to attend meetings in every epistle she sent, to stay the course. Like the letters Paul sent to the Thessalonians and the Philippians, her letters helped me keep faith. I asked Katherine if such a place might take someone like me? When I phrased such a question to her I am quite sure we both read "gay." Or we might not. It was a blurry subject. She wrote back and told me Harvard Divinity School was founded by the Unitarians, who practically believed and did not believe in everything. The door was wide. That comforted. On top of that, my poetry comrade Nick had been accepted there and wrote and encouraged me to consider it. Annie Dillard's command to study something other than creative writing also prompted me. The unsayable preposterous idea beneath these prompts that I couldn't bring myself to share then was that I wanted to *be* Herbert.

Harvard accepted me. The acceptance to the Divinity School wasn't anything remotely as impressive, I felt, as getting into the college. In fact, I had the sneaking suspicion the school accepted everyone in such a secular time. Two years of theological study lay ahead. I took the train from York to London to share this news with my parents, who had come to visit me. The train flew past the British world of semidetached homes and slugs multiplying in the dark crevices. The train-window glass filled up with cows and then towns. I was one year sober.

The group told me the fact I'd stayed sober was a miracle. I'd asked the group if I should tell my parents. I was afraid of their reaction, I said. I wasn't sure it'd please them and, as they bankrolled me, I was earnest to please. And yet. And yet. Many of the members gave me their phone numbers and told me to call if anything went awry. "If you feel like drinking, call," they said.

My parents then were in their late fifties. They'd both put on a significant amount of weight. They were proud of me and excited for me to go to Harvard. They were drinking when I arrived. My father had a numb expression. My mother looked as if she might break into song. We three Americans sat in a London restaurant. We questioned. We gestured. We ordered.

"What do you want to drink?" asked Dad, drinking wine. A waiter stood at the table.

"Nothing," I said.

Mom said, "Is everything all right?"

The waiter looked awkward. "I have stopped drinking," I said. Like that. After one year. I had wanted to wait one year to disclose this fragile realignment of my soul to them. "I have joined AA," I then said, feeling as if I'd said too much. The waiter reorganized his pad and looked back into the kitchen.

"What?" Mom said.

"Loretta, let the boy speak," Dad said, in a rare moment of coming to my aid. But my mother never stopped when asked.

"Is it some kind of cult? I guess this means we have to pay for treatment. How long have you had this problem?" my mother said. My mother had more wrinkles, more makeup. I felt more alone then with her. The waiter looked sympathetically at me and bowed and left, clearly not wanting to get involved, which is how many before him had looked on us. My mother ordered her food and then sent it back.

Herbert's relationship with his mother sounded tranquil. He'd written her from college, swearing off erotic poetry, "my resolution to be that my poor abilities in poetry shall be all and ever consecrated to God's glory." Pure vows felt unattainable to me in the muddle of my new sobriety and my shadowy sexual life.

"I thought you might be happy..." I began to say to my mother, but I couldn't end the sentence. My eyes stung at their corners. All I hadn't said threatened to break loose.

36.

After England, I arrived in Cambridge, Massachusetts, and took up residence at Divinity Hall, an old brick building on a dead-end street. I had a faux-British accent from my year in England and had perfected my Auden haircut, but I didn't have a Bible yet. Down the hall, a plaque where Ralph Waldo Emerson once lived. I shared a bathroom with a Buddhist monk from Sri Lanka.

I quickly found the large AA meetings there in Cambridge, some of them one hundred strong, many of them with schizophrenics released from McLean under a new revolving-door policy where patients were released into the general population and trusted to take their medication. They did not. Many of these people showed up in AA. We met in dark, cavernous, Goya-like spaces, often church basements, where distinguishing the shadow from the person was a challenge.

As everyone announced their first names, I noticed an odd fellow. Dressed in a khaki suit, wearing a Tiffany ring, he looked sort of out of place; he said his name, Durell.

If you had put Durell in a lineup of people and told me that Durell would be the person to *save* me, I never would have believed you. He was, to use a word Bishop treasured, *unlikely*. In his sixties, overweight, wearing ties and tie clips and suits to the meetings, Durell sat apart from the rest of us. Durell was difficult, demanding. He was intractable, and underneath it all lurked the knowledge that he was homosexual. We did not speak of this.

Herbert wrote: "Blest be the God of love." Durell loved me in a way no one else could. Durell knew what I had suffered. He had suffered the same if not worse. I sensed this more than understood it, the way I loved a poem's sound long before I understood its meanings. Durell had a sound I gravitated towards. Durell had spent twenty years or so in meetings. I shared with him my dream of writing a book of poems. The dream felt fragile to share, it might shrivel. I didn't want the idea to be laughed at. Much of what I loved was laughed at.

Every day, after every rejection, Durell, who bizarrely hated poetry, encouraged me, telling me, "Your ship will come in." To share this idea of a book of poems in the large meetings where the schizophrenics shook and the homeless people searched for pennies seemed ridiculous. My dream I solely shared with Durell. The sound he kept making was one of acceptance. In meetings I sat next to him and between us sat my dream.

Harvard-educated, stentorian-voiced, Durell had trouble finding employment because he told everyone *else* what to do. His mother famously said, "Durell didn't need to go to graduate school, he went to Harvard." But the prized Harvard education worked against him. His superior intelligence he irrepressibly demonstrated. His arrogance made him unemployable. People distanced themselves from him. When he had a birthday that first year, I was the *only* person to celebrate it with him. I gave him James Merrill's *Collected Poems.* He said: "A bit difficult, don't care for them much!" Durell, a white male of Canadian and British ancestry, was poor and lived in a small studio apartment on 19 Garden Street, his rent cobbled together from government subsidies and money he weaseled out of estranged family members. He'd say things like: "I've been squeezing shit out of buffalo nickels all week!" He was sensitive, brilliant, and wickedly funny, giving AA members unforgettable nicknames: "Fried Egg" for the writer who had too much electroshock and "The Archangel of Death" for a member who kept bemoaning her tragedies too indulgently.

37.

Mr. George Herbert is here.

—JOHN DONNE

We have Herbert's one book of poetry only because his friend Nicholas Ferrar decided to publish it after his death. Herbert handed the book over on his deathbed, succumbing to consumption at forty. Herbert said he desired to have it published only if his friend read it "and then, if he think it may turn to the advantage of any dejected poor soul, let it be made public." Three hundred years later, that poor dejected soul was me.

I'd been waiting for him in the toolshed of the graveyard at Bowdoin hatching my suicide, when I could no longer blunder on with the unzipped sex of myself. The poems were stained-glass windows lighting my way up and up. The poems were saving me with their clarity, even as I was hardly clear with my sexuality; the poems were helping me navigate through life, through despair, through meetings, and inching me closer to responding to the sound of church bells.

While we'll never know the order in which Herbert wrote all his poems, there is one that feels like a last poem, even if it was not. "Love (III)" contemplates the afterlife. What would Herbert have to say to his savior were he to encounter him after he'd died? I wondered the same of myself. It occurred to me at some point I'd been talking to *something* for quite some

time. Mainly I'd been begging to be removed. The answer was
No.

Walking over to visit Durell one spring evening close to my
graduation from Harvard, I recited Herbert's poem, but quietly, lest anyone think I was mentally ill:

> *Love bade me welcome: yet my soul drew back,*
> > *Guilty of dust and sin.*
> *But quick-ey'd Love, observing me grow slack*
> > *From my first entrance in,*
> *Drew nearer to me, sweetly questioning*
> > *If I lack'd any thing.*
>
> *A guest, I answer'd, worthy to be here:*
> > *Love said, You shall be he.*
> *I the unkind, ungrateful? Ah my dear,*
> > *I cannot look on thee.*
> *Love took my hand, and smiling did reply,*
> > *Who made the eyes but I?*
>
> *Truth Lord, but I have marr'd them: let my shame*
> > *Go where it doth deserve.*
> *And know you not, says Love, who bore the blame?*
> > *My dear, then I will serve.*
> *You must sit down, says Love, and taste my meat:*
> > *So I did sit and eat.*

My soul, that strange invisible thing I'd managed to rescue
in AA, had drawn back much. And love, what did I know of it?
I'd loved my parents. I knew that, but now I felt myself drawing
back from them as the drinking built a wall between us. I loved

my brother, yet with all my bottled-up self-hate, my communication with him grew wooden. In Cambridge love seemed to move nearer to me. My first entrance in—the use of the words "love" and "soul" in a manner that indicated a solution—came to me through Durell.

Herbert's speaker is recounting a time when he talked to God about how he didn't deserve to sit at the table with anything remotely holy. When I said the poem to myself and moved closer to Durell I felt unworthy. Like the speaker, I dimly and regretfully sensed I'd been the unkind and the ungrateful, by turns one, then the other. Or simply unaware. I was a boy about to be a man: I was between the two.

Clearly, simply, Herbert in that poem was inviting me to live. This was now entirely different from Plath's great despair and the charge and charm in her verse that first unlocked poetry's kingdom, and different as well from Bishop's lovely Yankee "awful but cheerful" stance that beckoned me to look and look at the world with a useless concentration. This poem looked directly at me, like one of Vermeer's women, and in confidence, said, "Over here! Welcome. You are loved." *Love bade me welcome.* At the end, two people sit at a table and eat, one the character Love and the other the speaker. I felt the speaker surrendering his defenses and anxieties, the way I wanted so much to do in those Cambridge days.

All my years had added up to a great deal of "dust and sin." Yet unlike Plath, I did not choose to kill myself and say I was through. Instead I took notice of this poem that closed on the two simple action verbs "sit" and "eat." God was an agent of change in this poem. The speaker snaps to attention much as I had done in the AA meetings. I did sit often now and talk more frankly of who I was. Not all at once, but gradually. A sense of belonging began to come into my life, and knowledge that I was enough.

That tableau of two men sitting down together closely mirrored Durell and me in his threadbare apartment where the infirmary bed he found on the street stood in the middle of the room. Dressed in an ill-fitted poplin suit, breathing stertorously, he took me in and flattered me, mainly about my poetry, which is ironic because he kept going on about how little he cared for poetry ("Obscure," "What is the point of it?" and "May be a bit above my abilities").

His thick hair curled up in the front, which gave him the appearance of an overweight Kewpie doll. He showed me a coffee-table book, found at Salvation Army, of nude men and women. He said, "I'm try-sexual. I'll try anything once. Sometimes I look at the men, sometimes the women." He reminded me he'd been married once. Then in the next breath gently he referred to a handsome man he'd followed down the street. He did not pressure me to respond. Like the poem where Love sweetly asks if the speaker lacked any thing, he slowly turned the high-glossed pages like a docent in a museum. For the first time someone wasn't judging me. His tone was less flirty, more clinical. He was trying to draw me out. That wasn't easy.

I had a hard time articulating my emotions in person. I had the demeanor of an abused shelter dog. Sometimes Durell and I went to gay-specific meetings, but we did so clandestinely, as if we were identifying as possibly gay only for that one hour.

Durell supported my sobriety. My parents did not. The half-shocking retreat of my parents over my admission that I was an alcoholic made me turn to Durell all the more. He said, "I believe you will have long-term sobriety. I have been gifted with foresight and I see this." I didn't argue with him.

For the first time, somebody was addressing who I might become in a way that felt judicious, encompassing, kind, and concerned. Intuitively I knew he understood me in a way my parents couldn't. Still, I wasn't my own man yet. I relied on him for his judgments rather than taking action myself. If things didn't work out, I blamed Durell rather than owned it. As I evaded my choices, Durell went up on a pedestal. I know. I know. How little most thought of Durell. How little he thought of himself. And yet. And yet. In that imbalance, there we sat and consoled one another. The Herbert line came to me: I was starting to experience the "heart in pilgrimage." We were two closeted gay men, one young, one old. A reddish light faded over Cambridge, tinted our faces with brown shadows like the faces of the disciples at Gethsemane. Durell and I were going to one of our basement meetings. We'd later dissect what people said. We'd have fun.

To Be Brought Down

38.

I decided not to be a priest. I graduated from Harvard Divinity: those two words, I felt, yoked, canceled each other—an impressive school and a meaningless degree. After I placed the order for my cap and gown, a nun, a direct woman, militaristic, a fan of Mary Daly, asked: "Maybe a religious career is not for you?" It was not a question.

Spring in Cambridge, Massachusetts, alive with green grass, students caressing one another on the lawns with their new flesh exposed. All the old trees full of leaves boiled over with green.

Nick had become a Unitarian minister. He was visiting Cambridge and had lunch with me to celebrate my graduation. The restaurant had white linen tablecloths. He wasn't sure what he would do next. His hand shook wildly. I didn't ask him about it. He had two Band-Aids on his forehead. I didn't ask about them. We drank water. He didn't ask me about that. I was tentative about mentioning my sobriety. Nick mentioned to me he was submitting his book of poems. His clear blue eyes behind his glasses telegraphed hope about the Yale Younger Poets prize. It wouldn't take him long to get it published. I was certain.

I was *not* going into the religion business. Some part of me knew I wasn't mature enough to handle weddings or funerals, let alone baptisms or catechisms. And what was in my heart and head and groin was not connected. I was fragmented. I could not see myself in a pulpit. How Nick was managing it marveled me. I didn't ask him about it.

All seemed lost, despite daily counsel from Durell; I had no patience for what the future might hold, a common enough problem with youth—I wanted a defined line. My decision to attend seminary misfired. After having taken all the courses, I faltered. True, Durell, in the background, encouraged, *endlessly*. I had that. I had drudged through the theology courses. With my one elective I ran to the college and sat in Seamus Heaney's "British and Irish Poets, 1930s to Present." I came early, sat in the front, didn't dare introduce myself and took notes like a court reporter. Yes, I'd liked thoughts about liberation theology and bought a colorful cross from El Salvador in the Square to inspire me. But with every spare moment, I snuck into Helen Vendler's classes on poetry: she was at a lectern but it could have been a pulpit and one of her many texts the Bible before her, with me mesmerized in the congregation. I tried to pass for an undergraduate. I was far from ordination.

My college classmates succeeded. I stalled. Buzz was on Wall Street, announced his marriage in the college magazine. Jonathan graduated from medical school and announced his marriage. Nick was a priest and a poet. Everybody advanced on life's chessboard. I was an untouched rook.

I sat at my desk in Divinity Hall. Boxes all around me. Red tulips shot up like stop signs. The high elms on Divinity Avenue thrashed their branches in a commotion. Birds chirped like church ladies.

I was not opening a door at the end of my school work, but standing on a gang plank. I got to the end of the course work at Harvard and I did not feel capable of being a priest—too daunting. Should I stay Episcopal or go Catholic?

I was a failure. It was as if I had gotten an MFA degree in poetry and realized, degree in hand, I had nothing to say. To borrow from T. S. Eliot: I "had the experience but missed the meaning."

Behind all my neurotic hand-wringing brewed AIDS: that distant drum in college was now a fire alarm. The noise made it difficult to think. At that point, I walked away from a life in organized religion and turned, turned sharply, emphatically, inwardly, instead, to poetry. I did so without public declaration. So far my parents were pleased to speak of a degree from Harvard and end the conversations there, without querying further into what was to become of me. I knew more about the biographies of poets than I did about any of the characters in the Bible. I began thinking of writing a book of poems then and there, on Divinity Avenue, one of the few dead-end streets in Cambridge, in that three-story brick dormitory where Ralph Waldo Emerson had lived. I was choosing a moneyless art. The dead-end street, the laughed-at degree, poetry—where was it going?

I was seeking counsel, conviviality, a voice in the wilderness, something to counter the nun's voice. I needed a *living* poet, not any of my beloved dead ones. Over the phone, before I disconnected it, I suggested to Durell that I wanted to write Merrill, but Durell discouraged the idea. I was poor Verena Tarrant in Henry James's *The Bostonians*, passive and indecisive, controlled by difficult authority figures. Durell didn't trust gay men. He said it had to do with his experiences in the army. However, in that moment, I stepped away from Durell's dominant chaperoning.

"Katherine," I said on the phone, "do you have the address for James Merrill?" The woman who had pointed the way to the plastic crinkling sign with the bold-faced God words on it knew Merrill because he was the godfather of her sister and best friend of her father, Frederick Buechner. Buechner and Merrill had gone to prep school together at Lawrenceville. To this lapsed Episcopalian who received direction from the upturned teacup of a Ouija board, I turned.

"I want to send him my poems," I had said with trepidation.

"Dear Mr. Merrill, I have so enjoyed reading your poems. I hope you won't mind that I am including two or three of my own efforts here..." I typed out. Where was I going to go to make sense of being a gay man? It had been a failed enterprise. Durell and I had attended Gay AA meetings, but often in the background or as bystanders. I didn't feel I belonged. I was cagey. Gay groups were forming on college campuses. I was tentative. I gave Merrill my home address in Minneapolis.

39.

The family home my brother and I had grown up in, now hidden behind yew trees, had a FOR SALE sign in the front yard. Behind thick drapery, behind stained glass, behind statuary, my mother paced. My father was arranging for his new position in Oklahoma City. I landed among the boxes and began to help my mother pack things up. Without meaning to, I answered the phone for my father's medical newsletters, which week by week became my job. In the chaos of my mother's histrionics, my brother came home from Bennington College, his hair an explosion of blond dye and mouse, and told me in confidence he was gay. I had feared as much. His lack of interest in sports and bevy of friends who were girls pointed towards what I was keen to deny. I had hoped adoption might shield him from our gay hatchery. I was not comfortable saying the word "gay" or applying it to myself. Truth threatened me.

Two drunk parents downstairs, two fairies upstairs—a dead end of no grandchildren. Unkindered, our genetics flattened before us like whoopee cushions. While the sequel to *Who's Afraid of Virginia Woolf?* was unraveling, Merrill wrote back quick. "Dear Spencer," he wrote, "Let's use first names now . . . I can see from these poems that you have a certain finesse and ability with words . . . I am grateful for your letter and you are kind to say what you say about my poems . . . I hope to hear from you *soon* . . ." The response thrilled me. I wrote back quickly as my parents fought in the living room.

I existed on a meat hook of hate. I was sober, but my ability to navigate was questionable. Regarding the wilder emotions of passion or trust or confidence, I was closed. I wrote Merrill back about poetry but not about my family. Reckonings come to those who are forced into denial. Mine came.

I stepped onto the Persian rugs and said to my parents that my brother was gay. The marble bust of Mary Queen of Scots looked on from the dining room: her Scottish sternness matching my innards. Betraying my brother might stop his gayness and prevent AIDS from coming to him. Such were my intentions. My words went across the room like a hatchet. There were two wine bottles emptied on the Japanese tea table before them and the talk of what Oklahoma City would or would not be faded. They paused. I stood. They sipped. I paused. My mother's wine glass shook in her hands. What followed came in pieces. She yelled for my brother to come down to the living room. She questioned me like a judge at the Nuremberg trials. When my brother admitted he was gay she said: "If I knew you were stupid enough to have sex with this crazy boy in college I never would have adopted you."

My brother walked out, ran away from home, and stayed with Katherine Buechner in Florida. I did not call Katherine. Shame paralyzed me. I chalked up new reasons to off myself. "We must keep a high standard," my mother mumbled on. "We must remain private." My inability to love myself was now moving outward, destroying more. The house darkened. I regretted. I denied.

The next day our mother came in, mascara dripping down her face, looking like an extra from a bad B movie, and said, "Forgive me, you know I don't mean any of those things I say, you know I just can't help what I say sometimes. But..." The police were called to locate my brother. Our mother, with her gifts for welcome and hospitality, grew smaller. Fewer people wanted to be near her. The more she justified her cruelty the more people stepped back. My brother stopped speaking to me. I didn't know how to be a person in the world. All our rock villages turned to heaps of stone. My maps were lost.

I was Cain. *Then the Lord said to Cain, "Where is your brother Abel?" "I don't know," he replied. "Am I my brother's keeper?"* I had felt myself to be my brother's keeper. How had I managed to botch it? *The Lord said, "What have you done?"* I'd made a terrible mistake. *"Listen! Your brother's blood cries out to me from the ground. Now you are under a curse and driven from the ground, which opened its mouth to receive your brother's blood from your hand."* I'd caused more harm. I didn't know how to take back a thing once I'd said it. *"When you work the ground, it will no longer yield its crops for you. You will be a restless wanderer on the earth."*

40.

My sponsor, Tim K., a gay activist, had red hair and a loud Texas accent. He was tall and moved around the AA rooms like a security guard. I was afraid of him. I asked him to guide me in AA. I assumed he'd shake the truth into me. He was the editor of one of the first gay newspapers, where most of the ink would come off on your hands. He had weekly nude massages from an aging ex-model. When I visited him these sessions would be finishing up. The Puritan in me judged the transaction. Yet when my sponsor's cry of surrender came from the other room, I grew curious.

He had appeared on TV chained to urinals in protest of the University of Minnesota policing the bathrooms to keep gay men from cruising. I was drawn to him—I admired his openness, and yet was unable to achieve it myself.

When he appeared on the nightly news, I didn't mention to my mother I had any connection to him. I wanted her pleased with me. When I spoke to him of my mother's descent into madness, Tim K. said of her, "I guess she could go to Al-Anon if they'd take her."

What I didn't want to discuss with Tim K., or was unable to discuss, was my descent into a new revulsion—my complete inability to claim my ugly part in what happened to my brother—despite my regular attendance in AA. Behind that lurked the plank, the blood over the station wagon, my brother's scar.

I told Tim K. about my time at Harvard Divinity School. When I said the word "Harvard" I thought it might impress him. It didn't. He smirked. He was not impressed by the word that followed "Harvard" either, and joked about a candy called "divinity." While I didn't need him to appreciate my stab at ministry, his reduction of my degree to a bubblegum from the Great Depression made me feel the idea of being a priest was stupid.

41.

Eventually after months of refusing to lower her unrealistic high price for a house that was covered with knickknacks and had wooden floors stained beyond repair with the urine of bulldogs, my mother sold our house at a shockingly low sum. My father had already gone down to Oklahoma City. My brother inched his way back into their lives, less into my life, and headed down to Oklahoma to be with them, traveling into the wild empty parts of America with dimly lit exits and thousands of highway signs indicating thousands of tiny towns. Off they went, into the lonely American horizons, sadder and more broken than I'd ever seen them.

The new owners of the house hired the contractors the day after they signed the deed. Every yew tree my mother had cooed over was ripped out of the ground. The house was expanded and the backyard replaced with more house. Soon the neighbors would complain that no air could circulate into their yard. All the golden cloth wallpaper in the dining room was ripped off by men with masks on. The nooks where I'd sat were bleached. The rooms were all painted high-gloss white. A clean minimalism replaced us.

42.

Poetry is rarely lucrative. Or if it is—Longfellow comes to mind—the money and recognition seem to destroy its beauty in equal measure. I was not unaware of that. Yet poetry claimed me as my accidental commitment to the newsletter deepened. I loved this art that reversed capitalism. I moved to the farm my parents owned, thirty-five miles south of the city. I worked for my father, driving a car owned by my mother. I was in my late twenties. The medical newsletters made enough money for me to buy groceries but not much else.

I answered a telephone and wrote reviews of medical books. One day I interviewed Dr. Oliver Sacks on a radio station. In the tiny tank of the radio station, he spoke rhapsodically of Temple Grandin, who designed humane slaughterhouses. The circulation was limited to doctors, perhaps fewer than five hundred subscribers. I kept track of them in an old rolodex.

Meanwhile, from Oklahoma City, my mother emptied the medical newsletter account to pay for the telephone bill at her Cape Cod house.

"There is no money in the account," I said to her one day from Minnesota.

"I know, I needed it," she said without apology, a Bach prelude playing in the background.

"How am I supposed to print this newsletter without paying the publisher?" I asked.

"Just figure out a way. This is not your money. I needed it," she said, in a wild uncontrollable tone.

"But doesn't the money belong to the newsletter?" I asked.

"Well, then set up an account where I can't get at it," she said. She hung up the phone mid-conversation.

I moved the newsletter offices into a tiny moldy basement room without windows in the town of Northfield on the wide main street. The rent was one hundred dollars a month. The office was next to a junk shop. There I was, pushing thirty, shuffling papers, stamping receipts, answering mail, designing the newsletter with pens and graph paper. I went to the small church All Saints on Sundays and listened to a priest who confided in me in his tiny beige office that he was HIV positive. His face was crazed as Van Gogh's and the room vibrated with worry. "Just between us," he said. Classmates announced more weddings. Two classmates died of AIDS. I went to the wedding parties, alone. I brought flowers.

43.

Merrill announced he would come to Minneapolis and read at the Walker Art Center. I drove in from the farm. I rode up the elevator with him to the Walker's glass-enclosed rooftop café. I was nervous to be standing next to a published poet. I was filled with the desire to enter his world. All the doors to all the other worlds kept closing on me: churches, weddings, proper jobs. Minneapolis, with its conglomeration of skyscrapers, glittered out of the corner of our eyes like a jar of fireflies. Intimidated by Merrill's refinement, my Midwest felt provincial. I wanted to apologize for all of it and me and all we represented or what I thought we represented to him in his sophisticated gaze.

"I think I'll read 'The Broken Home' tonight," Merrill said. "It's my old chestnut." He had a surprisingly deep voice.

"Oh, good!" I said perhaps too quickly, saying the words before I could even recall if I knew that poem. Underneath my exclamation was perhaps a part of me that was beginning to feel as if I might already know too much about a broken home.

"I met a young man yesterday who wanted to talk to me. I thought he was going to tell me that he'd fallen in love with the quarterback from his high school: instead he told me about his difficult Chinese girlfriend," Merrill said as his eyes rolled. There was about him an intuitive grace you rarely see nowadays. It's gone along with black-and-white movies and the weird faux-British way Americans talked in those films. He talked like a dead movie star.

His smile was puckish: in his mid-sixties he had maintained a boyish Christopher Isherwood-type demeanor. He had a face that moved to teasing in seconds. His gray hair carefully combed with a part, framed a patrician face you might find in the oil portraits above the heads of students in dining halls in elite New England colleges. The playfulness, bordering on jaded, mixed with the landed-gentry look, created an alchemical spark that welcomed everyone. It was a face that said: *We'll abide by the rules of sitting at the head table while playing footsy throughout the meal.*

"Anyone special in your life?" he asked, solicitously. "No," I said, which was the truth: I'd fielded this question all over the place with various groups. I was a eunuch, neutered by AIDS. I was stiff that evening: I'd outed my brother and I remained closeted. On the subjects of sex and romance, my face pinched like the faces of fundamentalists I saw on TV.

Merrill, heir to the Merrill Lynch fortune, had been rich since he was born, "whether I liked it or not," he wrote. He was the product of the financier's second marriage. In that glittering night, he glittered. He wrote to Edmund White about a poetry enthusiast, "Why does he want to meet us in the flesh? Doesn't he realize the best part of us is on the page and all he'll be meeting is an empty hive?" But the poems came to life meeting Merrill. The poetry business buzzed next to my face. I wanted to feed off the honey. He spoke in his cultured Upper East Side accent, colored by four years at Amherst, years living abroad, and a mother from Jacksonville, Florida. His eyebrows arched. He doled out barbed zingers softened by a Southern chivalry.

On the table, tea candles glittered. Merrill read beautifully to a full house.

Tonight they have stepped out onto the gravel.
The party is over. It's the fall
Of 1931. They love each other still.
She: Charlie, I can't stand the pace.
He: Come on, honey—why, you'll bury us all!

The soft half rhymes of "gravel," "fall," "still," and "all," evoked the melancholy in the Minneapolis fall night air. Half rhymes rather than true rhymes made the sound of their meeting evanescent. I thought of my own parents. I was the child in that poem witnessing the grand mysterious drama of parents, a "marriage on the rocks." The story of his parents ended badly, as I feared my parents' story would, or at least, my story *with* my parents. Despite calamity there was a distance with his language. Detachment had been hard for me to come by with my parents. I was *in* the marriage rather than witnessing it. I sat there hearing of this detachment, more decorously rendered. I was drawn to the grace of his approach. Although the tone was conversational, it was detached, not the intimate "Daddy" of Plath, but instead, "Charlie"—there were other options for me. However, accessing a true voice in the closet was going to be difficult. I could just write poems that had nothing to do with me and escaped self-disclosure.

I called him James, rather than the more endearing "Jimmy," which those closer to him used. That night he made every attempt to blend in. He wore a secondhand green blazer and Birkenstocks that camouflaged his aristocracy. Maybe his deference in manner and dress was partially a result of a life devoted to poetry: what shrives one of excess like poetry, the most money-repellant and fame-discouraging writing life of all?

"And isn't it astonishing," a suburban Midwestern doyenne muttered under her breath, "that a man with so much capital on his hands devoted his life to poetry, when he clearly could have done many other things?" But then, if the muse of poetry laid claim on you what else could you do? My own sense of being claimed was more provisional, and larger uncertainties haunted me. If pushed, if pinned, I'd say I loved poetry more than most things. But I couldn't articulate why or how.

Merrill had the subtle guardedness of someone who "never had to make a living," as he said. Because his living had been made by his father, he possessed a paranoia that most might hope to make their living *off him*. That was a tyranny. But with poetry, he was Benedictine. Poetry had no monetary charge. I steered clear of sounding needy.

44.

Nick Thorndike died. I read the notice in the alumni magazine. I called Nick's mother. I had never done that before.

"I just wanted to call, Mrs. Thorndike, and express my condolences."

We talked about Nick's poetry. His poetry manuscript remained unpublished she thought. "Nick always talked about you, your talent to write poems. I guess it is up to you now," she said in a wistful tone. She didn't want to stay on the phone. Over a divide, miles apart, I said to the phone funneling with grief, "Nick was a great poet."

I called the school, the director of alumni affairs. "What happened? Nick was only thirty or so." All the way from Maine, the line quieted. Then the director said in a hushed tone to me, under those giant white pines, "AIDS, Nick died of AIDS."

Maybe I'd marry. Maybe I could escape gay life. Plath and my father changed their accents. Could I change my sexuality, like a moray eel?

45.

Rich, eccentric, acerbic, flirty, childlike, Cary Grant-suave, worldly, mysteriously living in several locales around the world, fluent in modern Greek, winner of all the poetry prizes one could name, indifferent to religion: Merrill came at me like an evangelist cloaked in nonchalance. This nonchalance was courtly and reminded me of what the sixteenth-century Italian diplomat Baldassare Castiglione wrote in a book on courtesy, "Practice in all things a certain nonchalance, so as to conceal all art and make whatever one does or says appear to be without effort and almost without any thought about it." Merrill was exactly like that. I have a guess where this nonchalance came from.

Years before, the young Jimmy Merrill, wearing his horn-rimmed spectacles, invited Elizabeth Bishop to lunch at a fancy restaurant in New York City. He wanted to talk about her poems much the way I was doing now with him. He naively thought he could spend most of the lunch telling her how wonderful he thought "The Fish" was. There was an awkward pause. The waiter came and went. Bishop didn't want to talk about poetry. She spent all her hours *thinking* about it, she told him, and now she wanted to talk of travel, opera, just about *anything* but poetry. Merrill pondered if it wasn't some kind of superstition that she didn't want to make much of her poetry—that talking about poems jinxed them. That stuck with him.

Merrill was John the Baptist. What was coming after him

would be a larger story. He would disappear. He would not see me enter into the bright world of poetry. Merrill told me, generously, all he knew. He stood before me with high standards and a Mozart-like virtuosity. Such good news. The River Jordan grew wide.

46.

My parents' choices, eroded by drink, got sloppier. My mother lost more friends. Bills went unpaid, houses sold at auction. Frequently creditors called. My mother said in a loud voice, "Don't answer." Any delusion of family inheritance was replaced by news of bankruptcy and foreclosures.

"I'll be going down to Key West soon," Merrill said.

"Oh, my parents have a home down there, I might be going there too," I said, mentioning the home casually, offhandedly, the way rich people did. Would an upper-class stance help me with him? I was willing to try it. It was a half-truth.

"Maybe we can meet then," Merrill suggested. I nodded, but I was unsettled. I was coming to represent the opposite of inherited money: none.

How willing then was I to follow my art? The art that made as much fiscal sense as pastoring? Would I be willing as Herbert was with his priesthood to go and live simply in the country? Would I be willing to wake at four a.m. like Plath before her babies woke to write the poems that made her name? Probably. Probably I would. I couldn't articulate it then but I was in love with poetry. When you fall in love you sacrifice everything to keep love alive.

47.

The day after that reading, we drove to the farm where I lived at the time. The humble Minnesota landscape delighted Merrill. The Midwest hooted and shifted with unseen creatures: foreboding, ominous, capable of sudden, blinding darkness, elms and maples and poplars big as opera stage sets. We lunched and sat out on a small screened-in porch attached to the front of the one-hundred-year-old house and ate stromboli and drank Orangina. He liked the house. He said, "How marvelous, to have this house!" I didn't tell him that the house was built on my mother's financial quicksand.

The farm was no longer a working farm. The government at the time had a program that paid people who owned farms to let them lie fallow so the grain bins wouldn't overflow. This farm fell under that luxury. My mother had befriended a lesbian from the University of Minnesota who on her off days sought to bring the bluebirds back from Mexico. The fallow fields were dotted with several of these bird houses, and in the distance a troop of thoughtful, bird-loving lesbians in hiking boots with binoculars around their necks made bird calls in the weeds. That was going on in the background as my much-desired conversation with Merrill continued: we were in an Iris Murdoch novel.

Merrill spoke of the New York City ballet, his old friend Frederick Buechner, and the virtues of contact lenses. He sensed, perhaps, how defended and self-hating I was: it must have been like being with someone with a bomb duct-taped to his chest. He was ginger in his gay references. Dutifully and ceremoniously, he signed all the books by him I owned. Before leaving, he walked some of the property. Cresting the first knoll, he was out of breath.

"Can we go back?" he said. I took him back into the city. On highway 35W, he shared with me he was deciding whether or not to let his poems *be* in a "gay anthology." The man who'd written elsewhere that the closet had dissolved around him, hesitated to place his poems in the company of others who had left it too. He shared Bishop's dislike of labeling the work.

The Midwest blurred by us: a suburb, a farm, a cow, an elm, another cow, another farm, and one more cow. He wondered aloud about the memoir he was writing and pondered the frankness that prose brings, the unabashed nakedness of it.

"The publisher is saying it might sell millions of copies, much to my mother's horror!" he said. Poetry rarely struck fear into anyone. But memoir? Autobiography? The nakedness of it caused people to react viscerally. Had anyone ever said, "It's just a memoir," with a shrug?

Ariel came out quite quickly: 1965. But US publication of *The Bell Jar* was withheld until 1971. Plath's mother and Hughes argued that the book was a novel, but it backfired: people were convinced it was autobiography. It didn't help that Plath published *The Bell Jar* under the pseudonym of Victoria Lucas and she originally told editors that she wanted the main character to be named Victoria Lucas: she was one step away from naming the character Sylvia Plath. When it was published, Aurelia, her mother, had a heart attack.

I returned to the farmhouse. As I entered the kitchen, I realized Merrill had left his rainbow-colored wool scarf behind, a gift from the poet Mona Van Duyn.

When I called to tell him, he said, "This is good luck; it means we will see each other again." He wanted to connect with me. That meant much. I couldn't articulate that to him. But it kept me going.

48.

Gay men looking like Christ on the cross, eyes turned upwards, mouth a funnel, breath desperate, appeared everywhere. Crowds of beautiful men trailed with their IVs. The dead piled in heaps at the San Francisco morgues. Americans began to speak of their sexualities. Televangelists proclaimed God was punishing gays for their sins. Another former classmate Laurence was in a wheelchair. Another went blind. Another jumped off a building. I did not date in these years. Instead I ordered more magazines in wrapped cardstock covers so the postman could not see the male nudes inside. I feasted on the nudes, devoured them and memorized them like a fanatic with a Bible, and then destroyed them in the guest bedroom at the farm. My sexuality occurred in one wild flurry like a chicken having its head twisted off.

I started to go to the tiny Episcopal church, about the size of a tugboat, in the town of Northfield. I felt comfortable with Episcopalians. Catholics felt strict and dogmatic. My brain needed to roam the way Emily Dickinson's did. In the end, the Episcopal Church was what I knew. Whether they would accept me or not, there was confidence in recalling when to genuflect and when to sing the hymns. At coffee hour the warden said to me: "We have to be careful. They say now you can catch the virus from a toilet seat or from the communion chalice, so we have wipes in the bathroom and we are only dipping our wafers now." I nodded.

I sent letters with my poems to show Merrill, asking for "his surgery" as Dickinson had with her poems on the rare occasions she sent them to Thomas Higginson. It is entirely possible he did not care for my efforts, as I think back now. His responses were circumspect, although they ended with the rallying cry: "Keep writing!" He was a formalist, resurrecting sestinas, villanelles, pantoums, and hundreds of other metrical patterns, and this approach sounded natural in his voice and came to him as easily as tying his shoes. The rhyme schemes were embedded in Merrill like his upper-class accent. Many accompanied him: J. D. McClatchy, Alfred Corn, Marilyn Hacker, Mary Jo Salter, Brad Leithauser, Richard Wilbur, Richard Howard.

Although I would learn from form, I broke my molds. Encouraged by Merrill, I ordered several books on how to write forms from a crazed woman who ran the Grolier bookshop in Cambridge, Massachusetts. This ambassador of poetry was odd. The Grolier, the size of a broom closet, was one of the only all-poetry bookstores in the world. If you went there in person the woman aggressively accused you of shoplifting. Sales were questionable. I ordered books that showed me the forms. Then I practiced them like Czerny scales. With their aid, I worked on forms for years, playing the typewriter a la Frank O'Hara, starting with horrible villanelles on the seven deadly sins and the seven virtues. To encourage my industry, Merrill sent a Smithsonian engagement calendar, inscribed with the rhymed couplet:

> *What does the new year hold for Spencer Reece?*
> *Poems at dawn and nights of stellar peace.*

49.

I confided in Merrill as the situation with my parents worsened: my dependence on them living on the farm, the bank accounts draining, the mortgages mounting. From my heavy rotary dial phone at the farmhouse came tunes of entitlement.

"Oh, dear, that is too bad," Merrill said, when I confided in him after another phone call with my mother—raging into the phone, demanding money from the newsletter accounts. At her suggestion, I'd now hidden the money from her, which she herself had requested. The rupture between who my mother had been and who she was becoming widened: the voice and tone were unrecognizable from those I knew as a child.

Merrill sympathized, but was there fear that *I* might turn to him for money as many had done? I was determined with every fiber of my being never to be a person to ask anyone for money. I was seeing my mother do it with anyone who walked in front of her, and the request was awkward for everyone. I swore never to make people squirm like that. At night, I wrung my hands. Durell coached me on how to get through another day over the phone.

Merrill sent a letter:

> Your good long letter—"awful but cheerful"—is here and I grab the opportunity to send you a shorter one in return. Speaking of awful but cheerful, you must know that is what Elizabeth Bishop wanted on her gravestone. Now a young friend of mine made a pilgrimage to the

Worcester, Massachusetts, cemetery, found the family plot in which he was assured Elizabeth had been laid to rest but no trace of her name on the handful of stones that occupy it. At this point just like that Christopher Robin poem about the King and the Queen who asked the Dairy Maid for butter, my friend telephoned me, I telephoned Frank Bidart, Frank telephoned Alice (Elizabeth's relict) in San Francisco, Alice gave a shamefaced laugh and said, "O, I've been meaning to do something about that"— "meaning" for fifteen years!—so now it seems that the engraver will have to approach the polished backside of Elizabeth's parents' stone which is probably all to the good, since "awful but cheerful" can now appear without any reflection upon them.

This was the story of a relative. I was connected to *something*. Poets formed their family tree based on their art—from Bishop to Bidart to Merrill to me.

50.

Marriage is like a cage.

—MICHEL DE MONTAIGNE

I saw Merrill again in 1993. I was thirty, which made me think of Plath's choice. I marveled at what she'd created in a short time. In comparison I had nothing to show for myself. Merrill was wintering on Elizabeth Street in Key West, near a Black spiritualist church. He invited me to visit. I flew down to spend the spring holiday with my parents in a home soon sold. Mom spent her time in a bathing suit, her skin slicked with suntan lotion, and was on the phone arguing with bill collectors from morning until afternoon. They drank every night. The house where Merrill stayed was owned by his companion of thirty years, David Jackson. The house was a Bahamian shotgun house. Palm fronds brushed against the screens, painting their green blurs. Neighbors were flush with one another. Propellers zoomed overhead, interrupting conversations. In the background, the sound of neighbors loving or fighting or both, and behind that sound, spirituals vibrating the floorboards like tuning forks beneath our feet.

Merrill wrote a poem called "Clearing the Title" about that house. The poem, shot through with the ambivalence connected to his relationship with David Jackson, begins:

Because the wind has changed, because I guess
My poem (what to call it though?) is finished,
Because the golden genie chafes within
His smudged-glass bottle and, god help us, you
Have chosen, sight unseen, this tropic rendezvous
Where tourist, outcast and in-groupie gather
Island by island, linked together,
Causeways bridging the vast shallowness—

This poem describes a gay marriage before that term could be said casually. The title puns: is this a real estate title he is after or is there an allusion to the title change that occurs with a marriage license? Is that not the title that needs to be "cleared" up? I have often wondered. Merrill's epic poem *The Changing Light at Sandover* channels spirits through his Ouija board, and the marriage of Jackson and Merrill is writ large as they are the two men following the upturned cup on the board. Thom Gunn said the poem is "the most convincing description I know of a gay marriage."

This poem is its prelude. Gay life was anything but clear. I looked to Merrill as a pioneer, a man who had cleared some of the way ahead. There I was in the house built by a gay marriage. Would I ever have such a thing?

Merrill liked to remind me that the word "stanza" in Italian meant "room." A poem, then, was like a house. He himself had built a small housing development of his life, using all his forms, with such grace. His life went into his rooms. "Clearing the Title" is a big house of thoughts and sentiment: nineteen stanzas of eight lines each; the first line of each stanza rhymes with the eighth, which gives the reader the impression of the material being bookended. If this poem had an interior decorator the style would be chic clutter. Merrill is barely able to include all the things he would like to put into these rooms; they are packed with artifacts, no wall space is left available, much like the actual décor of his home. The rhyming words in this poem—"behaving" and "waving," "matter" and "patter"—verge on the comical. Later in the poem the rhyming words will be "dead" and "led," "oblivion" and "done," "clean" and "scene": starker words registering another emotional spectrum.

Emily Dickinson once described her thoughts as running around like squirrels, which could apply to this poem too: Merrill, here, discusses interior decoration, alchemy, stray cats, the hippie festival dedicated to the setting sun in Key West, the practice of burying the dead above ground due to the coral rock and the Greek mathematical invention of the Archimedean screw that twists and raises water. But surrounding all the objects and discussion are the two men. Two gay men who have become more roommates than lovers.

Langdon Hammer's biography of Merrill states: "Sexually he was more than a little promiscuous—from say the late 1960s to the late 1970s."

Michel de Montaigne, a sixteenth-century philosopher whose *Essays* merged anecdote with autobiography, wrote: "The ceaseless labor of your life is to build the house of death." At the time I met Merrill he must have been thinking along such lines. I hear this solemn note now in the poem as he starts with his chummy humorous welcome, then lightly refers to something more troubling, then thinks about death.

"Clearing the Title" ends:

(Think of the dead here, sleeping above ground
—Simpler than to hack a tomb from coral—
In whitewashed hope chests under the palm fronds.
Or think of waking, whether to the quarrel
Of white cat and black crow, those unchanged friends,
Or to dazzle from below:
Earth visible through floor-cracks, miles—or inches—down,
And spun by a gold key-chain round and round . . .)

Whereupon on high, where all is bright
Day still, blue turning to key lime, to steel
A clear flame-dusted crimson bars,
Sky puts on the face of the young clown
As the balloons, mere hueless dots now, stars
Or periods—although tonight we trust no real
Conclusions will be reached—float higher yet,
Juggled slowly by the changing light.

Vatic-voiced, the last words of the poem lightly reference his greater, longer work. The speaker observes the clarity of the setting sun and it reminds him of a young clown juggling. The sky wears a mask: a curious metaphor, a clown juggling the whole universe. Merrill's poem is personal until the personal burns off: life's tragedies are greeted by a red-nosed clown; the camera focused on the small drama in the little Bahamian house pans out. What it reveals, by the poem's end, is a long-term gay union, ambivalent in its triumphs. Life is rich and complicated, with space for all. This is the message shot through the hallway of the poem.

"I just finished reading Evelyn Waugh's *Brideshead Revisited*," he told me.

"It's more like a poem than a novel," I said, feeling in the moment that commenting on this lush British homoerotic prose would help unlock the door to more information, more clues I needed to live my life. I thought I was one of the privileged few let into Merrill's inner sanctum. Later I learned there was a horde of acolytes. He'd had the same conversation with Henri Cole.

"Yes, yes, it is," Merrill said in that surprisingly deep voice. I boasted about how I'd just won a poetry prize and read with Galway Kinnell.

Then I said, "But I don't think Galway cared much for me." "Of course not," Merrill said. "What do you mean?" said I, shocked. "You're not twenty-five years old with a wet—" here he referenced a female body part, using a word I knew but could hardly ever bring myself to use. The use of the word was in stark contrast to the elegant forms he trotted out. The word shocked my Midwestern sense of propriety. He said this word with a deadpan expression, pointedly bringing to my attention that it was not anything to do with my poems but my sexuality or my sex that had no interest whatsoever before the handsome lumberjack Lothario Kinnell.

"Right," I said quietly. "There's *that*." The bald comment made me blanch with its frankness. Merrill was touching on my conundrum—me. I was neither a young woman nor a straight man, which offered, I inferred from Merrill's look, no chance to connect to Kinnell. Being marked as different in a way I did not want to be different made me hate myself for what I could not ever seem to undo. Why couldn't I just say it? I was not heterosexual. How difficult some words were for a person devoted to words.

While Merrill was befriending me, his personal life was in

shambles. Because he was reticent, more in life than in the poems, I vaguely sensed this. He said, "There have been a few scenes at home." This reticence I respected. From the accounts we now know Merrill called J. D. McClatchy in New York one night around this time: "Can you come over here now?" When McClatchy arrived, near midnight, the apartment was in ruin. Furniture upended, pictures thrown from the wall, Merrill's bedroom door smashed in, broken lamps all over the place. Peter Hooten, Merrill's new boyfriend, was red in the face, frothing at the mouth, ranting about how bossy Merrill was. Hooten said he'd commit suicide.

In Florida, after my parents drove me into Key West, and I passed all those little mangrove islands Bishop had commemorated in her poem "Little Exercise," Merrill showed me the collection of *OED*s he'd inherited from Auden. "I am sending them all to Sandy McClatchy," Merrill said.

Merrill and Jackson, lived on opposite sides of their house. Chain-smoking Jackson's fingertips had yellowed. Once, long ago, they had been in love. Now Jackson was lugubriously transmogrifying into Miss Havisham out of Charles Dickens's *Great Expectations*: the bride jilted at the altar who wore her wedding dress every day into her dotage. How expectations did indeed smother and disappoint. I encouraged myself to learn from this. I hoped to keep my expectations low with regard to love. Jackson watched cartoons all day, and called in prostitutes. A neighbor dropped by and said in hushed tones, as if speaking of the dead: "He was once an accomplished concert pianist!" Behind the closed door, talk shows, a canned laugh track.

Earlier that year Allan Gurganus introduced Merrill at the 92nd Street Y and said, "He admits without confessing." So he was with me. He was busy with a literary seminar wholly devoted to Elizabeth Bishop, the first of its kind—and he was more intent to talk of Bishop than himself.

I said, "It feels like Bishop's star is starting to rise in the literary firmament, eclipsing Anne Sexton, Robert Lowell, George Starbuck, W. D. Snodgrass... What do you think of Plath?"

Merrill made a face, disapproving.

"What did Bishop think of Plath?" I queried further.

"I remember she was at Harvard then, and she had just read *Ariel* and felt she needed to jump into the pool at Harvard and wash it off her... It was a little too intense for her..." Bishop couldn't embrace Plath's "Beware / Beware. / Out of the ash / I rise with my red hair," and would instead write about "when emotion too far exceeds its cause."

"Be like Keats," he said. "Tuck your feelings into the landscape."

51.

In 1985, my mother bought a home on Cape Cod in a community called Menauhant. She achieved her long-held dream of assimilating into WASP culture. She never qualified for those letters, except the first. She wore a straw hat with flowers in it. Her brother, prompted by a case of beer and the sounds of John Philip Sousa marches, stood on the porch and shouted, "It's all about freedom and don't you forget it!" He'd fought under General Patton in the Battle of the Bulge. He'd freed the camps. What did their Jewish father have to say about that? While her brother shouted, the summer help brought a plastic bucket beside him saying, "Are you gonna be sick?" My mother read her books next to the Knock Out roses. A ferry inched across the horizon to Martha's Vineyard. Waves persisted like the sharp cries of gay men in porn videos. By the time I met Merrill, the five-bedroom oceanfront house sat on the auction block. My uncle was blind from drink. The mortgage payments not met. Sometimes my mother hung up the phone on me in the middle of the conversation. I didn't tell Merrill about any of this.

52

Mary Jo Salter said at the event that night: "Bishop was my teacher at Harvard. She had always called me 'Miss Salter.'" Merrill wistfully chuckled. This proper address was fading from the culture. Salter said, "Bishop wrote on my last assignment, 'I hope Miss Salter will continue to write.'" That brief human contact and encouragement again, a bidding. Salter was writing many poems at the time in various forms. She produced for Bishop a perfect metrical poem about a ballerina. Upon seeing the poem Bishop praised her and then with a pause asked Salter if she might "smudge it up."

The image of the smudged ballerina stayed with me. As I worked and reworked my poetry, as I pulled sheet after sheet from my typewriter, my own poems became a troupe of smudged ballerinas. The smudging, the blurring, aided my art, reminding me nothing was perfect, not any poem and not anything it might describe.

Later, Merrill dedicated a plaque to Bishop at her home at 624 White Street: "it is Elizabeth Bishop's human, domestic presence we need to feel this morning. We who loved and revered her miss her keenly still. And now even the stranger passing through Key West may feel pride to find a great poet's residence so lightly yet so decisively commemorated."

After the commemoration, we went back to his house. Merrill said, "We rather like what Mary Jo is doing these days . . ." The *a* in the "rather" was drawn out: ra*aaa*ther. I feared he probably would never say that about my poems. We had tea and biscuits and he made me practice iambic pentameter by reciting Bishop's poem "One Art." We looked not unlike a bishop and an aspirant to holy orders: the one settled, the other inquiring, wanting to impress. He'd done the same thing with Henri Cole I would learn later. "Go on," he said. My persistence had led me to that moment and I knew, for certain, whatever the outcome, I had been *seen*. I felt seen speaking words written neither by him nor by me.

There was power in what was not said. Much of his gift to me was what he preached without words in the church of literature. He took time with me. "The art of losing isn't hard to master," I began. "So many things seem filled with the intent / to be lost that their loss is no disaster." He stopped me, "To *be* lost," he said. "The accent falls on *be*." I squeamed. I did not like being corrected. But as with most public corrections, I never forgot again where that accent fell. Of the poem, he said, "I just recited it at a funeral."

Because of Merrill, I memorized the poem to keep it closer to me. The more such formal poems I read, the more I saw that these repeating lines and words were difficult to pull off—the poet had to make the writing seamless and effortless and not come across as a dance student trying to count out the beats for the Charleston. Dylan Thomas had written "Do not go gentle into that good night" about his father's dying, which has a beautiful cadence, but upon multiple readings its impact lessened for me, unlike the poem Bishop wrote. Curiously, I read, she wrote it more quickly than most of her others. I couldn't forget that notorious story that it took her two decades to finish "The Moose." And Merrill often reminded me of that story. "One Art" ended:

> *I lost my mother's watch. And look! my last, or*
> *next-to-last, of three loved houses went.*
> *The art of losing isn't hard to master.*
>
> *I lost two cities, lovely ones. And, vaster,*
> *some realms I owned, two rivers, a continent.*
> *I miss them, but it wasn't a disaster.*
>
> *—Even losing you (the joking voice, a gesture*
> *I love) I shan't have lied. It's evident*
> *the art of losing's not too hard to master*
> *though it may look like (Write it!) like disaster.*

"Shan't." That construction had become antiquated by the time she wrote this poem. Trying and failing to hide behind the past, she used a word that was fading from use. This may be the very last time an English-speaking poet uses "shan't," I thought. I loved the complexity of thought and emotion threaded through simple words. Like Herbert.

Poetry, I was beginning to feel, needed to have everything at stake. Each poet achieved this in his or her own way. Plath's clearing her throat in "Lady Lazarus," "Gentleman, ladies / These are my hands / my knees. / I may be skin and bone," is the circus barker, beginning her act. Bishop, with this prim form as her corset, can barely keep emotions contained. Line by line, I felt "master" winning over "disaster," as the meter grew shaky towards the end: only someone with Bishop's confidence could break this form by adding her parenthetical (*Write* it!). She's making fun of the fact that with her villanelle she must write the repeat line but also that she must write the closest she could come to the truth, something she strove for all her life. Part of what gets her close is that the poem also records the act of not getting closer. The merciless repetition that must take place in the villanelle works to repeat her claim that losing things is not a disaster, with each repetition reminding us that losing things *is* a disaster: and who knew that better than an orphan? She breaks her lines in the middle and uses "or" as one of her rhyme words, hiding the formal mastery that is at work here. I felt Bishop be as vulnerable as she could be. As my poems progressed I'd need to do the same. I'd have to keep trying until I got there.

Out the window, the daylight broke apart across the water like confetti. Night fell. The island shimmered like a tin ornament. In the auditorium that night, a crowd surrounded Merrill. His bemused head tilted back. His eyes filled with joy at the celebration of Bishop: "Of all the splendid and curious work belonging to my time, these are the poems (the earliest appeared when I was a year old) that I love best and tire of least. And there will be no others." Joyful, then. Joy stirred in the barn the way it must have stirred in the stable in Bethlehem. Annie Dillard and Mark Strand and Richard Wilbur looked on. The joy was contagious. I looked forward to writing Merrill more about this joy. Joy, a word he said was "rusty with disuse," "deserved and pure." From the darkened balcony that evening, I looked on.

53.

I read his obituary in the *New York Times*. It was February 1995.
Valentine's Day around the corner. Northfield, Minnesota.
I'd received a brief postcard from Merrill in Arizona. Then
I'd heard nothing. Teenagers climbed ladders to Scotch-tape
streamers in gymnasiums for school dances. Lovers placed
boxes of chocolates onto double beds. The newsprint tidily
summarized Merrill's life. Paul Monette, the poet, AIDS chron-
icler, and activist, died four days later. I read *Becoming a Man*
in one sitting. A frankness about being gay kept shocking me,
kept moving closer to me.

Five years with Merrill: the letters, the visits, the convivial
apprenticeship to the obscure art of poems. No more subtly
nudging me with his deep voice that patience was a virtue each
time I reported in on another book competition rejection. He
had the gift of age that is hindsight: he'd seen poets publish
with haste to produce works that shriveled and disappeared.
He did not want that for me. Ever so gently he would suggest
I might not regret waiting to publish. "Elizabeth published
late, and little," he said. No more of his winks that there was
nothing wrong with delay when it came to poetry and being
"between covers," as he referred to publication. Even though
he himself had published young and much, he seemed to value
Bishop's scrupulosity and measured approach when it came to
publishing her work. No more of his recalling Bishop and his
imitations of Lota's heavy Brazilian accent. I would miss much.

Not long after Merrill's death, I read his poem "Christmas Tree." I remembered Merrill saying, "I think I had a bad experience with nature and so I feel a little guilty I've written so little about it." I recall I saw the poem in the slick pages of the *New Yorker*, which had consistently rejected my poems now for over a decade. Yet it actually appeared in *Poetry*. Still my memory places it in the *New Yorker*.

I saw the poem looking like a tree in the way it was typed— nature contained, screwed into a stand, decorated and indoors. The odds of failure are great with any concrete poem but this one, in the shape of a Christmas tree, spoke to me. Artifice did not obstruct meaning.

This stanza was a viewing room, Merrill looking at his own dead body. In that way, the poem was not unlike the poems Plath wrote towards the end of her own life, except Merrill is more withheld. Now more than ever, order and structure provided a strange consolation, as he adopted his measured poise.

The poem went:

★

To be
Brought down at last
From the cold sighing mountain
Where I and the others
Had been fed, looked after, kept still,
Meant, I knew—of course I knew—
That it would be only a matter of weeks,
That there was nothing more to do.
Warmly they took me in, made much of me,
The point from the start was to keep my spirits up.
I could assent to that. For honestly,
It did help to be wound in jewels, to send
Their colors flashing forth from vents in the deep
Fragrant sables that cloaked me head to foot.
Over me then they wove a spell of shining—
Purple and silver chains, eavesdripping tinsel,
Amulets, milagros: software of silver,
A heart, a little girl, a Model T,
Two staring eyes. The angels, trumpets, BUD and BEA
(The children's names) in clownlike capitals,
Somewhere a music box whose tiny song
Played and replayed I ended before long
By loving. And in shadow behind me, a primitive IV
To keep the show going. Yes, yes, what lay ahead
Was clear: the stripping, the cold street, my chemicals
Plowed back into Earth for lives to come—
No doubt a blessing, a harvest, but one that doesn't bear,
Now or ever, dwelling upon. To have grown so thin.
Needles and bone. The little boy's hands meeting
About my spine. The mother's voice: Holding up wonderfully!
No dread. No bitterness. The end beginning. Today's
Dusk room aglow
For the last time
With candlelight.
Faces love-lit,
Gifts underfoot.
Still to be so poised, so
Receptive. Still to recall, to praise.

I loved this poem! It was a shape poem like Herbert's "The Altar," but modern, and just as satisfying. The spirit of the tree coalesced with the spirit of Merrill—"the stripping, the cold street, my chemicals / Plowed back into Earth for lives to come"—all this could've been Merrill, with the Christmas tree and a family tree all ending on the page.

I saw three bachelors—Merrill, the tree, Christ—well, four, if I included *myself*. Merrill's death pushed me to say, "I am one too." Subtle, stoic, Merrill never talked about his hidden diagnosis with me: it did not "bear, / now or ever, dwelling upon." The tree spoke in a way he never could in life, thinly and artfully disguised as Bishop was in "Crusoe in England." Merrill often said how sad he found that Bishop poem, a dramatic monologue about Crusoe, musing on a terrible moment in which intense isolation charged his life. Merrill's poem carried sadness, hidden behind another voice. Merrill pushed closer to memoir in this poem than he had in his *actual* memoir. The tree started with the greens and lights and a star on top. The poem ends at the stump.

The tree's stump got my attention: "today" breaking into "dusk," "time" ending a line, "love-lit" breaking into "gifts," and "so" breaking to "receptive." Simple, one or two syllable words, the grammar truncated, consisting of ten sentence fragments, mimicking shallow breathing. The "to be" verb greeting me at the top of the tree punctuates the poem's end through its absence: "The end beginning. Today's / Dusk room aglow / For the last time / With candlelight. / Faces love-lit, / Gifts underfoot." I count four missing "to be" verbs; "to be," the basic verb of existence, became a ghost right before me on the glossy magazine page.

I wanted to publish poems. I wanted in. I wanted *to be*. In his conversations with me, Merrill expressed hope in ornament. Here, the surface jarred with what was contained inside the tree: his death sentence. "The point from the start was to keep my spirits up," the tree said. That Merrill did.

"Christmas Tree" ended with a sentence fragment: "Still to recall, to praise." "Recall" and "praise" are verbs well known to any Episcopalian. We say them in the doxology and the Eucharist: "*Praise* God, from whom all blessings flow" I'd heard a million times along with "*Recall* his death, resurrection and ascension." What a strange pilgrim with his Ouija board! I thought of Thomas Merton who wrote that faith required "the complete forgetfulness of ourselves." Merrill forgot himself in this tree. Death was pushing him closer to his faith, whatever it was, not anything organized like the Episcopal Church, but *something*. Death was bringing his thoughts sharply into praise.

Langdon Hammer wrote that there was something "high stakes" about Merrill's spiritual beliefs—he was inventing a place for himself. Perhaps *I* might invent a place for myself *within* religion. *Still to be so poised, so receptive.*

What I didn't know: in the time I knew him Merrill had gone to the Mayo Clinic and learned he'd tested positive for AIDS. He'd kept it to himself. He helped me without complaint. I never forgot that.

54.

Snow fell across Northfield. The snow piled up just like the white rejection slips I received from Yale, the Whitman award, the Four Way Books contest. "Try us next year," some anonymous reader said. When I wasn't picking up rejection letters, I was going back to the church basements with their Styrofoam cups and their heroin addicts chewing their lips.

"Christmas Tree" lingered with me. When I went back and reread it twice and thrice I felt I was in the church of poetry. I thought of the poem as I knelt in my pew in All Saints, where the priest preached on Luke, the story of Zacchaeus, the short man. My mind wandered. I wondered how long before the priest showed spots? Christmas had ended, dead trees were pitched onto snowbanks like skeletal steeples. Odd story about Zacchaeus. Odd detail that he is short and rich. The Bible is sparse that way. You have to fill in the portraits yourself. Zacchaeus climbed up the sycamore tree to get a better look, because he did not, apparently, *have* friends to help him. He wants to see Jesus, talk to him, connect, like in an AA meeting. He persisted, alone, was odd, had been rich, made haste, wanted in, wanted to connect, wanted to live. Merrill's "Christmas Tree" poem was that sycamore tree for me. I was Zacchaeus. I wanted a better look. Merrill helped me get there.

"*Holding up wonderfully!*" says the mother in that poem, which resonated with Merrill's mother, who would remain unaware of Merrill's diagnosis. She lived six more years after

Merrill died. As "The Broken Home" eerily predicts, she buried her son. Off and on, Merrill alluded in that lunch in Minnesota with me to the guilt he felt in not having produced grandchildren for his mother. His comments echoed the sentiment he'd rendered in his earlier poem "The Emerald," where he and his mother descended into a bank's basement. The mother wants to give Merrill a ring Merrill's father had given to her. She says "For when you marry. For your bride. It's yours." I knew that expectation and the failure I represented. In the Christmas tree, I saw it again, the disappointment with having a gay child, the genetic end of things, a tree cut down. Nowadays gay men have children. Breast milk can be delivered to your doorstep packed in dry ice. But that was after Merrill.

What remained in my head was the fact that before my parents had moved to Oklahoma City, I had bought a basset hound, a long roll of brown and white fur and love: I named him Bishop after Elizabeth. My mother said, after her fourth glass of wine, "Well, this dog is the only grandchild I will ever have."

55.

In All Saints, the priest swayed in the pulpit. He sweated. He closed his eyes. He looked brittle up there. We all looked on. Parishioners kept singing the hymns in the comfy pews. In the vestry meetings, a church lady argued vociferously about the liturgy being sloppy, people standing instead of kneeling. People took sides as if their lives depended on it. The priest looked distracted. The church shipped him away before he got too sick. His sister, who came to collect his belongings, told me he'd gone to live in a nunnery, where the Anglican nuns were looking after him in a hermitage until he was ready to pass. She didn't offer an address. I didn't ask. One year later, he died.

Keep Fast Hold of Your Parents

56.

At four a.m. I was admitted into the locked ward. At five a.m., in the murmur of the mental ward, the city glittered beyond the sealed plate-glass window like a set of keys. I heard the nurse say, "Harold, put your clothes back on! Harold! *Put your clothes on!*" I hardly slept in that place. I had entered a dead end. I greeted the morning sun: it expanded through the locked glass windows filling us up with yellow. The visiting doctors trudged in and poked me. My blue paper pajamas ripped as I crossed my legs. The air smelled of Windex, bleach, plastic bags, and hospital food. We ate lima beans the color and texture of old chewing gum. A plastic wristband indicated that I belonged.

A nurse entered. "Hello," she said, "my name is Martha Arthur." Uttering her name, she smirked. "My name always sounds so funny to me; my name is a sort of linguistic tongue twister!"

Gray-haired, in her sixties, Martha had a feline quality about her and enormous blue eyes that rolled around comically in her head like the marble eyes of a ventriloquist's dummy. She sat down on the bed with her clipboard. There was something comforting about her.

"I am sorry," I said, as the orderly passed by with pills.

"Why are you sorry?" she asked.

"Oh, I don't want to take up any of your time... I..." I couldn't finish my sentence again. All Reeces had trouble looking at people.

"Would you like to hear a poem?" I said, because I wanted to derail the conversation from the personal and how I got to where I was, which was somewhat ineffectual as she had all my information on the intake form.

"Oh, yes," Martha said, almost childlike, "I love poetry." Suddenly I was back in Ms. Young's English class. I began to recite Bishop's "One Art" as Merrill had taught me. *The art of losing isn't hard to master.*

To tell Martha with her rolling kind eyes that I was a poet with one hundred book rejections to my name seemed unwise. I finished the poem, "I shan't have lied. It's evident..." "I am a crier!" Martha said, pulling out wadded-up balls of Kleenex from her jean jumper.

The following day I was instructed on the art of making moccasins in group occupational therapy. I began to tell Martha the story of how I got to the "sad hotel" as Anne Sexton called mental wards. The story jigsawed the air, as I spoke pieces fell into a coherent scene: "My parents have been drinking so much, so we decided to have an intervention. My aunt and uncle had contemplated such a thing with my cousin, but it didn't work then either. It was a bad idea. I don't know. Maybe I've never had one single good idea in my entire life. My father has gout, my brother helped me, we had the aid of some professionals, I don't know. Maybe it wasn't the right thing to do... But I couldn't go on... It has all been a house of cards, someone was saying. I feel like a failure. I—the thing exploded." Here I stopped sewing and looked out the window.

I went on. I spoke of lawyers, real estate agents, screaming, fighting, my parents' fighting, no longer turned on each other, turning on me. My parents wanted nothing to do with sobriety. I spoke of food on their faces after they ate.

"Where are they now?" Martha asked.

"In Oklahoma City." I'd visited once shortly after they moved there. The visit had been like landing on the moon, the city big and flat, no people milling on the streets, Chickasaw and Choctaw and Arapaho stuck on those reservations made me nervous, all the years of false promises over their land, the lakes all man-made, all murky and brown. I grew separated from my parents, felt as if they were going down. Couldn't fix it.

"Oh, I see by your intake form you come from Northfield. That is where I live some of the time too!" she said tentatively. It was a risk for a nurse to locate her residence with the mad.

"Oh," I said, thinking in that moment of my dog, my cat, and the ringing telephone. "My brother," I went on, connecting the dots from the botched intervention to becoming very alone to my hives to no money to not sleeping to wanting to die once more. I pulled one last thread through the bright beads on the moccasins.

"I am not crazy," I said to Martha. The bell went off for lunch.

57.

Quickly graduating from locked to open unit like a star pupil, I was allowed an electric typewriter, which had to earn the approval of the doctors; there was some thought if I was *still* suicidal, I might swallow the keys. The medical team asked me if I wanted to go on medications for the depression. I declined. I did not feel what was wrong with me was biochemical but situational. The poet John Clare wrote to his wife from the asylum that everyone he was meeting there had "brains . . . turned the wrong way." My brain was turned wrong.

Reciting the poem by Bishop stabilized me. The days out the window showed a city and people moving in it and a set of large elm trees lining a street ready to show the world their résumés. The people on the street looked natural—they had jobs, agendas, cars, mortgages. Bright inhabitants of Saint Paul went by like construction-paper cutouts. How was I going to be a part of it?

Martha said to me, "How is your plan going?" The nursing team kept asking me for "a plan." I needed a plan. The day before they'd whispered behind the nurse's station about my case: one nurse read off a clipboard citing the need for twelve-step groups and a program called Al-Anon. I overheard. There wasn't much privacy on the unit. The nurses knew little about Al-Anon. I was surprised. I was not surprised. I knew about it, but I'd largely avoided Al-Anon, believing one twelve-step group was enough.

"What is Al-Anon?" Martha asked the next day. I was prepared. I'd gone to the in-hospital AA meeting the night before and read a pamphlet on Al-Anon. I, too, was curious. I was open. I did not want to return to my hospital bed without something to read. There were no books in the world of broken brains.

"It sprung off from AA. AA was started by two men, Bill W. and Dr. Bob. Then Lois, the wife of Bill, started to find she *too* had problems . . . So she started forming groups for dealing with those who had been affected by someone else's drinking. It got its name from truncating the two words 'alcoholics' and 'anonymous' . . . They were going to be called 'AA Helpers,' which would have been a ghastly name." I said the last bit with humor, which encouraged me. If I could laugh again, I might get back to the world.

"Well, maybe that is a good idea," Martha said, she smiled at me the way a new friend does.

What was my plan?

"What is your plan?" said Martha, the day of my discharge.

"I will go back, go to meetings, carry on," I said. I did not sound convinced. I sounded brittle. I needed to move on, the insurance companies didn't allow people like me to dally in mental wards the way they used to, in the days of the Confessional poets. Lawyers and real estate agents swarmed over the farm property. I folded my underwear into a plastic bag.

"I don't normally do this, but here is my number in case you should need it," Martha said to me, whispering so the staff couldn't hear.

58.

Emily Dickinson didn't like being noticed. And yet she wanted very much to be seen. These two opposing impulses were always seesawing in her brain. Dickinson, that Amherst sphynx—I thought of her stoic stance when anonymity enveloped me in quicksand and every attempt to be known snapped off like another vine that wouldn't acknowledge me. When she finally sent her letter off to Thomas Higginson, she said, "Are you too deeply occupied to say if my Verse is alive?" Higginson had published an article in the *Atlantic Monthly* encouraging young writers to come forward. Higginson was a Unitarian minister, an abolitionist, and an author. A correspondence began. In a following letter, he asked some about her life. Just how alone was she? She wrote back:

> You ask of my companions. Hills, sir, and the sundown, and a dog large as myself, that my father bought me. They are better than beings because they know, but do not tell; and the noise in the pool at noon excels my piano.
>
> I have a brother and sister; my mother does not care for thought, and father, too busy with his briefs to notice what we do. He buys me many books, but begs me not to read them, because he fears they joggle the mind. They are religious, except me, and address an eclipse, every morning, whom they call their "Father."

Dickinson needed family as she was rebelling against them—her alienation was bound to and twined *around* her family, a distinct helix of support and isolation, she needed to write what she wrote. I understand that.

The gay organist (was every church organist gay?) came in to pick me up and take me back to Northfield. In my humiliated state, I felt I could trust a gay Christian more than anyone else to pick me up from the doors of the insane asylum. I was trusting him to keep this to himself and not turn me into church gossip. He had a bald head, large horn-rimmed glasses, and a thin wrinkled neck. He looked like a turtle. We did not speak all the way home as we drove into the empty Midwest countryside. On the long drive home, I thought about the aunt who'd lived her whole life separated from the world in a mental institution. Lowell and Plath and Sexton had made much poetry from their mental stays. I would not. The stories of McLean had riveted me in my youth, imagining my mother walking past Plath with a chart or a pill tray. But now I knew what it felt like to be turned inside out and have people see that, and I never wanted to experience it again. I had more compassion for the inconsolable. I was now more likely to change the conversation if the topic came to mental illness than to delve into it. Something of that world might enter my typewriter, but I felt tentative: the days there were *not* romantic or poetic, and I could not find any winsome enthusiasm to speak to the organist about it. I was glad to have left it. I would be happy never to see it again.

The farm with its seven outbuildings sagging had been waiting—the granary, the machine shed, the barn, the outhouse, the chicken coop, the garage, and the wee house. The house was yellow with blue shutters and a red roof. The house made me happy. It was like looking at a Christmas tree orna-ment. The farm! In the three years I'd sequestered myself there, many poems had come to me. Being alone suited me, as it had Dickinson, yet, also like Dickinson, I was tethered to family. Like Dickinson's parents, mine not only tolerated a poet in their midst but made allowances.

The farm then had one hundred acres of rarely explored nature. The nature inspired me the way a church might. Dick-inson wrote her famous little triplet:

> *In the name of the Bee —*
> *And of the Butterfly —*
> *And of the Breeze — Amen!*

This benediction Dickinson winds up like a toy to crawl across the floors of anthologies: its simplicity belies its com-plexity. She's genuflecting in the name of nature. She's a priest in drag, irreverent and reverent in the same breath. I'd seen such raw nature in those years on the farm: snakes had come out of the heating grates one spring like strings of spaghetti; I'd heard wolves howl; I'd encountered a deer in a clearing that had actually let me touch it; the land oozed God. I'd have been quite happy never to see the inside of a church after a spring there. I felt at home there. This was a raw hospital I wanted to be in. Bats had cradled and crammed their families into the timbers and crevices of the buildings. They bleated at twilight in all the nooks of that place. Their urine and feces caused all the roofs to sink in the centers, which gave the place an ambi-ence of inertia. I'd die happy there.

Dickinson wrote:

The Meadows — mine —
The Mountains — mine —
All Forests — Stintless stars —
As much of noon, as I could take —
Between my finite eyes

Mine, returning from the city, as the car crested the top of the drive, all the raccoons, squirrels, muskrats, moles, voles, chipmunks, field mice, badgers, weasels stopped and noted my return. I put down my luggage and greeted my cat, named Frank, after O'Hara, and my basset hound Bishop, after Elizabeth. I loved my sanctuary.

The phone rang. "We are selling the property," Mom said.

"But I thought this was to stay in the family," I said. "I thought that—"

"It was," said Dad, also on the line.

"Not anymore," Mom said. "How many times have I said we are private people? That kangaroo court you put us through was the last straw."

Mom, unhinged, sliding down the walls, unbalanced, wringing her hands, tulips waving from the basement window—that is what I remembered of her. My heart plummeted.

"What is your plan?" Martha had asked.

"To keep the farm," I had said.

Once more, I argued with my parents. I lost ground. Illogical haranguing depleted me beyond measure. Bishop had once said, "I've never seen the point of, or been able to endure, much argument."

59.

Early evening darkened the kitchen. Bishop blew through his jowls and looked at me with satisfaction. He stepped on his long ears and tripped. Frank looked at the two of us with detachment, fat and gray, more like an owl than a cat. Had they talked to one another in their animal language and agreed to watch over me that night? I sat at the kitchen table in tears. I was having trouble sleeping. I was having trouble not sleeping. I paced the rooms. I did not want to commit suicide. I picked up the phone and called Nana back in Connecticut knowing her dementia kept swallowing her brain.

"Nana?"

"Hello, darling, is that you?"

"Your daughter is doing terrible things," I said.

"Is this the police?" Nana said.

"I can't stay on the farm much longer, Nana," I said.

"Is this the police?" asked the old voice.

"I love you, Nana." I said, and hung up the phone. Darkness covered the kitchen floor and Bishop and Frank kept vigil over me one more night. Both slept next to my body during the night as I wept. The tears were not for me.

60.

I called the secondhand bookshop in Northfield and asked the owner to come out to the property. I sold every book I owned and my mother's recipe books from which she had made her merry meals. Selling my mother's books turned my entitlement into a bayonet. I didn't grasp that yet. I put the money in my wallet. "I *love* that dog," said the bookstore owner as we carried out our transactions and he packed up the truck with all my books of poetry—the collected Frank O'Hara I got at the Grolier with the olive-green cover, all the edges of the cover missing like an old Giotto fresco, Elizabeth Bishop's slim *Geography III* with the edges turned up like the corners of a kitchen linoleum floor when one has spent years walking across its surface, Plath's *Collected* with the copper curlicue cover, Theodore Roethke's book with the primary-colored tree cover, Galway Kinnell's Klimt cover with his line repeating, "When one has lived a long time alone," James Wright's *Collected* with the "I have wasted my life" poem, an anthology of younger poets with little black-and-white headshots of Carolyn Forché, Rita Dove, Cathy Song, David Wojahn: I'd memorized their biographies the way boys used to with baseball cards, all of them. I smelled like the books and the books smelled like me.

The owner again looked at the dog. Behind the truck of books, the empty iced Minnesota rivers shook like drawers of knives being pulled open and closed. "Would you like the dog?" I said. The sky above big and cold. The trees were bereft.

The bookstore man paused, and he said: "Really?" "Yes," I said, "I can't take him with me where I am going." He pulled the dog into the front seat. Bishop's eyes tracked me. I looked away. The bookstore owner drove down the gravel road shaking his head and singing. Bishop bounced among the poetry books. Bishop bayed. Bishop grew small among the huge gray hills, some Indian burial mounds, and the steel blue lakes. Winter was coming. An hour later I gave Frank away.

I stood in the empty kitchen with the uneven floor. I felt uneven. I couldn't go down emotionally now, I said to myself. I looked at the paper with Martha's number that I'd left on the fridge with a magnet. I held my breath. I called Martha Arthur. Into the white rotary-dial wall phone in the kitchen of the now empty house, darkness coming on, I said: "I can't stay here any longer."

"Well," she said, "Robert and I have a room here. It isn't much, but you are welcome to it."

"Can I come now?" I said. Upstairs the rejection slips settled into the wastepaper basket. The black embers of the *Playgirl* magazines rustled in the fireplace.

"Now?" she said, children in the background, grandchildren, a TV on, someone playing the piano, a house with life in it. She did not pause.

"Yes," I said. It was one of the few deliberate decisions I had made.

"Come now," she said. I took nothing.

61.

I went to church but I couldn't see myself a part of it. The hymns cheered me. Robert Arthur, Martha's husband, British, had gone to Keble College, Oxford, and was a Quaker. He looked like an eagle, sharp blue eyes that surveyed social situations searching for spaces where he could hold forth and speak. He was the best talker I'd ever met: he could talk about anything from business to poetry, history or physics. He liked me for some reason, and he loved to talk about both world wars and a new life in America and his children and many other subjects. I loved to let him talk, because I had little to say, but occasionally he made space for me to recite memorized poems. He liked it when I did so. He had a birthday once in a hotel and I was the featured performer. I did William Blake's "Jerusalem," William Shakespeare's "Sonnet 18," and Jane Kenyon's "Let Evening Come."

I fastened on to Robert and Martha in those days without my family. A legal battle ensued over my unemployment benefits. I had worked for my father for three years and now they did not want to pay out benefits. After the intervention, they'd wanted me fired. Robert paid for the lawyer to defend me with a major firm in Saint Paul. At this my parents backed down and let the benefits stand. This money saved me in days when I had little. The insurance companies would carry me just ten days on the mental ward and I needed a much longer recovery from grief. Robert and Martha made that possible. I laughed with them. We went to concerts together. The Arthurs had six children and a string of grandchildren between them—it was a second marriage for both, and somewhere there in the family photographs you will find me, bespectacled, tall, thin, having just left the house of madness.

The Arthurs kept a distance from All Saints. I encouraged them to go: I intuitively felt they'd fit. Martha and Robert *took* to the place, joined the choir, sat in the front row. One day, after dinner, Martha said: "Robert and I went out to Valley Grove and we bought grave plots. We bought three. Three spots. One for Robert. One for me. And, well, one for you . . ." Three spots, under a maple tree, in a graveyard out of town, on a hill, with two churches, abandoned, that faced each other, like two old people talking in a nursing home.

The Arthurs never said anything about my sexuality. They must have speculated. I could not bring that part of myself to public utterance. Dickinson wrote in her letter to her brother's wife, Susan Gilbert:

> Now, farewell, Susie, and Vinnie sends her love, and mother hers, and I add a kiss, shyly, lest there is somebody there! Don't let them see, will you Susie?

I appreciated deference.

62.

During the days I took many long walks. I'd go for hours in that melancholy college town, walking without speaking, past comfy homes, families, dormitories, little coffee shops. I walked. I walked. On one of these walks I befriended Karen, in a copy store in town. A drifter like me, she had moved to the town from Virginia on a second marriage that faltered, had a kindness, had a Southern sense of suffering, had the generosity the poor possess in large quantity, had smoker's eyes that squinted. "There's a space here if you need to write," she said.

At her invitation, I took up part-time residence in the copy shop. The copy shop was a makeshift, prefab building that might have been a gasoline station beforehand. The floor plan made no sense: a large room, followed by a triangular room. I worked in the back, drank as much coffee as I wanted, and once more began to work on my book of poems, on a computer large as a bee box.

I sent the poems out in batches of three or five, folding them twice, attaching paper clips and enclosing an SASE or an IRC ("international reply coupons"). Someone, I hoped, opened them. Someone I hoped read them. Someone then sent them back in my envelope I provided and I was never sure if they were read or not: often attached was a xeroxed rejection slip. Every single one of those envelopes came back to my continued dismay—month after month, year after year, like dutiful homing pigeons.

Out the window the Cannon River tumbled, glinting, rushing. We sat with our coffee, for business was never quick, and pondered life without saying much. There was a boss who occasionally visited. Somehow the boss accepted me as part of the business he bought. I typed up poems, some of the same ones I'd been working on at the farm. The sun set early there, gently covering the little town's brick buildings in orange. On the graveyard on the hill south of town, elms and oaks and maples shuffled their leaves in a dim light. Inside the graveyard, those two churches stood abandoned and collapsing. A place for me. A place to be "called back" as it is written on Dickinson's gravestone.

63.

After three gentle years living with Robert and Martha, I found wee bits of work here and there on radio stations and for newspapers. Robert patiently coached me about job interviews, spoke in his caricatured British accent, which included his *r*'s rolled. "Now, my dear boy," he began. I loved that he loved me. Some missing piece of me was filled in. We rehearsed my interview for an English teacher's position at my old high school.

"You're applying for the English position?" said a chipper woman. Ms. Young had married, had a child, her life long flown from there.

"Yes. I . . ." I said.

"You know you have to be tough with these kids," said the woman interviewing me. She was saying something else instead of that, she was doubting I could handle teenagers. *I seem fragile*, I thought.

"I have this poem I like . . ." I said. Outside the football team grunted. Students passed by. I got the creepy feeling they were laughing at me. I felt out of time. I was the leper from the Gospel of Mark, caged in smelly skin. My head flooded with images of John Steven, bloated and purple. Nick Thorndike covered in cancer spots waved from the window. I began:

I'm Nobody! Who are you?
Are you — Nobody — too?

Then there's a pair of us
Don't tell! they'd advertise — you know!

That Dickinson tune: almost all her words here are one syllable, lonely notes, true notes. We know she loved to improvise on the piano and she took some of that energy when she came to improvising her hymns. They have the habit of changing meaning, suddenly "nobody" takes on an authority I never thought it had before. I realized as I sounded out her score no one was going to be advertising *me* any time soon. I felt dizzy. Why couldn't I fit into the world? I had enough paranoia to think the lady interviewing me knew I'd been in a psychiatric ward. I wondered if I gave off a scent of the mad or half-mad or post-mad. I paused too long after the first stanza. The interview was not going well. Questions were asked. I grew stiff. The lady looked over my shoulder at the clock.

"We'll get back in touch soon," she said in a wooden way as the bell rang and the currents of children streamed by, nimbly advancing to their futures.

I went back to Robert and told him things had not gone well. I printed out a new set of résumés in the copy store with Karen. With less than five hundred dollars in the bank, I had my name listed at the food pantries. I had radio work. I had invitations to AA parties with the plastic silverware and paper plates and the sugary frosted cakes for anniversaries. Such was my estate. I knew the government subsidies and Karen's largess couldn't hold forever. I drove to the Mall of America thirty-five miles north of the town: woods and cows and farm fields replaced by big slabs of concrete, parking lots and office complexes for medical practices. I'd driven Merrill right by these same scenes: we'd laughed about poetry and how cozy I felt in the world then. Now there was no money. Or little. Less than four digits on any given inquiry. Now there was no time to imitate Merrill's upper-crust accent.

The manager for Brooks Brothers, Mary Beth, lived in Northfield. She had said to me on numerous occasions in the coffee shop to visit her if I ever needed work. When I showed up, résumé in triplicate, she asked: "Why are you applying for a job here?" Originally from New Jersey, she had a delightful smartass way about her, professional with a wink.

She said, "You went to Wesleyan and Harvard."

"Because I need to leave this building today with a job," I said.

"Just for the Christmas rush," we both agreed.

64.

Continually getting rejected from book competitions, about ten to fifteen times a year, I started working then in the Mall of America, the world's largest mall, a battleship stalled on the prairie. I became a boarder, renting a small room. I drove my beat-up car into work and it looked like a rowboat against the mall's gunwale.

Most days, I spent my whole working day next to Ralph, an effeminate sales clerk I'd brushed up against in high school. When Dad and I bought shirts before I left for college, Ralph waited on us. In high school, I hoped I would never resemble anything close to this man with his multiple gold bracelets, his foundation makeup smearing the phone receivers. Now we made a father-and-son team.

The numbing feel of the mall, the smell of the industrial carpet, the endless glass fronts, the merchandise, repelled and comforted me. The mall world felt stilted, arranged as a terrarium. I missed the farm. Rem Koolhaas, an architect, called such places "junk space." Junk space it was, no redeeming aesthetic anywhere. I was part of the junk. But my bills were paid.

Mark Spencer Reece at your service. My first and second names echoing Marks and Spencer, which then owned Brooks Brothers. My name predicted my career.

We, the retail workers, moved around the cramped, windowless back of the store breathing in recirculated air as if we were on a submarine. We worked under great stress. Usually the customers forgot who had helped them, our names, our look, our gender. Many customers came from my old country club neighborhood.

"How am I supposed to remember if the person that waited on me was a man or a woman?" an exasperated customer yelled into the phone. That caught my attention. Arthur Miller's line from *Death of a Salesman* came back to me, "Attention must be paid." I jotted down notes about the place, about Ralph, on the backs of receipts.

65.

In my off hours, I hung my dress slacks over the chair. On the desk, my piles of poems, which I kept in a black three-ringed binder—my cathedral of toothpicks.

Dickinson wrote not long after the Great Awakening and during the time of the Second Great Awakening, two waves of a religious movement that spread across America, as Mormons and many other groups began to question organized Christian ritual and ceremony. Revival tents in the woods. People spontaneously converted. People wept the moment the preacher George Whitefield said the word "Mesopotamia." The sounds out Dickinson's window echoed with religious fervor. John Wesley had people preach who were not ordained. The Second Awakening reached out to the unchurched. Mormons and Seventh-day Adventists came into their own. In all this swelling of spirit, Dickinson, unordained, began to have her own open-air services attended by none but she. Working on the poems I felt that self-appointed industry she felt, an unwatched pleasure.

Months before she died Dickinson called herself a "Pugilist and Poet." Her "I" wore boxing gloves into the ring of her poems. She expended a tremendous amount of effort to go it alone. She had lived a hermit's life, like the fourteenth-century beguines, medieval laywomen who formed their own monastic lives and owned their own houses up until the French Revolution. She took to wearing white dresses. Some categorize her as eccentric, others neurotic or agoraphobic. Yet when women were invisible, Dickinson's aloofness gave her the space and time to write her titleless, dash-laden, unexpectedly capital-ized poems. Eighteen hundred in all. These existential hymns with their menacing, nursery-rhyme tone buck the Church, disregard authority, and are on the whole unfazed by Christian salvation. She sang to me.

66.

"What are you doing here?" said Mrs. Lyman from Country Club.

"I needed a job."

"But you went to Bowdoin, right? Our son went there too."

"Yes," I said.

"Well, why are you here then?" she persisted.

"I had an intervention on my parents and it didn't work, and they live in Oklahoma now." As I told this story my manager's eyes were on me to sell something. My own voice repulsed me. I needed a *new* story: I was sick of apologizing for my existence. Mrs. Lyman went off with her packages.

I worked shift after shift with Ralph. I worked there one year and a half. Ralph had been the top seller for twenty years, but I put him into second place. I could sell. I realized if I talked about everything but the clothes I could hold the interest of the customer. I asked about their families and their jobs. I acted the way my mother did in a cocktail party: she was a great listener in those days. Why did I work so hard, pick up extra shifts? I needed to prove something in that hospital of clothes. I went through three pairs of dress shoes and worked double shifts. Anger and self-hate drove me. I out-fairied the fairy.

After the conversation with Mrs. Lyman a voice in my head said, "Time to go." Was that God's voice? Surprising. Minneapolis is a rooted community, families stay there for generations, go to their cabins, live in the same house forever. But we weren't *from* there. We had been impostors: we had tried desperately to fit in. We had failed.

After that long year and a half of double triple shifts, I went into the backroom where we counted the money and looked at the laminated list of stores for Brooks Brothers across the country from New York to Los Angeles. All places in wealthy communities from Atlanta to Kansas. I'd probably seen the list a thousand times but never looked at it. I now had this skill that identified me and was more valuable than literary talent, which the regular arrivals of anonymous rejection slips suggested I might not possess anyway.

On the list was Palm Beach, which I associated with F. Scott Fitzgerald. Store 28. That night I consulted briefly with Durell by phone. He okayed this idea of moving. Ten minutes later I contacted a friend in Delray Beach who'd been encouraging me to visit. He said I could stay in his spare room for ten days. Then I contacted the store and they said they couldn't promise me a job, but if I showed up they might have an opening. I mentioned to Mary Beth and Ralph I was considering this move, but as happened in retail, they were busy with lines of customers: my news barely registered. They nodded. Flimsy as it sounded, I pushed ahead.

The following day on my dinner break, I altered my life. I bought a one-way ticket to Palm Beach County International Airport. I felt as if I'd jumped off a building. "One way?" said the clerk.

Before the break was up, I said into the phone to Durell from the back of the store, "Store 28: Palm Beach."

"That sounds good," Durell said. He breathed heavily. He sounded distant. He'd stopped going to meetings.

"I bought a ticket. I'm going," I said.

"You can't keep a good man down," Durell replied. He sounded wooden, changed, bereft. He had mentioned recently that his eyesight was failing and that he wasn't always making it to the bathroom. Nurses had been coming to visit. I wanted to ask why wasn't the golden promise of happiness of AA he'd told me so much about working for him, but I didn't.

Then he said: "I am a little short on money this month." They paged my name. A customer was waiting for a trouser fitting with a special-order suit that had gone terribly wrong. I ignored the page and kept talking to Durell.

"I don't have that much myself," I said. Ralph lit a cigarette and looked impatient—it was time for his break.

"That crazy man is out there waiting for you," Ralph said. What awaited me was an eighty-year-old cantankerous man shaped like a pear who was trapped in his suit and stumbling around the fitting room as if he was in a game of Twister. My name kept being paged. "Spencer to the floor . . . Spencer to the floor . . ."

"After all the time I have spent with you," Durell said, bullying. "More than a therapist would spend with you." I looked at Ralph, looked at the clock. I did not want to be abandoned.

"I'll get something in the mail to you this week," I said.

The following day I gave Mary Beth my notice.

67.

Good-bye. Good-bye. Never had been to Palm Beach or the famous Worth Avenue, but I figured there might be more air and light, even if between the cracks of mall doorways and out back doors for receiving merchandise. I sold all my winter clothes. I packed two suitcases. Good-bye. Good-bye. Said good-bye to Ralph and Mary Beth, emptying my tiny locker next to the lunch room. I said good-bye to Robert and Martha, which was difficult. Good-bye. Good-bye. Left the key on the entry table to the room I rented. Made reassuring sounds, I'd see you or you or you soon. An old friend from prep school drove me to the airport. Good-bye neighborhoods of Minneapolis, with streets whose names I knew by heart: Browndale, Bridge, Moorland, Bruce. What would be at the other end? Time to remake myself. Good-bye. Good-bye. Like that I was gone. Twenty-five years in Minnesota, the burial plot, the farm, the house in Country Club, the orange school bus, all gone. Good-bye. Good-bye. The airport buzzed, planes ascended, planes descended. I boarded my plane. I fastened my belt. We catapulted into the atmosphere. Minneapolis shrank, Minnesota shrank.

Minnesota, clean, practical, with cold streams and canoes and pines and hockey teams. Good-bye. Good-bye, green squares that make up that deep rich land, a square where once I nearly poked my brother's eye out.

Dickinson wrote:

The brain — is wider than the sky —
For — put them side by side —
The one the other will include
With ease — and you — beside —

Her brain her sky. Thoughts skimmed across her mind like flat rocks thrown across its surface, her dashes emphasizing her rapid skips. Dickinson stayed in her house. Her poetry achieved an astonishingly wide circumference inside her home. What would losing my home do for my art?

68.

The Florida sun sizzled the dew on the puzzles of the ficus hedges. Bright-green parrots in the gumbo limbo trees sang. The sea sparkled in the bright light like crushed glass.

I interviewed for store 28 and they *did* hire me. I was Peter in the boat: I had to look ahead and trust and trust, holding off any false tremble of fear, or I'd sink in the water. But hadn't my life been built on such unlikely improbable physics? Accidents formed the best of me.

I began work in Palm Beach County, Florida. I found a modest apartment in Lantana after one week. My whole apartment could have fit inside Dickinson's bedroom. The tiny kitchenette, sitting area, and bedroom were in one of those old Florida motels. "State with the prettiest name," Bishop said, in her understated way, about perhaps the most overstated state in America. People make fun of Florida: Disney, heat, no culture. I called Durell every other day or so, between my shifts, giving him updates on how my Florida life was going, how happy I felt in this strange and tropical world where the people made up who they were. Sometimes now I regretted calling him because it had become a recital of complaints followed by requests for money to be sent. When he mentioned his estranged brother and sister now, he cried. I didn't think anyone had heard this man cry.

I settled on that peninsula of flowers and bees flamboyant as a million Liberaces. Improbably, there, between all the strip malls and strip clubs, I began to entertain the idea of Christ as a companion. Durell encouraged this investigation. He'd attended church in youth, had played the organ, but in the intervening years he'd grown estranged from the Church. Our unspoken difference from the heterosexual world had everything to do with it. The idea of Christ as something I could meld to my life, something practical, began to make sense to me. I started going to church on Sunday. I sat in the back. I didn't have a Bible.

69.

What was I doing in retail? Years mounted. Fifteen times each year, the book of poems got rejected. I worked long shifts at Brooks Brothers. I ate a sandwich on my lunch break in the windowless room behind the store. I went to AA. I did not speak to my family. My face fixed into broken sadness. On Sundays, I went to church. My approach to the Church was like Dickinson's: I was outside it, looking in. Her church was in her head, not at a pulpit. Religion failed her, and for a long time it failed me.

In Mount Holyoke Female Seminary, where Dickinson spent one year, the young women were divided into three self-designated categories: "no hopers," "hopers," and "Christians." The last group was the largest; they were women who testified to a certainty for salvation. There were 230 Christians, fifty hopers, and the remaining thirty were "without hope." By the end of the year many of the thirty no hopers found hope, but not Dickinson. She wrote: "I am not happy . . . and I regret that . . . I did not give up and become a christian." Of all the words she capitalized, here she failed to capitalize "christian." The Bible was read at great length in her house. She will quote the Bible in her poems and letters more than any other work.

If religion failed her, she remained industrious at home with her writing about all things Godly. Although fewer than a dozen of her 1,800 poems were published in her lifetime, she sent out 575 of them in letters. She wanted to share those poems. I wanted to share mine too.

I went up to Palm Beach for church, where the rich ladies nodded their heads with enormous hats. I wore cream worsted-wool trousers. There was lots of decorum, and Christ mainly felt decorative. Like Dickinson I could grab on to the idea of his suffering more than any promise of salvation. I was not convinced he would want to save me. Maybe these nice rich ladies, but not me.

Left to myself when the shifts were done, I snapped at coworkers or customers who alluded to my being gay. Was I nothing more than an irritable closeted effeminate retail assistant manager estranged from family who had a passion for poetry—ridiculous peacock with a thousand Brooks Brothers ties fanning out from me?

70.

Durell was admitted to Brigham and Women's Hospital in an ambulance. Then the apartment building evicted him. Rent control ended in Cambridge. He remained in the hospital bed and then he moved to a ward somewhere. He had no phone. A social worker called me as I was listed as next of kin. The social worker said Durell was bedridden, close to blind.

71.

Years zipped by my Lantana mirror. I was on a carousel. Each time I rounded another year on my plastic horse I was balder and more worn-down. I circled the months and years with a routine of driving to work, working shifts, going to the gym (one of the main cultural activities in Florida, where "body-sculpting" was a verb people put into sentences seriously), paying bills, riding my bicycle, walking the beach, reading books, writing book reviews for the local newspaper, and writing poems that collected in the apartment like desiccated moth wings. Predictability created a certain solace in me. I was suddenly forty. Or was I forty-one? I shrugged, realizing then I was done applying to the Yale Younger Poets prize: the cutoff was forty. At that moment in time I had submitted my manuscript, revising constantly, about three hundred times to national book competitions. I had become a sweet machine, a poetic baseball-pitching machine, my manuscript catapulting onto anonymous desks across America. From time to time I'd receive xeroxed rejection notes and *sometimes* even the xeroxed note had actual handwriting by a human that said, "Enjoyed some of these!"

Folding down the sale cashmere-sweater table after Christmas I told myself sternly that I needed to give up: "You don't know anyone," I told myself. "You've given this poetry publication thing more than a reasonable try and it is time to forget about it." I convinced myself that day to apply for the manager job in Bal Harbour, although my heart was not in it. My heart hadn't been in it for a long time. I sent the paperwork off.

I drove home in my blue Dodge Neon with the hand-crank windows rolled down: the AC had gone years ago. I chewed gum to stay alert. I whizzed by strip malls, pawn shops, sex clubs, down into Lantana, which sits south of Palm Beach, a community of servants and workers who cater in one way or another to the rich. I spit the wad of gum out as I made the final turn off 95W. Parked in the big parking lot, walked up the outside staircase to my apartment. Palms blew. My feet ached from my dress shoes. In my hand my keys, my mail containing credit-card bills I couldn't pay off and a bag with a new Brooks tie. Management from New York had encouraged us to wear more Brooks ties. Kicked open the door and microwaved dinner. On my answering machine, on the unfinished door from Home Depot that served as my desk, a red light blinked. Stacks of poems around me.

The message played. "This is Michael Collier. I am calling for Spencer Reece. If this is the phone number for Spencer Reece can you please call me back at your convenience? I am from the Bread Loaf Writers' Conference." Played the message again. Then a third time. A fourth. And a fifth time. Maybe ten. The train went down the tracks and shook the apartment. In this room with the lime-green shag carpet was a poster I had framed of Lance Armstrong. He was my hero. His perseverance.

I held myself in check. Disbelief. Apprehension. They were calling me because I was the runner-up. Isn't that what they did? If you won they'd just send you a letter. I could not assume I had won after fifteen years of waiting, only to be told the following morning I did not win.

Dickinson wrote in poem 112:

Success is counted sweetest
By those who ne'er succeed.
To comprehend a nectar
Requires sorest need.

Not one of all the purple Host
Who took the Flag today
Can tell the definition
So clear of victory

As he defeated — dying —
On whose forbidden ear
The distant strains of triumph
Burst agonized and clear!

I'd counted and counted my rejections from magazines, from contests, from grants, from prizes. I felt a complete failure.

I played the message again. It made me—I'm hesitant to say nervous, because that sounds negative, and what was in me was nerves, yes, but also excitement. I took a bath to soothe my aches. I didn't sleep much. By four I was wide awake and thought of how Plath had written much of *Ariel* at that hour in cold London. Bless Plath. She was with me.

The morning before my shift the sun laid down its bacon strips across the bright sea that sizzled into another Florida day of sweat and tang and salt. I made coffee. People started going to work in my neighborhood: keys clanging, kids sighing with backpacks, van doors sliding shut. Lance Armstrong on his bike stared at me from the poster. I talked myself into behaving as though this was any other day. I dialed the number.

"Hi, this is Spencer Reece, is this Michael Collier?"

"Spencer Reece?" said Michael in an affable way, like the guys at the fraternity parties who used to throw me out when I got too drunk.

"Yes, it's me," I said, waiting.

"Well, you won. We're calling to say you've won. Louise Glück is the judge and she wants to know if you are willing to work on edits with her before the book goes to press." Pause. Silence. I stood. I did not know what to say next. *Are you nobody too? Then there's a pair of us.*

This moment. The nectar of acceptance, the flag of victory. In that moment, my Florida was a church. Stillness in the air. Time slowed as it must have for Lance Armstrong on that bike, his bike chain clicking. Silence had been a faithful partner to me, more than any man I attempted to date. I thought of my compatriots in the nuthouse. Were they making moccasins? I thought of Martha Arthur. My plot. I thought of Robert Arthur, tutoring me before interviews: "You can do this, my dear boy!" The streets where I lived in Lantana accompanied me. The sun expanded, yellowing things.

"Hello?" Collier said.

"Yes. I am here."

"Well?" he asked.

"Sure, sure, I will speak to her." I smirked as I said this because my perverse sense of humor imagined myself saying, "No, that's okay, I'm happy to wait here in Lantana another fifteen years."

Fifteen years I had waited for that call—in the cell of myself, as Dickinson waited, as Julian of Norwich waited, waiting in the corporate conference calls with New York on why we weren't "making plan," waiting in the business meetings for AA and Al-Anon and deciding whether or not we could take coffee into the church room with the carpeting. I'd waited evening after evening in that apartment and listened to the freight trains click-clack down the tracks, the way Dickinson had heard the train hooting near her home in Amherst. As so many characters do in the Bible, from Adam and Eve to John waiting for revelations in his cave, I had been waiting, like everyone who waits in that big book. Faith lurked. Spirit. Something of a communion with others, a change Dickinson never knew. She said once that publishing her poems would be like publishing her soul. Well, it was. Scab ripped off. What life looked like after that Dickinson never would know. I would.

I slid down the wall in the second bedroom with the ugly green shag carpet the same way my mother had slid down the wall in despair when I was young. But now, hope—feathered, fluttered. Hope was in the air. This fundamental recognition, which Dickinson pondered and scoffed at in the same breath, was now coming to me. Was it a grace I was older? Probably. Success can surprise us with its challenge when we're accustomed to failure. I was in waters Dickinson never charted. It remains sad to me that Dickinson never knew she would be cherished.

Dickinson had written back to Higginson, with more insolence, once she realized he wanted to tidy up and change her verse:

> If fame belonged to me, I could not escape her; if she did not, the longest day would pass me on the chase, and the approbation of my dog would forsake me then. My barefoot rank is better.

You think my gait "spasmodic." I am in danger, sir. You think me "uncontrolled." I have no tribunal.

Would you have time to be the "friend" you should think I need? I have a little shape: it would not crowd your desk, nor make much racket as the mouse that dents your galleries.

She would go it alone. I would not. I felt some luck in that. Elizabeth Bishop had commented on Dickinson to Robert Lowell in a letter:

I never really liked Emily Dickinson much, except a few nature poems, until that complete edition came out a few years ago and I read it all more carefully. I still hate the oh-the-pain-of-it-all poems, but I admire many others, and, mostly, phrases more than whole poems. I particularly admire her having dared do it, all alone—a bit like Hopkins in that.

I had dared much alone for a long time and now that was at an end. I placed a call to the hospital where Durell was. *His heart is giving out*, the nurses said. *His leg is all gangrene*, the nurses said. I called the nursing station.

"Can you leave a message for him?"

"Yes," said the nurse. "He keeps talking about you all the time," she said.

"Tell him the book has won, and I am catching a flight to come and see him and celebrate it." Dickinson: *The distant strains of triumph*. Yes, they did feel in that moment distant, and they did "burst agonized and clear."

72.

Phone calls began. Louise Glück became Louise quickly. Ring, ring. "Hello, is that you?" "Yes, it is I," Louise said. Louise spoke in a unique manner. Cultivated, Northeastern—there was something unusual in her cadence. She never said "um." She spoke in fully formed, complete, complex, laser-like sentences. Her tone was the sound of brilliant originality and unrolled from the phone like ticker tape. My own English tightened to keep up. She spoke. I took notes.

Had Gabriel swooped in, wearing golden robes, to take up residence in my stable? Usually we would go for two-hour stretches. Sometimes I simply wanted to know more about poetry, the world of it. "What do you think of this poet?" I'd tentatively ask. "Tell me about that poet," I'd beg. She told me she had just run into Mark Strand and that he'd just gotten back from Madrid where he'd fallen in love. Traveling to Europe, let alone falling in love, these possibilities shook my brain's confines, which had been groomed into submission by over a decade in retail—mistakenly or not, I'd felt my world limited to folding seminars, time clocks, no time to date and only three weeks of accrued vacation, which could not be taken all at one time. Now, in these conversations, which were the opposite of gossip, which I might call illumination, poets I'd met only in word were becoming flesh. Possibilities were filling my guest bedroom as if it was a crowded airport lounge. Louise welcomed me.

Other times I heard the pages of my manuscript moving rapidly through her hands, it sounded like a gold prospector shaking the pebbles in the riverbed. I jumped as she mentioned specific poem titles and images. Adjusting to the fact she'd *read* the book took some time for me. When not on the phone, I worked my shift at Brooks. I told no one for several weeks what was transpiring at my house. I was engaged in an affair of the mind like none other I'd known. I thought no one cared much about poetry: my fellow workers needed to pay their mortgages.

Several weeks into the edits, the cords and wires of our two landline telephones were alive with the black-and-white heated crackle of poetry. Her input and my output charged our talk, her insights electrifying rapid rewrites. She prodded. She prompted. She joked. She whispered. She cajoled. She bolstered. She marveled. She protected. In a poem "Memoir," Glück wrote, "A few words were all I needed: nourish, sustain, attack." Her fierceness and her love wound round that telephone line. I erased. I tossed. I pulled. I rearranged. I rethought. I sighed. I thanked. I stalled. I praised. I rewrote again. The poems fell into place, reordered, refined, readjusted, cleaned and set, like a dining room table where soon a reader would be welcome to sit and eat. As they began reading it, Louise and I would exit stage left. There was a mysterious hush sound as I set down the phone for the final time. Her visits had been a great fortune: her sensibility suited to me and mine to her.

I had been roosting on hopes, and little hatched for so long, working, bowing my head, dealing with customers, waiting for the store door to be locked, driving home, paying my bills, hammering away at poems, going silent much of the time, and now, suddenly, that was at an end.

A book!

A book looks like a door as you open it, with hinges. I'd made a thing: a few people were going to walk across its threshold. Not many, after all: it was poetry. Perhaps that was the art that most suited the public declaration of a Reece. But what I didn't and couldn't have realized was I had carpentered that book, all those long years, so *I* could walk across its threshold.

73.

Louise said: "So few of these poems are published."

"Yes," I said, "just a few, one in a high school magazine."

"Let's send the title poem to the *New Yorker*," she said in the tone I associated with wizards in fairy tales.

"I've tried them for nearly twenty years," I said, a hollow sound to my voice.

"There's a password," she said. I could see her smile at the other end of the telephone, even though I'd never met her in person. "The Clerk's Tale," the title poem that I'd spent nearly seven years on, trying to pay as close attention as I could to Ralph and our life, ran on Father's Day in 2003. The poem wholly concerned my working at Brooks beside Ralph.

74.

I'd informed the work staff a book of mine was careering into the world. I had spoken rather stiffly to the Florida manager, store 52, in her office, saying, "Something has occurred," as if I was talking about a brain tumor. My manager was one Ellen Morris, an indomitable Welsh woman who had trained for the shot put, the discus, and the javelin for the Commonwealth Games. She'd been the manager a good ten years and I worked as one of her assistant managers. At that point in time I had worked my way up to management and spent most of my days in the back, doing work schedules, calculating store plan, receiving shipments, and addressing customer complaints.

We toiled in an office the size of a broom closet. She was a wonder, and when talking about store issues or "making plan" she'd spit on me without realizing it, like a Shakespearean actor. Gently I would push the spittle away and stand at attention. She rolled her *r*'s as Robert Arthur had. As she spoke to me that day she was circling her lips with red lipstick as if wanting to emphasize her mouth was the giant bull's eye I needed to focus on. I loved her, and she remains the only woman who at my six feet two inches, made me feel small. Whatever mother issues I had, God sent me a female with a big blue bow on her head to smooth them out.

Pages went off, including, "Spencer to the front, customer waiting," and "Molly Fisher is here," which was code for a suspect shoplifter. Our two heads bobbed like woodpeckers as we tried quickly to communicate information. Between each loud interrupting page I told her the book would come soon.

"A book of *what?*" she said, applying more eyeliner, like a Zulu warrior going into battle.

"Poems!" I nearly yelled, as we dashed to the front of the store, looking like soldiers ready to dive into the trenches before a bomb went off.

75.

One day at work Ellen looked at me officiously and said, "I need you to stop by my house tomorrow night, regarding work responsibilities here." She'd never spoken to me so seriously. I began to wonder if I'd be asked to leave now that poetic engagements might interfere with my managerial responsibilities. Driving to her home the following night I noted the small Florida street was full of cars, more than usual. "There must be a party somewhere," I thought. When I opened Ellen's door, there they all were.

Ellen had gathered thirty or forty Brooks staff members from stores 28 and 52 and God knows where else. I was wrong in my assumption that they did not care. Wrong. They cared. The tailors, sales and shipping staff, all lined up and not a dry eye among them. There was a giant cake and many cards. They were proud to be seen through poetry.

Dickinson wrote:

> *This is my letter to the World*
> *That never wrote to Me —*
> *The simple News that Nature told—*
> *With tender Majesty*
>
> *Her Message is committed*
> *To Hands I cannot see —*
> *For love of Her — Sweet — countrymen —*
> *Judge tenderly — of Me*

I could see the callused hands of my countrymen and countrywomen, I could see they were patriotic for poetry. No accident Dickinson repeats "tender" followed by "tenderly" in the second stanza. Poetry is tender.

76.

The *New Yorker* staff, a week before the poem ran, asked me to call Ralph and make sure that it was all right with him that he was anonymously, or somewhat anonymously, referred to as "the old homosexual."

The call went like this:

Me: "Ralph, this is Spencer."

Ralph: "Oh, hey, kid, how are you?"

Me: "Ralph, you remember that I wrote poems, right?"

Ralph: "No, I don't, kid." I could see his smile, all the teeth beautifully capped. I knew he was surveying the room for sales as we spoke, I could hear it in the tone, you'd have to have been a salesman to know it.

Me: "Well, I did, and I do."

Ralph: "Oh, that's nice."

Me: "Well, I wrote a poem about you."

Ralph: "Oh, that's nice." I could hear him rustling bags and ringing the register.

Me: "Well, they are going to publish it!"

Ralph: "Oh, that's great, kid, listen I better go, I've got three customers here. We miss you! Mary Beth says hello." I think he thought I meant a local newspaper.

Me: "Ralph, there's one more thing. It's going to run in the *New Yorker*."

A pause. "Oh, you better read it to me, kid, let me take this in the back." I heard him hand off his customers to the others.

I read him the whole poem. The poem mentioned he took a trip to Europe and that he had a bunion on his right foot. After I finished, he was quiet for a moment and then said, "Oh, kid, that's so nice." He did not object to being called an old homosexual at all, but he did say, "There's just one thing, I never went to Europe and the bunion is on my left foot." We agreed to let the details stand wrong.

Later Ralph handed out magazines in the store, saying, "It's me, I'm the old homosexual. See, look!"

77.

The livelong June Florida day came when the poem ran. The morning felt wild and strange. I went to work that day for the early shift, seven to five. People started calling me from around the world. The poem landed on doorsteps and in beauty parlors. I was dizzy.

When I got home, I took off my dress shoes and listened to all the messages on my answering machine. The last was from Durell's sister. She said, in a brief message, she was sorry to call with the news but that Durell had died that day at two p.m. A heart attack. The heart burst its valves.

I never did celebrate with Durell. The flight had been booked to Boston. His sister and I, instead, buried him. At the funeral at Saint Thomas Church on Fifth Avenue, which was ridiculously rich and large for our humble moment, I recited the Elizabeth Bishop poem as Merrill had taught me, with the accent falling on the right syllables. Hardly anyone came.

78.

Above me hung the Florida sky, day after day. The huge bright blue infinity flecked and flocked with gulls. I was looking out the window at this sky one summer night, listening to the news of a shooting on the radio, as I sat in a white suburban Toyota Highlander driven into the heart of Palm Beach by Mary Jane Zapp, my new Al-Anon sponsor. A new century had begun. FOR SALE signs were stacked in the back, her car full of real estate calling cards, photographs of houses sold or needing to be sold, crinkled xeroxes of listings, secondhand scarves purchased at World Thrift, pamphlets for the twelve steps, one faded fire-engine-red pamphlet that read: *ALCOHOLISM: The Merry-Go-Round Called Denial.*

It was off-season in Florida—my favorite time. Maybe it was June. I love a place after everyone has left: Florida in the off-season had that spooky feeling of a stage set struck, the audience gone, an undocumented Honduran gardener or two chitchatting with each other in beautiful Spanish, trying with every syllable to root themselves into a place through language. Florida in summer and I was finally at ease there.

Then, in seconds, the sky transformed to dark purple and brackish blue, flared with yellow and green, a storm sliding in. "What is the difference between a friend and a sponsor?" I queried Mary Jane, who was both my friend *and* my new sponsor, as we pulled into the parking lot and the heavy summer rain started pulverizing everything, shredding the hibiscus. Florida summer rain comes at you sideways and up into your armpits.

I had asked Mary Jane to sponsor me by default. I'd asked another man in the program a few weeks after Durell died; he had declined but said Mary Jane was available. Something about Mary Jane intrigued and scared me. For one thing she was in Al-Anon, and I had a hunch there wasn't a pamphlet in those meetings that didn't relate to me. I'd been gently encouraged to go to Al-Anon by numerous individuals but always begged off committing. Wasn't one twelve-step group enough? I'd already done the steps. Why did there have to be more wrong with me? I complained at times that Al-Anon gave me a headache. Plus, I was somewhat hesitant to work with a woman in the matters of my soul, but then again I began to have a hunch that there was more healing that I needed to do with women than I realized. I've a theory gay men often have more problems with women than with men. My theory goes that for a gay man to be whole he must smash his mother-hate. While some gay men love drag, it did not intrigue me. Nor did it embrace the femininity I needed. I needed reverse-drag: I needed to be a lesbian without the sex. I needed a sister. This theory was burgeoning in those days. So I'd asked Mary Jane and she'd said yes immediately and then later had said she'd been watching and waiting for me. She'd said to herself, "He's mine."

"A sponsor takes tweezers to your bullshit," Mary Jane said. Then she and I ran for cover, the two white car doors like stiff wings of a gull slamming back into her hard body. We dashed into the Jewish deli TooJay's, where she had once been a waitress.

Mary Jane was a real estate agent in her early fifties, the age Dickinson was when she died. She had a vague feel of the old hippie about her: she had moony watchful Joni Mitchell eyes and long blond hair.

A few days before, she told me she had been so depressed after her second marriage ended that she made plans to swim out into the Atlantic and swim and swim until she drowned. Because she wasn't melodramatic this statement stuck out, like her teeth.

"I don't know if I can reconcile with my parents or my brother," I said abruptly, my glasses still covered with rain drops. "What do you want?" she said, smiling her big-toothed smile.

Then Mary Jane added: "And once you know what you want, what are you willing to do to get it?" She spoke directly, in lightning bolts, as if her last name, Zapp, from Transylvanian relatives, was bestowed upon her to emphasize her head-on style.

"I want . . ." I said. I felt awkward. For so long I'd talked around the margins of myself. Perhaps that is why I started writing poetry in the first place, as a Reece I needed to speak around myself. The speaker of the poem was always separated from the poet, Ms. Young had taught me, and this created just enough of a thin membrane for me to move about. And what art is more indirectly direct? No one loves a disappearing act more than the poet does. We tolerate and expect these sleights of hands in the art. Prose explains. No Reece possessed the directness of Mary Jane Zapp.

"I want to try to reconcile," I said, quietly, maybe even surprising myself somewhat, for there was a part of me that was afraid of this idea. What kind of poetry would I write if I began to contemplate forgiveness? Yet hadn't Louise pushed me to change? As we laid that first book to bed, she said through the wires, "Now comes the real challenge, to make something new again." The damage I'd catalogued lyrically in my first book brought me into print. Now what? More damage? Or? Or what?

"God gives you more than one chance," Mary Jane said, staring at the waiter. "Now that's finesse," she said, commenting on how the man traveled through the deli with plates in his hands. "That's the sign of a good waiter. Always have something in your hands. Never leave your station without something in your hands." The rain drummed like a typewriter on the windows.

"I want a world that is expanding," Mary Jane said. When she smiled in TooJay's her overbite increased, revealing a large top gum. The lower jaw was smaller than normal, the top part adult, the bottom child.

"Do you want to be right or do you want to be happy?" she zapped me. That rainy evening in the deli, the two of us wet as the newly baptized, my anxieties diminishing as I let go of the justified anger left, right, and center, I commenced once more my great tragic story, the gigantic taproot of my misery.

"Where to start with my parents? Ten years without speaking to them. My brother's not being in touch with me. I'd been mad for so long, now it all seems ridiculous." I sighed. My sigh cooled my chicken noodle soup with matzo balls. I'd refined the recital of my family dramas masterfully: the drinking, the estrangement. Wasn't it tragic? I wanted a sober family hugging each other in church basements, collecting coins and cakes. I raised my head. A tear fell out of my eye. I'd gone to the nuthouse, worked in retail for over a decade, and been disinherited.

Here Mary Jane stopped me. "Disinherited?" I did not like being stopped.

"Yes," I said, "disinherited."

She tweezed. "Your parents went bankrupt after you ceased speaking if not before, so *you* weren't disinherited. That's bullshit. There wasn't any money. And it wasn't your money anyway. That's entitlement. Finally, inheritance concerns money given to you after someone has died, and they aren't dead." Her teeth gleamed.

I paused, annoyed. How dare she interrupt me! But I proceeded despite the slap, seeing now a distinction between friend and sponsor. I resumed. I laid down my victim cards before Mary Jane, one by one, as if I had a tarot pack: "See this!" and "See this!" and "See that!" Dickinson wrote:

> *Pain — has an Element of Blank —*
> *It cannot recollect*
> *When it begun — or if there were*
> *A time when it was not —*

That seems exactly right. I'd gone blank, and the idea of constructing meaning without this despair seemed impossible. As I got to the part about my mother, some egregious slight of hers I thought worthy of justifiable anger, Mary Jane stopped me. Midsentence.

"Your job," she said, "is to leave other people alone." Her gums and teeth bloomed. I stopped. Miffed.

"I'm a scary bitch," she said. "Do you hate me?" I paused too long. No, I did not hate her. Yet what followed was an awkward pause. I was annoyed, yet a small part of me knew I needed rearranging, and well-meaning friends weren't going to pierce or strike like this. So many had let me go on for years. No one's fault but my own.

"You know," Mary Jane said, in the quietest voice, "I know

I have bad teeth." What was she doing? Changing the subject on me? Yet an eerie charge filled the air as if she was bending spoons before me.

"They're not so bad," I said, softening her frank assessment, but I knew I'd been staring at them.

"The boys in high school used to harass me for being ugly. They used to call me an ugly bitch and then I would pray for the ground to swallow me up." I knew the desire to die in high school. "People stare at me, you know? Kids laugh at me in stores. All my life. When I was in high school a dentist kept pulling my teeth out. My jaw was too small, as you can see, so they figured they needed to make space for what was there. This went on for many years, years and years. The dentist would keep saying to me that he was going to make me a pretty girl. The prettiest girl in Long Island. That is what he kept saying to me."

The deli got quiet. "After about ten years of being in surgery with my jaw I told the dentist to fuck off. That dentist wanted to break my whole jaw apart, reconstruct my face, so I ran out of that office in Long Island, ran and ran, graduated from high school, got married. But I wish to God I'd listened to him now. It's too late now, I think." Here Mary Jane's regret was palpable. "But now, well, I think I am getting used to these teeth, this mouth."

"We better go," I said. "Aren't you chairing the meeting?" Off we went. The sky putty-colored, every trace of thunder and rain gone. The Flagler Memorial Bridge thumped behind us like a beautiful heart, the FOR SALE signs slid off the back seat, and down South County Road we went, date palms swooshing. The sea going in and out, the palms waving. Florida, Florida, your insistence followed by release.

79.

Nothing can be changed until it is faced.

—JAMES BALDWIN

I had trouble saying "Gay AA." That glob of a tripled-up diph-thong! Behind getting the back of my throat to work, I kept hearing the damning voice of my mother, in a self-pitying tone in front of guests: *We are such a small family, I had hoped for grandchildren.* Over forty, I needed to face men. If that meant putting a name tag on me, so be it. I needed to *try* to date. So I went to Gay AA—a subset of a subset. There in the middle of Gay AA I saw P.—intelligent, butch, legs spread wide, a fine blue vein ridged across the top of each bicep, an engineer in the construction business. To his straight talk and sports updates, my talk of poetry and landscapes.

The clubhouse on South Dixie Highway where we met was called COMPAS, an unassuming building that had been a gas station. The title COMPAS stood for *something* that I can't recall now—however, it was symbolic, as if the needles in my compass had finally set me off in the right direction. P. was the first man I *ever* dated. The men in the circle supported and gig-gled. They knew we two were destined for one another. That felt odd and good. Joy rippled through the meeting when I wore his sweatshirt that advertised DRY WALL FOR REVERE BEACH. A timid lesbian who taught math encouraged us. We represented success to her. She shared that she sat at home every night with her algebra tests when not watching women's basketball, afraid to pick up the phone and date.

These circles of Gay AA meetings warmed us like a kiln. P. was better looking than most people but he never thought much about how he looked, which increased his handsomeness: eyes blue and forlorn, eyes that said a lot about Boston—growing up tough and Irish, with those Catholic nuns and their admonishments, P. wishing he could be part of Harvard but knowing he'd never be part of Harvard, closest he got was washing dishes in the student union. Oh, and of course, there was his Boston accent—the *r*'s sinking into the cave of his mouth, the constant nasally swear words, the expanding vowels that gave me a hard-on. Thick gray hair, drill-sergeant walk—God was he something. Most people thought so. His Irish charm had an element of detachment so I was never sure if I knew him. Did I? He was jokey and unknowable. He was older: fifty-two to my forty-one. He'd lived in the closet his whole life. Butch/fem, Ireland/Britain, left-brained/right-brained—we snapped into each other like puzzle pieces.

My love story is not extraordinary. It is only extraordinary because it happened to me. P. liberated me and liberty bears repeating. He arrived at the same time as I was resolving deep estrangements with my family. He came through the door as the door of poetry opened. Love is the most important emotion. I wish it for everyone. He was my bee and my butterfly and my breeze.

We sat on a bench by the sea. The waves like a poem that was getting rewritten over and again.

"You never played with a doll or dressed up as a girl or ..." I asked. The sea roiled.

Dickinson, wrote, madly in love, perhaps and probably with her neighbor and sister-in-law, Sue:

> *Wild Nights — Wild Nights!*
> *Were I with thee*
> *Wild Nights should be*
> *Our luxury!*
>
> *Futile — the Winds —*
> *To a Heart in port —*
> *Done with the Compass —*
> *Done with the Chart!*
>
> *Rowing in Eden —*
> *Ah — the Sea!*
> *Might I but moor — Tonight —*
> *In Thee!*

I'd found my man. I rowed to Eden knowing how Eden ended: if expulsion was the price of admission, I would pay.

"No, I just wanted to work with my father's tools," said P.

So he smote me.

80.

It was a sorry business to see him change as he progressively died.
—JULIAN OF NORWICH

As the book went to press, Louise Glück was named poet laureate. She invited me to read from the book in Washington, DC. I went from standing behind the cash wrap at Brooks with receipts in my hand to standing behind a podium at the Library of Congress with my poems. Afterwards, people asked for signatures.

When I got back from that trip, Martha called to say Robert stubbed his diabetic toe back in Minnesota. Martha reported that the toe was green. A few weeks later doctors amputated the leg up to the knee.

After the surgery he called me. "Spencer, dea*rrrrr* boy," Robert said, the sounds of nurses and hospital pages behind him.

"Yes," I said, smiling, customers floating by my counter.

"Martha and I are indeed proud of you and we wish to visit you," he said. I knew what he was saying to me. He was saying, "I want to see you before I die."

With my sharp tailoring scissors I cut the alterations ticket from a set of linen slacks and covered them in a plastic bag and handed them to the customer with the phone in the crook of my shoulder.

Martha was on the phone: "He won't stop talking about it. He says he must do it."

They came. Robert and Martha talked softly in the next room of that tiny apartment, unpacking their suitcases. There was pride in their voices. I held in my hands the *New York Times*. The smell of the ink and the paper were a fine perfume. We were startled they'd written me up that week, in the Style Section, and startled by the photo of me on a table with an umbrella in hand. I looked like Mary Poppins. The reporter talked about how I had jettisoned out of oblivion. He had an angle that meant to spotlight my isolation. That *was* right. That was *not* right. What wasn't in that article was the many who had shepherded me, the margins of that newsprint teemed with my shepherds.

I began writing sentences on scratch paper to honor what was missing in the newspaper. I started dryly, at some remove, veering towards the academic. But I was a poet and I thought like one. Poems were what I loved most.

Dickinson wrote:

> *I Dwell in Possibility —*
> *A fairer House than Prose —*
> *More numerous of Windows —*
> *Superior — for Doors —*

To claim my ghosts, I wanted something closer to newsprint, yet lively. I wanted the fact and the fun I felt, a contrapuntal tune, like a Bach prelude, two harmonies going at each other, between myself and them. How would I manage it? "True Poems flee," wrote Dickinson. I knew what she meant. Poems were hard to catch. What would true prose do? What could I nail down?

That evening Robert and Martha slept in my twin beds. I slept on the fold-out couch in the living room. Through the door opened a crack, before I turned off the lights, I saw the artificial leg, the straps.

81.

"I can't fucking walk," said P. a few months later on the phone. We had been seeing each other at meetings. Whispers went on that we were dating. Were we? I wasn't sure what to call it. My gay brethren applauded us. We went to AA conventions. We slept in a hotel room in separate twin beds. We hadn't kissed deeply. We went to lots of meetings. We mainly spoke. We were Victorian. P. called a trans woman from our group "Big Tits Randy" and I told him to lower his voice, scolding. A lover's scold. We'd hardly touched.

One night, in my humble second bedroom with the lime-green shag carpet, we kissed. He said, "Haven't done this much." He backed off. Looked scared. A horse not broken. Quickly he went home. I watched him go. My Florida town went on and on. The Walmart in the distance. Kitchens full of the sound of plantains frying, a hissing mixed with tsking. I wanted a life with P. in one of those little kitchens with the Walmart in the background.

Then came a call, piercing through the salty jalousie-window slats. "Can't fucking walk." He had spine problems. Some said it was emotional. Others said it was related to his obsession with windsurfing. P. loved windsurfing. He loved to be on the sea, writing his body's instincts across the surf. The intense pressure of his upper body controlling the sail took its toll. Or fifty years of repression pinched every nerve. Or both. For decades, he'd been poised like a question mark.

"I can come and help you if you need it," I said. My heart thumped just as tires thumped over the drawbridge's meshed mouth on Flagler Bridge. A proposal. A pause. "Well, I have an extra bedroom here," said P.—close as he got to asking me to stay with him. And so I moved in. Like that. One day led to three. Three days led to five years. For five years I stared out that window and smelled the sea, heard its murmur and saw its striptease. I smelled the cleaning products that P. liked to use, scrubbing down his kitchen and the bathrooms.

P.'s interior was masculine and simple: blue carpet, white tile in the bathroom and on the kitchen floor, tables of blond wood, and a sectional couch in blue. A bookcase with more family photos than books, one photo of him bare-chested on a beach in Cape Cod that made my knees weak. We lived at separate ends of the house for the first year.

P.'s back got better through acupuncture. One night after the last of the pins had been removed, we decided to sleep in the same bed. That solemn night something sacred stirred in the room. There was no bed frame. The walls had no pictures. There was a mirror without a frame. The lamps could have been taken from the showroom. I thought of a porn set.

P. said, "I have nev-ah slept through the night with someone."

"Never?" I said.

"Once when I was eleven, Jimmy Sheehan had me over for a sleepov-*ah*, but that was it . . ."

P. had paid young men to sleep with him, but none of them ever slept through the night. We lay. Two men, two men, side by side, in boxer shorts with T-shirts. I did want to touch him, but if I did, what we had might collapse. So we talked and said good-night like two night watchmen.

He said abruptly: "Goddamn insulin." He looked at his

waterproof sports watch and jumped out of bed. I stared at his beautiful body close up, its rough musculature.

P. was diabetic. Since his thirties he had required two shots of insulin, one at night and one in the morning, pricking himself and checking monitors for his sugar levels and writing them down on sheets of paper. Long curled-up sheets of paper that he examined. Because the science of monitoring his sugar levels and the amount of insulin was inexact it frustrated him. He pricked himself with one of his needles, pressing down on his vein the way I had pressed down on the paper to write a poem. Back to sleep we went.

Around four in the morning everything turned upside down. His body flipped around in the bed like a porpoise. Coated in sweat, his eyes dilated and rolled into the back of his head. I thought he was having a heart attack. I called 911.

By five in the morning, firemen and ambulance drivers and EMTs were in the bedroom with us. They strapped him into a stretcher, gave him adrenaline. I stood beside in my boxer shorts. The firemen chuckled.

"He's diabetic," I said.

"And what is your relationship?" said the fireman, repressing a smirk.

"We are . . . friends," I said.

The EMT worker said P. mixed up his insulin and took the short-acting one instead of the long-acting one. All these years living alone, he had never done that.

When P. woke in the hospital the nurse told him I'd saved his life. When she left and pulled the blue curtain closed, we held hands and looked into the distance, not at each other.

82.

Dickinson felt publishing her poems ruined them:

> *How dreary to be Somebody*
> *How public — like a Frog*
> *To tell one's name — the livelong June*
> *To an admiring Bog.*

Like Dickinson, I was not drawn to self-aggrandizement. The school of anonymity had taught me much and continues to. Yet there I was, in the world with my poems now, and hadn't I wanted that, sending them out all those times? A part of me did. I wanted community. As did she, however briefly. Sore need I had for a long time without the nectar. The silence in which I had carpentered had been long and given me solace, like an invisible church. But now, no going back. I was visible. Customers came into the store and asked about my poetry.

I kept working at Brooks Brothers. I accepted reading invitations to San Marcos, Texas, and Los Angeles, California, for the fall. I would travel as I had longed to do for years in retail but had been unable to because of lack of money and the limited vacation time my job allowed. Or was that not right? Had I created an atmosphere of lack so deep and thick around me, regardless of limited funds, so I knew only deprivation as a way of seeing the world? Could I change that? When I was young I had traveled with my parents and loved the adventure of it, and especially the humbling sensation that an entire community carried on without any knowledge of me.

"What will you do now?" people asked. I was not sure what I would do. I sat. I waited. I traveled. I went onto more and more college campuses. Knock, knock: it's me. I told audiences that came to readings, especially aspiring poets, that I had thought the contests rigged. I emphasized Louise did not know me or even the screeners that screened for Louise. It had been blind. Blessed are those that do not see.

I went back to retail work. I'd spent the last decade now in Palm Beach County, the narrow strip of wild land that squiggles down the side of the state—a ragtag collection of coral rock islands and isthmuses and half-formed mangrove clumps. Florida was becoming home to me—my "admiring bog."

Usually by the time I headed to work my parents had left several messages. They called five minutes after I arrived.

"We need money," my father yelled into the phone. "You owe us!" he yelled harder. They spoke as if they were having seizures. We fought without meaning.

My mother yelled in the background, "Tell him, tell him . . . TELL HIM!!!! We paid for his goddamn education. Tell him he *owes* us, he goddamn owes us every nickel and dime we paid out for him . . . That is what any normal child would do. Half that grant he won is ours!"

I hung up the phone. I worked. I slept near or next to P. I worked on poems. I never talked much about the poems. My art left me inarticulate. I'd cultivated it alone for twenty years.

Yellow and orange and light pink colored the hours. Lavender and violet were rubbed in. In that little white cottage not far from the mall, P. and I found two dogs from a shelter—"faggot children" someone from Gay AA said, smirking. I grimaced. Above us that sky, before us that sea—a jaw, opening and closing the days. The octopuses floated in the deep with their multiple hearts that circled around their throats like necklaces. The two dogs snored.

83.

Two years passed. P. and I were practically married. Sometimes we held hands under the wild oaks, scrub pine, and the gumbo limbo trees.

At a restaurant, P. said: "I am not physically attracted to you."

Confused, I said: "But you said you love me."

"I love you *spiritually*, but I am not attracted to you. I am attracted only to men in their early twenties," said P.

I ordered key lime pie. Flat, flat, Florida flattened in the twilight. Undocumented workers from Honduras returned to their trailers. In the brightly lit lonely restaurant, we'd come for the early bird special.

I said: "Did you take your insulin?"

We drove home. The sea grayed with garbage and sharks. The two dogs looked at us dumbly. Then we began to argue—like my parents. I did not want to remain virginal. Irish Catholic celibates had created in his mind and soul a world of extremes: I was on the shelf of adoration with votive candles, covered in robes and never to be thought of in the nude.

Dickinson wrote in a letter to Sue:

> I have but one thought, Susie, this afternoon of June, and that of you, and I have one prayer, only; dear Susie, that is for you. That you and I in hand as we e'en do in heart, might ramble away as children, among the woods and fields, and forget these many years, and these sorrowing

cares, and each become a child again—I would it were so, Susie, and when I look around me and find myself alone, I sigh for you again; little sigh, and vain sigh, which will not bring you home.

I was losing him. We argued. How long could I call home home?

84.

I stood at a crossroads after my first book of poetry was done: I was not sure if I should stay in retail or perhaps search for a job teaching poetry at a college. Or what? I'd seen a few of these colleges and their jobs. At times the poetry professors looked as if they were sucking on lemons all morning and had been trapped into a Kafkaesque existence of killing poetry through teaching indifferent undergraduates. Bishop said flatly, "not my line at all."

I drove the car to hospice. Why? Why did I do this? Not sure. Puzzled by my choice, I trusted it, the way I'd learned to dive into the mystery when I wrote a poem. I'd grown up in doctors' lounges with ER intercoms and sanitary wipes. Felt familiar. Yet my résumé showed ten years of retail. I didn't feel credentialed for the work. I was a homosexual cliché: the thought of that almost stopped me from walking in the door. But something pushed me. God? Hospice took me. After an initial training course, I started rounds.

"Follow me," said Frank, the head chaplain, well dressed with his name tag, looking like a banker. "You don't see this often." I'd braced myself for all kinds of versions of people on the brim of the abyss—after all my father had been a pathologist and when I was a boy he took me to the morgue where he did autopsies—but what I certainly was *not* expecting to find was a baby. The baby, born without her brain's frontal lobes, gurgled on the nurse's chest. The baby was living longer than the doctors expected. The face the size of a sonnet. "Our little bundle of chocolate love," said the nurse, patting the soft cranium where the brain was missing. The family of the Haitian baby was unable to care for the child in their home. Machines surrounded the baby's body like a city. Fugitive thing, I would come in to see the baby, with my Brooks Brothers khaki pants and my rep tie with a clipboard and a stack of poetry books, and sit clueless, unmonitored. Silence. What was I doing? I prayed. Nothing. Many Christians love to convert, but that strikes me as arrogant and not my nature. A revival tent pitched next to the oxygen machine felt distasteful to me, aggressive and pushy and presumptuous.

That's when Nana's ghost came to me. In the years of family estrangement word came that she had died on her nursing-home cot, melted into the mattress like snow in spring. I'd avoided the funeral, unable yet to face my mother. Now Nana was next to me. The most anonymous undetected evangelist. We began to talk more than when she had lived. I saw her more. Her quiet religion I modeled.

The baby died. Words failed the nurses. Words failed me. My faith felt fuzzy. I thought of Dickinson. As Charles Darwin published *On the Origin of Species* and Henry David Thoreau *Walden*, she sat behind her locked bedroom door and at the height of the Civil War wrote nearly a poem a day. Trunks and drawers filled with the poems. In a letter she commented, "But we thought Darwin had thrown 'the Redeemer' away." But it was she who flirted with tossing off redemption. In the poems she called Christ her "tender pioneer." I identified.

Could I become (here in my thinking, I paused and said something so quietly to my mind and to Nana's ghost that even I had a hard time hearing it)—could I ponder being a priest *even* with my doubts? I'd discounted this thought as foolish in my twenties. The thought came again. Could I salvage the Redeemer? Could I redeem me? Could I follow that tender pioneer?

85.

I came home, placed my plastic name tag with the sensor on the kitchen table and said to P., "I think I want to be a priest."

"What are you talking about?" he said, having finished masturbating to videos of young men ejaculating.

"I think this is what I have been moving towards for a long time," I said. I said it like a dare, to provoke him.

"But it is like a calling, isn't it?" P. said. As he spoke he became part of my past, inanimate and two-dimensional. P. transmogrified: his mouth flattened into an em dash. I would write of him.

P. turned away, walked out the back door and did not touch me. I worked my shifts. He worked construction. On my days off I went to hospice. The truth: we loved each other. We'd cracked each other open like eggs—our passions launched and spent, falling back with animal exhaustion. That had finally happened. Not as much as I would have liked, but occasionally, and in an attenuated manner. Yet. The lie: we loved each other. No matter which way we came at it, P. remained sealed, hard-boiled, impregnable, not mine.

At hospice, the sky swallowed the months like painkillers. A room at hospice filled with life, and upon my return it was scrubbed down with the bedsheets hospital tucked—a new name on the door.

Out the window, beyond the cars swooshing, the sea pushed and retreated, pushed and retreated. Florida. A coming in. A going out. A coming in. A going out. *I'm Nobody. Who are you?*

86.

One rainy day in Florida, my aloe-spiked town oddly intro-
spective, Mary Jane came by the house while P. was away on
his construction site. I spoke to her about my brother.

"Do you want a relationship with your brother?" she said
suddenly. After many conversations about my parents' failings
or injustices, we'd left my estranged brother alone.

"I don't know if I can. I am so busy. With readings," I said. I
spoke with conviction. I stood on the cliff of a fib.

"That's not what I asked you. Do you want a relationship
with him?" she said.

"Well, yes, I think I do," I said vaguely, yet knowing I missed him.

"But—" began my brain. The dog lay down on the white tile
with a clatter of bones and sighs like a bag of tools. So simple,
the dog: his desire, his life. How had things become so complicated for me?

"Then what are you willing to do to get it?" Mary Jane said
again. I took less offense to her frankness. She said, "Write him
a letter and we'll send it, but don't send it before I've seen it."
She said this like a character in a fairy tale. The sea glistened
outside the window. I remembered again Herbert describing
prayer as a "heart in pilgrimage." It began to come to life for me
there in Florida with Mary Jane. I wanted to be a pilgrim of the
heart. I needed to journey back to my brother now. I prayed.
A blank prayer. I kept repeating my brother's name to myself:
Carter, Carter, Carter.

The following week I fingered the poem about my brother on the plane up from Florida to New York City. As we flew into LaGuardia, I thought, "My brother is here. Somewhere." New York City hummed. Possibility moved like electricity in the bones of the buildings, possibility moved in the complex networks of plumbing, possibility clung to the moldings and the window frames, possibility went up the chimneys and down the laundry chutes, possibility bumped along with me as I peered out the window of the taxi.

Interviewing me on New York public radio, Leonard Lopate asked: "Would you like to read a poem?"

"Yes," I said. "It is about my brother."

The poem closed:

another year passes still no word from you.

Eight million New Yorkers. Some listening to Leonard Lopate on public radio for those rich five minutes. One was my brother, working in the backroom of a florist shop, arranging pussy willow stems in a glass vase for the rich, the people we used to be. My words vibrated in my brother's eardrum. Lopate announced the reading's time and location. My brother came. I saw him across the sea of people, standing at the back of the room. A forlornness in his eyes. My brother, in the line, buying the book and slowly putting it under his arm, waited for me to sign it. The crowd emptied. He came forward. He said, "Don't stay angry."

87.

Mary Jane sat across from me at the kitchen table. P. on his job site. The two dogs slept like disciples. "Are you going to show me the letter?" she said.

Several weeks had passed since the uncanny encounter with my brother. Had my wish to amend things with him called him into real time? "Yes," I said with resistance, *I* was the writer, I had won a prize, won a grant: I knew how to *write* a letter to my brother. An awkward silence. Mary Jane was a real estate agent. Not the writer. Dogs snoring. The sea said something we couldn't hear.

"You can't send this," Mary Jane said after she read it.

"What do you mean," I said, irritated. I hurried to get something done, but where was I going? Why was I being difficult when I asked for help? Why was I defended?

"You are justifying all your behavior in this letter, you don't own *anything*, you use 'but' all over it, which negates all your apologies, you don't want to change anything," Mary Jane said. She was not afraid to say ugly things. Where did she get this courage?

"But. Well—" I stumbled.

"What is your part?" Mary Jane insisted, putting her finger on that nerve.

"I . . . He is just not a letter writer, my brother." I looked over my shoulder as if someone was going to walk through the door.

"I don't *want* to hear about him," she said. "This is about you, *your* part."

Why was it challenging to get to my story? "Okay, years ago," I began the story of how I had outed him and how he ran away and rarely spoke to me. Like when the gospel is done, and the priest returns to his seat and the congregation settles into their pews, there sat between us silence.

"*That* is your part," she said. "You were a shit."

I sent the letter, revised, with resistance at first. I wrote to him I had been afraid, I wrote to him that if I had known what I knew now I would not do what I did then. I would've found a counselor. Mary Jane would not let me use "but" once. She said that negated everything. I did not buck her. Once the thin letter drifted into the world, I waited. Waited. Waited. Waited. Seasons passed. Hurricanes came and went. Christmases passed. I worked. P. and I slept in bed, apart. Nothing from my brother.

"Can I call my brother?" I asked Mary Jane.

"No," Mary Jane said in the Jewish deli, biting into her pastrami and rye. She smiled. Strings of sauerkraut dangled from the edges of our mouths.

88.

Love makes one generous.

—JAMES MERRILL

My mother read the poem about Ralph in the *New Yorker* while getting her hair set. In the Mall of America, Ralph received audiences and signed copies of the *New Yorker* between his shifts. Later she called me. This time, I softened. Not sure what or why. Maybe it was the love I had felt with P., a handsome man who had been vulnerable with me. I'd taken Mary Jane's suggestion to do "anger work." Maybe that? I'd gone into quarries and smashed quartz boulders and yelled "Fuck" to release pent-up anger over family. Maybe all these things? Maybe it was the poem? Maybe the poem realigned us? Maybe.

"No one's perfect," I thought. Truth was, when I asked myself why I was angry with my parents, what had happened in the home, the slop of drink drenched in forgetfulness of who harmed whom, I could not, with time gone by, recall which wires to fuse together to jump-start the engine of my anger. A part of our discomfort was theirs. A part was mine. I'd never entertained that. I'd adopted the stance of a fundamentalist regarding my parents' drinking. I knew best.

I'd studied Keats's idea of negative capability—two opposing truths held as valid—but it had been abstracted. Keats made sense now. "Would you like to come and visit?" I said to my mother one afternoon after we'd had a series of these calls. I'd discovered P. was signing up for paid escorts. I did not mention this.

"Yes," she said, without hesitation. "How about Daddy and I come in March?"

89.

March came. After ten years of hardly speaking, I stepped out of the cottage to see my mother coming over the hill in a rented PT Cruiser. The make of the car gave the scene the effect of a Disney cartoon. She bickered with my father. Her face was determined. It was the same expression she had when she entered the toilet stall with fresh trousers in a grocery bag when I was a kid, after I'd wet my pants.

P. agreed to join us. We four sat on the light-blue sectional couch. We looked like contestants on a game show. Outside, the kerfuffle of waves was our murmuring audience.

"Here we are," my mother said. Pause.

"We are so proud of you," Dad said. I looked away. Mom led the talking as she always did.

"Tell us about your job," my mother said to P.

"I am a manage-ah on construction sites, I'm a field engine-eh." She seemed at home with his Boston Irish accent, although she had adopted an upper-class Connecticut sound.

"How long have you lived in Florida?" Mom asked.

"About twelve years now," P. said. The strong Florida sun came through the venetian blinds underlining our aged faces. My mother surveyed the spotless living room: the minimalist décor with the carpet combed in rows caught her attention.

"We're not cleaners!" Mom said under her breath, after P. got up to go to the bathroom. "You weren't raised this way." She took pride in our mess: I recalled the interiors we'd lived in, a mad nest of newspapers, drinks, antiques, and books—a Greek Orthodox church with an explosion of images, throwing the eye into paroxysms. P. returned from the bathroom, his hands smelling of soap and disinfectant. I recalled my dad's pile of books, on top of the pile a pumpernickel sandwich with mold.

"So here we are," I said.

"So here we are," Mom said.

"Yes," I said.

"Yes," said Dad.

"We are so proud of you," my mother said. We looked away. We looked away. We kept looking away as people do in the waiting rooms of hospitals. We four went off to dinner for the early bird special.

90.

The next day my parents came to hospice for my pastoral care class. As we tentatively walked down the hallway, my agnostic, Southern father said quietly to me: "I am glad to hear you have let go of your anger, Spencer, there is nothing worse than an angry religious person."

Down the hallway, the patients, like fish thrown on a dock, with oxygen tubes hooked into their noses, gasped.

Dickinson:

> *This is the Hour of Lead —*
> *Remembered, if outlived,*
> *As Freezing persons, recollect the Snow —*
> *First — Chill — then Stupor — then letting go —*

Letting go, letting go, from the mouths of hospice to my insipid judgments, my heart widened, my fist flowered, my tongue a spigot, my love hot metal.

91.

I was forty-five. In the churches, a committee of priests questioned me between my Brooks Brothers shifts. The policy in the diocese of southeast Florida was that if you were gay you needed to be single—no attached gay men allowed. Gay partners were not allowed into the process. Things with P. unraveled. "That works out rather nicely," I said to Mary Jane.

One Episcopal priest, married, questioning me, asked: "Now what happens if you meet some man in seminary and fall in love? Are you willing to drop out of the process?" Odd constricted man, his face pinched, he loved floral arranging and read *Southern Living*.

I said: "We will cross that bridge when we come to it." Deacons and priests around the kidney-shaped table picked up glasses of water, moved stacks of papers and opened Bibles.

I needed to be prompted prior to these meetings. As in my early days in AA, I memorized responses, I was a fairly empty vessel when it came to church business. I had to talk the talk before I knew the talk. I had, much as Plath and my father or my mother had done, to provide an accent that would be acceptable. My accent needed to be Episcopalian. I learned to say priests have a passion for the ABCs: absolve, bless, and consecrate. We become priests to be conduits as we perform our shazam number over the bread and wine. I enjoy this moment in the church now that I am a priest, but I didn't know that then. I had to guess at it. By the end, they decreed I return to seminary for three full years.

"Do you think this is crazy?" I asked Mary Jane after the final session, while eating a Rueben, juice dripping from the corners of my mouth, in the deli before Al-Anon.

And she, a disaffected Catholic, said, "Oh, yes, I see this, I can see this. If God wants this to be, there's no stopping it. God has your back..." Together with our matzo balls and sauerkraut, we were moving along in the heart's pilgrimage.

At home, in those days, P. was rejecting me.

"It isn't you," P. said, in despair. He resolved himself to his attraction to the young. P. had a strange look in his eyes, as if he had decided to enter a barrel and go over Niagara Falls.

"I am standing in your way of loving the person you are meant to love," I said. "You need to go out there and find this young man, this mythical young man, make him three-dimensional, I am never going to be that person for you." I sounded as if I was reading a technical manual. Some of my language came from our sessions with a sexologist in Fort Lauderdale. Despite exercises, homework, and multiple sessions, we failed.

"No one has to know, if it makes sense to us, we can still have sex," said P., bartering. The two dogs looked at us.

"But you aren't attracted to me," I said, hoping he might counter. He didn't.

92.

I disappeared into New York City one weekend, zigzagging through the masses of humanity, layers and layers of humans. I was giving a reading with the poet Ilya Kaminsky at NYU. Kaminsky, a tall bespectacled Russian immigrant who was partially deaf, held sway that night as he chanted his beautiful poems. He looked like Nick Thorndike. Despite deafness, poetry touched and healed him like one in Jesus's healed throng. Kaminsky inspired me. What might poetry do for me? What had it already done that I'd been dimly aware of through those years of silent toil?

Afterwards I had dinner with my brother. At Two Boots, a pizzeria in the West Village, close to ten p.m., after I had surrendered the idea that my brother would ever address my apology, with the charged intimate Village streets ambushing us, my brother said, suddenly, out of nowhere, "You know that letter you sent." I paused. Two or three years had passed since I'd sent my letter. My brother and I had seen each other a few tense times. I had to practically bite my tongue until it bled so as not to ask if he'd gotten the letter and what he'd thought of it. Then something quite astonishing happened.

Neither irritated nor rushed, he picked that moment at Two Boots to address me. Where was Mary Jane? "The letter you wrote," he began, as I sat poised at attention. So things could change. Something was finishing along with the daylight. Greenwich Village was listening to us the way my grandmother

266

once did at her kitchen table in the north end of Hartford. Greenwich Village was wearing that ruby-colored terry-cloth bathrobe and smoking. The Three Lives bookstore closed its red door. Gay men in the Village retreated, returning to their intimacies.

A golden light shaded my brother's face. My brother had grown more handsome as he had aged. He had a full head of sandy-blond hair without any gray and a full beard of a slightly darker shade. His enormous hazel eyes caught the attention of most people in the pizzeria. He had become a quiet solid presence in the world, preferring jobs where he was found behind the scenes. He had a droll sense of humor that could make me move towards a laugh without sound in minutes. We shared a perverse sense of the world. He didn't want to be made a fuss of, which made him more intriguing. If I was out front and on stage, he was off stage and happy there. I knew little about his personal romantic life and questions from me on the subject were gently rebuffed. There had been one or two long-term boyfriends, but they hadn't ended well. Now he was alone. I didn't want or need to know any more. I simply wanted him near. He loved cats more than any other animals and his demeanor resembled a cat's: cool, watchful, self-sufficient.

My brother continued: "That is the first time anyone in our family told the truth." The wood plank closely missing his beautiful eye flew over the cornfield. The scar branded my awfulness. The half-moon scar orbited me, the lights of New York illuminated it, where the stitches had been. I looked at the scar. Looked out the window. Then back at the scar.

"I'm so sorry about the scar . . . throwing the plank," I said, the words hurling out of my mouth. I floundered.

"Oh, please," he said. "Don't even think about it." He released me. Like that. He threw our greasy paper plates in the garbage.

I had outed him. Why? Fear? Hate? Love? Maybe all three had been the recipe for my poor choice. Behaving like my parents, but worse. To regret or feel guilt wasted the moment now. Choices led to the life lived. I was I as a result of heaps of choices. Some reversed me, others advanced me. The enormity of Carter's forgiveness filled Two Boots. My brother, adopted, was a gift that intensified with time: My parents' generosity lived on and in and through my brother. The years of destabilizing finances left me and my brother more stable than I thought possible in Greenwich Village that night. God, I was glad not to be an only child: some I'd met were solipsistic and unaware of others. The space my brother took up in the world made certain I'd share more, listen more, pause more, and the more I aged the more important that became. I sat next to my brother. I was close. Lucky me.

When Dickinson lay dying her brother wrote, "I was near." So with me. I was near. I was near. I was near.

93.

"Mom? Dad?" I said into the phone from Florida. I had not slept all night and waited until the somewhat reasonable hour of six to place the call. I'd never called anyone at six.

"Yes, darling," said my mother, private Connecticut in that voice. How like a mother not to be bothered by a six a.m. call from her son.

"Sorry to call so early," I said. My words stalled. "My relationship is over. We decided yesterday. I will leave on Friday. Some friends are coming to help," the words leaden in my mouth. Silence. The sun rose. Gulls dropped their clams on the rocks, eating the goo of the mollusks. I could hear my father on the other line, rustling, breathing, not speaking.

"We're sorry to hear this, he was so lovely," said my mother, circumspectly: she made a sound of concern for me I hadn't heard before, the sound of someone who knew what a broken heart felt like when it rattled inside one's rib cage like a dying animal. Then a diplomatic pause. "It is okay, darling. We're here. Best to leave quickly," said my mother finally.

"Come home, son," said my father, and the clarity of his demand broke my idea that I knew more than these people. I was humbled. That I had spent a great deal of time judging their marriage embarrassed me. I knew little about little. I shrank to a mustard seed.

I never "came out" to my parents. Yet, here I was, telling them my gay marriage was finished.

We were a family. I had them now, more than ever. My anger

had not broken the bond. Queer. Was my reserve cowardice? My sexuality went from unacceptable with my mother to acceptable: Maybe dignity was in the ellipsis? Queer. I'd said "I am" about other things easily: "I am an alcoholic," for instance. "I am a Christian" was difficult to say, like "I am gay" and "I am a poet." Christian, gay, and poet were things understood more than said. "I am an alcoholic" needed to be said to live.

I didn't come *out*. I came in. I came into focus. I came into myself after being long outside myself. I came into AA. I came into my body. I came into the Church.

Perhaps the most important things of one's *very existence*, if they didn't get said at a critical moment, never got said: they got, instead, assumed. In that dark hour with my parents over the phone, out the open window, the sea soothed me, abandoning its arguments on the knees of the shore.

And Durell was dead.

Lavinia Dickinson wrote in a letter, after her sister died and she was alone in that house, parentless, "Keep fast hold of your parents, for the world will always be strange and homesick without them."

I was going home.

94.

Friday appeared on the calendar. I retired from Brooks Brothers: all those years and years of circling a calendar with week after week of shifts. It was over. My Jamaican colleague said over her shoulder with her singsong accent, "Don't forget us now, you hear?" Time bent. There I'd been, waiting patiently, folding clothes, all those shifts, attending folding seminars with my plastic board, thinking I would be there in that shop *forever*. We had spent much time together. Twelve years, day in and day out, punching a clock, taking messages, answering the phone, standing alert for corporate visits, firing employees for stealing, and here it was, finished. My last day after twelve years. Out I went.

Was it possible that attending meetings with Mary Jane, the way people attended Lourdes with their crutches, had healed me? Maybe walking out of P.'s house the week prior propelled me to keep walking? Or, no longer trapped inside high-end retail, with the recognition of the book, the book rising to the top of one thousand books, there had been a click, the latch of my cage unhooked. Sometimes the world conspires to push a person to change. Out I went.

My head turned up. My spirit lifted. The sound of the shoppers diminished behind me, the soft scrunch of the sneakers of the elderly walking the perimeter of the mall every day grew softer. The nonthreatening cheerful music piped in faded. Down the hall I went, past the security guards who knew me well and whom I knew well, I could hear their jangle of keys. The whiff of cleaning disinfectant that smelled sugary tickled my nostrils one last time. I pushed my hand against the shiny metal doors. Out I went into the parking lot, into the sunlight, the bright Florida sky that had watched over me. Out I went.

Out, out—and the unending line of retail work ended and I was now circling back to where I started. Saturday morning rolled in crystalline and fair across Florida. I headed out in the Mini Cooper the Guggenheim grant bought. The Atlantic on my right, the Palm Beach mansions on my left. Seagulls arranged and rearranged themselves in the sky. Over the Flagler drawbridge I went—thump, thump. Outside Orlando, I loaded the car onto the Auto Train passing the wild river in Saint Augustine where they drowned John.

The window scenes went by like the drafts of a poem: trees, then fields, then parking lots, then buildings, then cities, then neighborhoods, segregated neighborhoods—vast lonely America. I began holy orders on Monday.

95.

I'd picked up the gigantic Sewall biography about Dickinson with the pale blue cover. She died in 1886, four years after her mother died. After, she reversed her former critical attitude about her mother. She became haunted by that mother. She wrote in a letter: "The Month in which our Mother died, closed its Drama Thursday, and I cannot conjecture a form of space without her timid face." "Conjecture" is an odd word she'd have found in her father's briefs. It's the perfect odd word for her: an opinion based on scant evidence. Was that not the fulcrum of her poetry? Opinions based on scant evidence? Her mother's timid face was everywhere.

She had complained bitterly in youth that she had no mother. According to her, her mother was a simpleton. Then, in a late letter, she commented on a friend's mother's death with awe, unlike the stance she had taken with her own mother. To that friend she wrote, "To have had a mother—how mighty!" Mightiness jolted my heart: Perhaps I was not built for lovers to last. Or not yet. Now I stood strong, framed with family. I had them back. How mighty.

One of the things that kept us separated had been my friendship with Durell. My mother was convinced he'd brainwashed me to have the intervention. There was some truth to that, but as my salty AA pals would say, "Our brains needed washing." She attributed our reconciliation solely to his death. She made no apology for her gratitude over the news. I didn't correct her.

I didn't elaborate. I recalled my mother met Durell at my Harvard graduation: A quick awkward handshake passed between them, as AA bumped up against my mother, as two Americans born in the thirties, raised in the forties, products of the fifties, met, each having suffered their restrictions but having no compassion for the other.

Durell needled me to write a poem about him. "Will you write a poem about me?" he'd say. I deflected the subject. "I bet you'll never write a poem about me." These moments were graceless. Writing about him would be impossible. How to write a poem about someone who'd helped me and was to many unlikable? I paused. In some ways he and my mother had a few things in common: they were brave; they were difficult; I was I because they were they.

In the years after Durell died I began my weird long poem. I thought to myself, "Okay, my friend, I will try to write about you now." It took seven years to complete. Drafts and notes clung to me. I would write the same line a hundred times and not be sure of it. In Florida, I annually showed drafts to his sister, whom I'd gotten to know when we had Durell's funeral. As I had estranged myself from my family, so had she estranged herself from her brother. Did gayness breed estrangement?

She had a second home in nearby Boynton Beach, where she wintered. Introducing me at the country club always took a few runs at it before people grasped the relationship. On one of those last visits to her country club before I returned to the Northeast, I showed her a recent draft of the poem that had grown long; she paused between our blintzes. She said, "There is something you don't know." Ominous. I stopped eating.

She said, "I've never told anyone this before. Durell was gangraped in the army. No one knows. Not my husband, not my children, not my grandchildren. I'd prefer to keep it that way. I am telling you so you understand perhaps that's why he was the way he was." The way she said it shocked even her. Then she cried. Decades of estrangement dropped off her face. She grew closer to me or Durell or herself or God. Not sure which.

All his defensiveness, his need to make a better life for me, which was a daily battle cry, the inordinate amount of time he'd taken with me made poignant sense, it fell into place. If he couldn't save himself, he'd save me. Gratitude set in. Hindsight softened what time made hard.

"Oh, I see," I said stupidly.

"You know," she said, keeping her mascara in place, "you look a lot like my brother." Elegant, proper, private, old New Englander, her sad look buried him.

I knew I'd need to leave this out of the poem. I needed to honor this confidence by his sister. He was dead, but he wouldn't want that in his poem. His sister was alive. I'd need to reference it obliquely, which suited the subject, as the subject was an oblique cipher from start to finish. I tried to make a short poem of him, but the poem kept telling me it would be long. I needed to fill in so much of him that was left out. I attempted to make a monument of him no one could ever quite see. That, he'd like.

I thought of Bishop's famous exchange with Lowell when he began lifting directly from the love letters of his ex Elizabeth Hardwick in *The Dolphin*. Bishop was appalled by his action and said to Lowell: "Art just isn't worth that much." I wanted my art to continue a conversation with two people, Durell and his sister, one dead and one alive, both submerged and affected by shame. I knew that stance. I lived in that stance. Obfuscation made sense. I would please Bishop and not follow Lowell. I eclipsed the fact. For now.

96.

My belongings all packed up once more: how transient I was. Christening my latest departure, I read one of the last poems Dickinson wrote:

> *To fail within a Chance —*
> *How terribler a thing*
> *Than perish from the Chance's list*
> *Before the Perishing!*

Was "terribler" a word, I wondered. I liked its oddity. What seemed "terribler" was behind me: hangings, murders, black outs, estrangements, gang rapes. I grabbed on to my second "Chance," with Dickinson's uppercase letter. My family was back in my court "before the Perishing!" with Dickinson's exclamation point. We four were once more. I'd tried at love with P. and seen it fail. Or I'd seen love linger then crumble, but what in this world does not linger and then crumble? I'd believed that I hitched myself to something that might last me into my dotage. The parting was deep yet bitterness was not what remained— rather, I felt love that I had been loved and love that I had loved. If I was to rescue an emotion it would be love. The world was strange without the man I'd loved. Yet the absence of romance gave me a key into writing, and that opened a sweet cool place. What was more important to me? Men? Or the chance to write another poem? Poetry was a faithful bridegroom.

I headed off to divinity school. I headed home. My family loved me for who I was. I had the bounty of family support Dickinson lived to appreciate. *How mighty.* I stepped back. I leaped.

But Where I Say
Hours I Mean Years

97.

Could I be out and in? Committing to a religious life, I hesitated. Could I be me? Gerard Manley Hopkins said about Walt Whitman:

> I may as well say what I should not otherwise have said, that I always knew in my heart Walt Whitman's mind to be more like my own than any other man's living. As he is a very great scoundrel this is not a pleasant confession. And this makes me the more desirous to read him and the more determined I will not.

Was I a scoundrel? Rubbing up against a religious vocation, someone might take issue with who I was.

New Haven alleys were splotched with wet newspapers. Every room I walked into smelled of old wood paneling and fireplaces. I'd missed that scent. In New England, I went to the library the first semester of holy orders and couldn't read. I kept waiting for the phone to ring with a customer complaint. Handling difficult customers had addled my mind. Kept waiting to *fold* something. Maybe I wasn't going to be able to do this? That vaudeville hook lurked: would I be asked to leave because I was gay?

I called people from the committees back in Florida. All those priests encouraged me. My staunch agnostic family encouraged me without taking interest in knowing about the

Church. In some complicated way I barely understood, they were proud of me.

Seminarians crammed the week. Morning prayer started in Saint Luke's chapel at seven thirty a.m.: a motley throng of the pious, Southerners who had grown up on Bible bingo, androgynous organists smiling like courtesans, and young balding men with crumbs on their cheeks who talked of early church fathers, and then, well, whoever I was.

I took my straw-woven seat, genuflected, knelt on the Persian rug, embraced the other hopefuls during the peace. Psalm 34 went: "O taste and see that the Lord is good." I tasted and saw in that chapel. It had been a long time since I'd had the opportunity *to sit*. Those years in Palm Beach I'd been playing a game of musical chairs. Now the music stopped. On the wall, a Byzantine icon dedicated to Tim Dlugos, an American poet. In 1987 Dlugos tested positive for HIV. In 1989 he was diagnosed with AIDS. He'd come to this chapel wanting to be a priest. He was unable to complete his studies due to illness. Dlugos died in 1990. The icon was of Saint Luke, the healer. I stared at that icon. The icon stared at me.

98.

Instead of opening the Bible, I opened up a biography of Hopkins by Robert Bernard Martin: *A Very Private Life*. Hopkins's spirit was close to me in New Haven.

During his time as a Jesuit priest celebrating the mass, Gerard Manley Hopkins faced the altar. The bread snapped like a light switch and he saw no one. The lonely celibate priest in the sacristy haunted my mind as a likely paradigm. Towards the end, Gentle Hop, as Hopkins was called by his Jesuit colleagues, wrote the sonnet, "I wake and feel the fell of dark, not day." He was forty-one. Six in all, "the terrible sonnets," as they are known, were written, to use Hopkins's words, "in blood." He felt confined "in a coffin of weakness and dejection." The sonnets came to be known as terrible, because according to his friend, Canon Dixon, they crystallized his melancholy, a melancholy that had turned violent. Where had the ecstasy gone?

> *I wake and feel the fell of dark, not day.*
> *What hours, O what black hours we have spent*
> *This night! what sights you, heart, saw; ways you went!*
> *And more must, in yet longer light's delay.*
> *With witness I speak this. But where I say*
> *Hours I mean years, mean life. And my lament*
> *Is cries countless, cries like dead letters sent*
> *To dearest him that lives alas! away.*

Hopkins yokes "feeling" and "felling," echoing isolation. I hoped I'd left such loneliness behind me, but loneliness has a habit of waiting. The next line grows ecstatic. When he writes, "Hours I mean years, mean life," time bends, speeds. He slashes his "I" into the paper, unable to acclimate himself to Ireland, where he'd been sent to teach classics to large classrooms of diffident Irish students, cut off from his family, his workload heavy, he worked past midnight in a room at the back of the house off Saint Stephen's Green in Dublin. His sunken cheekbones looked like "harp frames," as he wrote to his mother. His chamber pot filled with diarrhea. His eyesight failed. His eyes bled. Migraines pounded in his temples. Estranged from family and himself, bound up by his religious calling, being a Catholic in a family of Anglicans, denying, displacing, repressing his attractions to men, he'd orphaned himself countless times.

Hopkins died in 1889. He was forty-four. Four years before he died, England criminalized unspecified acts of "gross indecency" between men, in what was known as the Labouchere amendment. This amendment led to the love that dare not speak its name being fog-horned in the Oscar Wilde trials. Wilde, in defense of his love for Lord Alfred Douglas, will cite the Bible's David and Jonathan, Plato, Michelangelo, and Shakespeare. "There is nothing unnatural about it," Wilde will say as they take him off to prison. His wife and two sons will change their last name and never see him again. Douglas will disown him, take an interest in Nazis, and marry. (*He'd rather marry.*)

Gentle Hop *did* fall in love once, maybe twice. The first time was Digby Dolben. An odd public school boy who burned the tips of his hair, refused to wear glasses so he was always squinting, and donned monk's habits and would run off to confessionals after he'd had trysts with Oxford boys. Hopkins's Anglican confessor forbade him to write or spend time with Dolben. He stopped drawing after he was too aroused by drawing the half-naked Christ. But it wasn't long after the two met that Dolben drowned in a freak swimming accident. Took them days to find the body. The body all bloated and unrecognizable. Purpled. Shortly after that Hopkins sought the Catholic collar. Much later, he said he'd always wanted to visit the site where Dolben drowned. *And my lament is cries countless, cries like dead letters sent to dearest him that lives alas! away.* The poem would like us to frame these sentiments thinking of God, but I read a reference to his suffocating closeted existence here. Hopkins never went to the spot. Similarly, I'd asked after the spot where John was murdered but never could bring myself to actually go pay my respects to it.

99.

"This is Michael," Edmund said, bright, young, and blond. He had befriended me on one of my first days at seminary and he called Michael "my partner." Michael had come to help him move in.

"Honey," said Michael to Edmund in front of a bishop, "can you pass me the sugar." Edmund and Michael were not anxious to pass as heterosexuals. Standing there, everyone sipping their coffee, I thought—we'd married women, lived double lives, extravagantly self-destructed. Young men now married their boyfriends and went on to serve prestigious Episcopal churches in Manhattan, had their wedding announcements published in the *New York Times*.

"When did you come out?" Edmund asked, kindly inspecting me, the way a child looks at an adult.

"Forty, I think," I mumbled. I wore a sweater with holes and food stains that smelled like moth balls. I had bad breath. My teeth were stained. I was jolted into a dizziness as my past slammed into my present: *But where I say hours I mean years, mean life.*

"How old are you now?" Edmund asked while typing out a text message, his two thumbs moving like lobster claws.

"Forty-six," I mumbled, as if swallowed under the sea of time.

100.

We aged. "This is an end game now," my mother mumbled under her breath. We were in the kitchen in Old Saybrook. Dishes piled up in a shipwreck. The light scarce, she'd shuttered the window, said she couldn't see well with her cataracts and diplopia. The kitchen floor dark and gray and caked with food scraps like the floor of the cage of an old gorilla. "No one touches me much anymore," she said matter-of-factly. I remembered her beautiful. Remembered her strong. Remembered her confident. Remembered her fierce. Remembered her. When we went into stores in Old Saybrook the clerks saw an old woman whom they preferred to ignore. Not what I remembered.

Someone was coming over to buy a Chinese screen, her wedding silver. The car got repossessed the morning before I visited. She had grown much smaller since I last saw her. Her toes went off in all directions now. Gone all the high heels. The toes were like talons or roots. The nails completely discolored, purple and brown, they looked like potsherds that an archeologist had carefully discovered with a toothbrush from a dig. Her wedding ring slid up and down her wedding finger like the latch to a door one is endlessly opening and closing: where once her skin had been tight on her hand now the blue veins looked like ropes and almost pulled away from the flesh.

Me, next to her, on my way to becoming a priest. Hopkins wrote, "The hidden life at Nazareth is the great help to faith."

Even if few noticed my declaration, maybe that would help. It wasn't anything unfamiliar: poetry is a hidden life. My faith was out in the open, but my mother and I didn't talk about it. Faith confounded her. Faith confounded me. I fastened to hidden lives.

My mother turned to me, using a language that had plastered over her first of Lithuanian. Shaking in her walker, she said: "Did anyone ever tease you or bully you when you were in high school?" She asked this without any expectation that I would answer her. All the neighbors carried on with their lives, taking out the rubbish, making to-do lists, pulling up the blinds, lowering the blinds, answering the phone, not answering the phone, taking the dogs out, bringing the dogs in. We didn't look at each other.

I lied: "No. Never." She knew I lied.

Tears in her eyes, she said, "I'm so sorry about those comments I made to you about not having grandchildren. I won't say it anymore."

I touched her swollen knuckles. I called a car rental agency. I needed to get groceries in the house. I needed to clean up the shit and piss. I needed to buy diapers.

101.

I like my queer public persona.

—JAMES FRANCO

In my second year, James Franco came to my seminary. He wanted to ask permission to film "The Clerk's Tale." He wanted to make a short film, fifteen minutes—a film in miniature. He came in a black limo. Suddenly, from the stacks and from the large wooden tables, we, the dandruffed theological students looked up, we pushed our greasy hair away from our temples, and we glued our eyes on him the way we usually did with obscure biblical criticism.

Handsome muscular man, Franco had gained a reputation as possibly gay, which seemed not to be true from what I'd read. Or read between the lines. Yet the ambiguity of his sexuality had generated a mystique for him as (what else to call it?) a sexual impersonator: Franco in person regarded it all as fun and not the ruin of his career as it would have been for Tab Hunter or Rock Hudson or Marlon Brando. A complicated (or faux-complicated) sexuality *bloomed* in Franco. He seemed at ease pretending to be gay, the charm of it, which did give me pause and left me wondering what it might be like to flirt with gayness without carrying the suffering. But perhaps Franco had suffered? People suffer in ways we do not know. Same-sex kisses razzle-dazzled him and did not stick to him with guilt. Lucky Franco, maybe, unless of course he wasn't even sure himself, but then I thought, sexuality is an idiosyncratic business—slippery, seemingly straightforward, but often it is not. To use Bishop's word, maybe there was something "undecided" in him? In any case, one afternoon, when I was sitting in my little attic room, Franco stood in my doorway.

"What is this like for you, this fame?" I asked him later as we sat in a restaurant. The nervous hostess put a screen in front of our table so no one would see us. As she stretched out the screen, fame encroached on our peace: this made me protective, in the neighborhood of paternal love.

"It's crazy, crazy," he said, looking caged.

Meaty and intelligent and fifteen years younger than I was, Franco had spent his life yearning to be captured on screen and had succeeded. His smile was large and unzipped his face with pizzazz, a mouth that had stretched across buildings and screens and multiplied itself in glossy magazines. Funny, I thought then, how I'd spent my life trying hard *not* to be seen. I reached for salt and pepper and thought of Daryl's mouth and the long string of blood swaying from it—*dearest him that lives alas! away*, Hopkins wrote. If the line refers to Christ, Christ is molded into a figure of loneliness and despair, something unreachable. I'd long ago had such a grim view on things, but something had changed with me. I felt like one of Dickinson's "hopers." There I sat at a table with my beet-and-goat-cheese salad, about to be a priest, representing Christ, across from a gay-talking, gay-acting gay icon who wasn't gay.

"I loved a woman once," I said. Why did I say this? To add complexity? To chime in and say that an undecided sexuality was not strange to me? I wanted Franco to find ease, for he seemed uneasy. Perhaps for the first time, I felt like a priest. Nick Thorndike's ghost was near.

"Oh, yeah," Franco said, looking over his shoulder. The waitress took our order. Her hand shook.

An odd tension vibrated between us: while his acting was driven by disclosure, in real life he was reticent; ready to be nude on film, in person he was guarded. He'd learned how to be there and not be there. While he hadn't invented an accent like Plath with her British accent or my father with his Northern accent or my mother with her Yankee accent, he had invented a whole way of being.

"It was a long time ago," I said.

Franco was curious about my decision to enter the Episcopal priesthood. I still had a hard time articulating why I was becoming a priest. Words failed me. But I thought I must try to articulate *something*. I pushed my brain. I pushed my tongue up against the back of my teeth and then released the muscle as if I was pressing on brakes.

Paul wrote in his letter to the Philippians: "Let this mind be in you, which was also in Christ Jesus." So what was that mind that I was hoping now to graft to mine? Herbert would say it was a mind of love. I hadn't known much about God's love in my youth, but the forgiveness and compassion that had worked me over in midlife gave me some awareness of the measure of God's love.

The choice to become a priest came from some place *beyond* words. Becoming a Christian had to do with unlatching my own cage. Somewhere below the crucifix around my neck, near the gut more than the head, lay the answer. I wasn't changing my accent or speech, but I was adopting a way of existence. I scarcely knew what I thought, why I'd been called to poetry or the priesthood. I was mute as my Connecticut grandmother.

That gray slushy New Haven day circled in silences: students burrowed into the library stacks, and few people were in the shops. The New England silence comforted me. Silence had tutored my priesthood. Had I been acting in a play and losing myself in the character until I became the character as Franco did so skillfully? Where did I end and the art start? I'd memorized the lines before I felt their meaning. Soon I'd be accompanied by a costume.

Was I hiding? The farm and Brooks Brothers had hidden me. I no longer had those. The church could serve to hide me. As calculated as Franco might be about his "queer persona," I'd been calculated about hiding.

I was the hesitant invited guest from Herbert's poetry who comes to sit down at the banquet. I had a place even if I felt unworthy. Even with doubts. I had a place as I had in church basements. I was the meek. Christ was not blocked to me. The way I sat with my movie star and his bleached teeth and sculpted muscles, I felt as if I didn't need to apologize for myself anymore. *That* had taken time. I wasn't sure Franco understood having to apologize for one's existence, but maybe he did. Gray salty Yankee light raked across my face. I had healed.

102.

That Connecticut spring, my final year in seminary, squirrels shook like mobile phones on vibrate. Nervousness grew in the shrubs and in me.

K., my old college girlfriend, invited me to give a poetry reading at Wellesley College where she taught classics. Dad went with me. Dad and I, the two of us, tall and silent, driving and getting lost in the little towns with their Robert Frost stone fences. Laughing. We look alike: it's not uncommon for someone to say to me, "Now you'll know what you'll look like when you get old." A relative had said, "Carbon copies, carbon copies!"

Silvery poplars and birches unraveled their green news as we zoomed past New England. Dad and I weren't part of this landscape: we were interlopers.

Smart, clear Irish skin, tall, K., my old girlfriend, was watchful, circumspect. The minute I saw her I loved her, loved her as I could. Guilt lingered: I could not fulfill a promise that burned within us when we had dated. I felt protective of her. The scales inside me tipped towards the old boyfriend role as she introduced me at the reading. I was surprised. I was not surprised.

After the reading, we went out to a Vietnamese restaurant. The professors were keen to talk. The professors mainly wanted to assess who had tenure and who did not. After that they seemed determined to outsmart each other with the information in their brains, which was impressive. They ignored me and pretended as if my father did not exist. My father had lived over eighty years, and to me it seemed that would spark, if not curiosity, then kindness. It did not.

Hopkins must have felt isolated as I felt that night. According to his biographer Paul Mariani, Hopkins had "a pronounced tendency to overelaborate, to go on at too great length, and so lose his audience." He didn't connect with his audience as an eccentric babbler. My church life did not connect to anyone at the table.

Despite graduating with a first from Oxford, Hopkins had barely passed his theological Jesuit exams, which prevented him from rising in the Catholic hierarchy. He went against the grain and then some. He was a pariah within the world he'd chosen. Being a poet in the Church I felt doubly odd and doubly close to Hopkins. I've been laughed at on both counts.

Painfully there is a story that the Jesuit fathers snickered knowingly during one of Hopkins's sermons to the point that Hopkins lost his place. He was an oddball. Ignored. Perhaps that is the space that created an opening where Hopkins could write those poems? The poems couldn't bring him into communion with others. Maybe poems needed loneliness? Hopkins's poetry drips with loneliness, the lonely syllables like church-candle wax splattering across the anthologies. The later poems are swallowed by loneliness. I knew loneliness. I'd known loneliness young, without a stitch of faith. Now I knew loneliness with faith and in the Church. Reading Hopkins made me less lonely. He was as weird as I was. Hopkins said to me, "I did this, you can do it too." Hopkins's loneliness comforts my mind.

As the pho soup steamed up over our faces, recalling who did what in *Middlemarch* trumped interest in my father. "The

Republicans want..." my father began, which doomed him from gathering an audience that night. I wanted to silence him but I didn't. K. squeezed in questions about our house in Cape Cod. I stared at my father across the table. I remembered us back on the Mississippi, how I followed him. Loneliness was woven into our nerves.

That night, after I'd washed out my father's two sets of underpants in the hotel sink and tucked him into bed, I said, "You know the woman that introduced me tonight?"

"Yes," Dad said with that soft voice he had used after he fought with my mother. He must have felt lonely with those arguments. To whom did he turn? If not a God then what? Drinks? His writing endless articles about the politics of being a doctor? All the articles adding up to trying to understand his life as I have tried to understand mine?

"She was my old girlfriend ... in college."

Pause.

My father and I ignored discussing my personal life. A lonely car stretched out its headlights, the beams fell across the hotel wall like two big warm arms. Then the arms disappeared.

"I felt a certain warmth at the table," Dad said.

With witness I speak this.

With witness I speak this.

With witness I speak this.

103.

Alas! away. Tucked into a labyrinth of vinyl-sided condos, behind books, and more books, ten thousand or more, shades drawn, drenched in the scent of old pages and dog piss and sticky old wine bottles with pencil markings from my brother's visits, my parents moved from room to room. Creditors called. The statuary was gone. The life-sized hand-carved wooden mandolin player boxed, crated, and sold. The carved whale from Nantucket vanished one week. All the golden candelabras gone the next. The eclectic collection à la Isabella Stewart Gardner was replaced by something closer to a flea market. My mother doted on each rusted teapot like it was a diamond ring. She was incensed when collectors offered two dollars for things she thought worth two hundred. My mother looked disoriented. The more objects that disappeared the more she disappeared.

The phone rang. "Don't answer!" she said. She had moss and twigs from her last fall in her dry, dyed-blond hair. We ate meals on trays. The TV blared. The phone rang again.

"Don't answer!" she said, irritated. I turned to see who was talking, and I saw what looked like a woman I once knew.

"How is school, darling?" she said.

"Fine," I said. She moved slower, used the walker all the time now.

She said: "Your mother isn't as young as she used to be. Do you have twenty dollars to go get us some bread?"

She watched her blue jays in her birdbath. She watched over

those birds like a mother watching over her bassinet. When birds came on the television, dying in oil slicks, she sobbed. She'd lost her sense of value in between the Republican political speeches she'd listened to and the mixed-up feelings she'd had about religion and her desire for clothes and antiques. There was less drinking but I didn't care anymore. I didn't want to know anymore.

Family photos—an old one of little John Steven, curled at the edges—fell all around my mother's feet like leaves of a dead tree.

The two of us and our long story, our long witness. Hopkins was with me in that dark Old Saybrook mortgaged condominium. Hopkins wrote:

> *And my lament*
> *Is cries countless, cries like dead letters sent*
> *To dearest him that lives alas! away.*

The long lament between my mother and me lengthened. I couldn't reach her. I hadn't reached her for a long time. Many dead letters had gone out.

104.

My mother swayed. She waggled. I grabbed her arm. Falling and more falling, her days were characterized by falling. My mother fell eight times before my ordination. Fell on the steps, fell on her back, fell answering the phone, fell in the garage looking at a childhood doll she was going to sell on eBay to get money for groceries that week. "The earth is calling me, darling," she said. The strident woman who planted tulips and had a strong tennis serve and bolted off international flights to London in heels hardly could stand. She wobbled and lurched. Falling and falling.

Dad fell in the garage. He whimpered. He had a massive heart attack, the large vein in the back of the heart burst. Afterwards he burped for three days. My mom called 911. He was rushed in with tubes and wires on a stretcher. As I arrived two nurses pulled back the thin blue curtain. "Give me a kiss, Loretta," he was saying to Mom as I arrived.

Mom kissed Dad gently, bending down with—there is no other word I can use here—reverence, and I thought then I didn't know much about love, for what I saw—perfumed by the sterile hospital air—was the most consistent love I've ever known, two people together for nearly sixty years— disappointments, failures, doubts, fights, surrenders—but they *abided*. What did I know about that? In the next bed a policeman was splayed bare-chested with enormous purple nipples that jiggled as he joked with my father about basketball and about how he used to hear my parents' wine bottles clinking away when they took their recycling out.

I stared at the cop's beautiful body: how at ease he was displaying his torso and how I repressed wanting to be his suckling. Hopkins wrote: "I think then no one can admire the beauty of the body more than I do." I felt like Hopkins when he described himself to his friend Bridges: "time's eunuch." Elsewhere he wrote: "All impulse fails me: I can give myself no sufficient reason for going on. Nothing comes. I am a eunuch—but it is for the kingdom of heaven's sake." That was then. Much had changed. My father's body pulsed before me. Next to him, pulsed the beautiful body of the cop.

105.

During the worst blizzard to hit New England, after three years at Yale, I was ordained to the diaconate, the first major step towards priesthood. Snows came down and down, filling windows and streets and doors. White on white on white. My brother came on one of the last trains to make it through the snow from New York City, smiling at me so his scar became a tiny dot. Friends from New York got out of taxis.

If loneliness came, as it would, I told myself to remember this moment. The snow-drenched mob clustering in the beautiful white Marquand Chapel, with its mullioned windows and Doric columns, was the opposite of loneliness. This was love gathering and expanding, bidden by my call. Love was multiplying like Jesus's loaves.

Mary Jane flew in from Florida with seasoning for the dinner on her lap. We were going to make a Cuban meal in honor of my Cuban American bishop. Mary Jane smiled so her teeth shone bright. I invited P. but never heard back. Alice Quinn, the poetry editor at the *New Yorker*, who'd brought "The Clerk's Tale" into print, got the last train from New York, her shoulders epaulets of snow. Next to her one of my mother's old friends who'd survived Bergen-Belsen. Next to them, my parents. Someone drove my parents in on a four-wheel-drive truck from Old Saybrook. Many stood. Stood strong. This is what we do for one another: stand witness.

Friend and poet Richard Blanco drove down from Bethel,

Maine. I asked him to read a poem in Spanish by Roberto Sosa, a Honduran poet I'd discovered. The previous summer I'd traveled to Honduras for the first time, with the impulse to learn Spanish. The country and the language and the poverty I'd seen clung to me. Sosa began his poem:

> *The poor are many*
> *And so—*
> *Impossible to forget.*

The poem was impossible for me to forget. In two summer months I'd glimpsed poverty beyond anything I could have imagined. I'd never looked out my kitchen window to see a baby eat garbage before. I was beginning to learn Spanish at a later age, yes, but I was also being shown scenes that would alter my direction beyond what I could ever imagine. A deep change had begun with that Honduran visit, and the poem, it turned inside me and warmed the cold winter twilight some.

Two hours before the snow ceased. An eerie quiet. Then came the ordination. That was where John's ghost walked in and patted me on the shoulder. Followed by Nick Thorndike and Nana. White high houses, covered with snow up to the first floor. As the service began with "Laudate Dominum" my mother wobbled up to the podium and read Jeremiah: "Then the Lord reached out his hand and touched my womb..." Snow covered New Haven. The rich incensed air between the readings was the atmosphere inside a bell after it has been rung.

I lay prostrate on the floor, my arms outstretched as if on a cross, before my bishop. The choir began to sing "Nada te turbe." Albs rustled. Heads bowed. All of us beckoning and ushering in that real thing of spirit that cannot be seen, that absolutely cannot ever be understood. Then I knelt before my bishop, the way I had for trouser fittings at Brooks, and took my vow of obedience. Then the Eucharist, and my parents held back. The ritual of a perfect circle held high and then broken. Bread and wine, bread and wine, mouths opening and closing like little chicks. Afterwards, I said, "I noticed the two of you did not come up for Holy Communion. You know you could have if you wanted to. You only need to be baptized, I think." People exited. Snow fell. The smell of candles snuffed lingered.

"But I don't think your father *is* baptized," said my mother.

106.

Had they been sitting in the same tattered wingback chairs all morning and afternoon? Several months had passed. That afternoon, I visited my parents, the house unbearably quiet after their last bulldog had died. Both of them smelled of urine. I came forward with fresh trousers and asked them to change. Around the edges of the house, the house wrens beckoned for their mates. Wrens filled up their nests with sticks and booty, such elaborate scaffolding for mating. All our lives—whether bird or human, wren or Reece—this singing and building, singing and building.

"The condo committee made us cut down the beautiful tulip tree," Mom said, speaking as if a relative had died. "It was so beautiful, *that tree*." Violence made her squirm. Hadn't Gentle Hop wept when he heard the Binsey poplars were being cut down?

> *My aspens dear, whose airy cages quelled,*
> *Quelled or quenched in leaves the leaping sun,*
> *All felled, felled, are all felled*

"I have been thinking," Dad said. Another pause. I lived in a Pinter play with my father. Pause. Pause.

"I want to be baptized," Dad said. Mom shook her head, "Yes, he's been talking about it for some time now . . ." Church confounded her. You could tell by her tone the subject interested her as much as cleaning their house. "I hate cleaning," she said, followed by, "Your parents are *not* cleaners." A small blue jay alighted on the tulip-tree stump. A rabbit quivered in the holly. Her hand tamped Virginia Woolf's diary.

"Why?" I said to my agnostic father. "Why do you want to be baptized?"

"I want to be closer to you," he said. Pause. We each stood back, surprised. Then I saw what I saw and saw what I'd never seen before. Tears for my struggle welled behind the dirty film of Dad's scratched glasses and then, immediately, behind Mom's new foggy bifocals—*what sights you, heart, saw*—the four sets of lenses were four bay windows that hadn't been opened in fifty years.

107.

I needed to help my mother with a clasp. We were going to church. I looked for the impossibly small hook to connect the string of secondhand fake pearls.

Their long-married argument ensued.

She: "There he is, sitting there and not talking."

He: "I never have a chance."

She: "Whole hours go by and he never speaks."

Me: "But aren't you both used to it now?"

She: "If you only knew."

He: "Ah, Loretta. I guess we're doing better than we used to."

Me: "You mean us? Or you and her?" Pause.

Me, again: "You mean us or you and her?" Pause. Nothing.

She: "He just sits there. Answer your son."

He: "Well, I would if I wasn't so monitored all the goddamn time."

She: "See, see how he talks to me. He's nothing but an old crab."

He: "God dammit, Loretta."

Me: "We better get going." And so it went. And so it had gone. And so it would always go. Their great long mysterious love to which I was tethered. And my witnessing it.

So it came to pass that I baptized my eighty-year-old father. Westerly, Rhode Island, gave us a day with tulips, garish and candy-colored, clowning in the circus of spring, blowing their horns. A gay couple, Roger and Dan, who had been in the church since I started there, agreed to be my father's godparents. Roughly my age, Roger and Dan had lived together since their twenties. They took to my parents and were as decorous as airline pilots, escorting my parents here and there. Dad began saying, "Where are my gay godparents?" Later my mother, father, and I attended their wedding, the first gay wedding in that church. Someone asked my mother at our table if *I* had met anyone "special." My mother said, "No, but we hope he will." I don't think we looked at one another, but we certainly knew how long it'd taken us to say such things.

A gigantic baby was baptized alongside Dad. The priest dripped water onto their heads in a big golden basin. I stood next to him. My father's bald head leaned into the baptismal font next to the bright pink orb of the baby's head. His scalp covered with basal cells and age spots like a wild map of an ancient country. The two heads shone bright and reflected all the light in the church. Two beginnings. You could begin at any time. It was never too late.

When Hopkins died of a virulent form of typhoid fever his parents came over on a boat from England, barely understanding who their son was: there had been much estrangement. The air smelled of rotten eggs from all the sulfureted hydrogen coming out of the factory stacks. The Jesuit priest gave Hopkins last rites and Hopkins said, "I am so happy, I am so happy." I'd outlived Hopkins now a few years. Happiness, that elusive emotion, was near.

After the rite, the family of the young big baby took out recording devices like a military flank getting into position. The mother took the baby into her arms and began to walk up and down the aisle. Then my father, unprompted by anyone, *also* began to walk up and down the aisle, accompanied by his two gay godparents. My father—tall, bald, Southern, conservative, Republican, basketball star for Duke, with his yellow teeth smiling, missing one upper incisor—looked as he did when we had walked down by the Mississippi. I watched from my pew and was not unaware of the ten years we hadn't spoken over—what? Monumental and unsolvable our problems, now there we were, father, mother, son, brother, proud, a part of something, finally, without tragedy, or carved more sharply by tragedy, and now joy. Round and round the church Dad went, round and round, dripping with baptismal water, looking in demeanor and carriage like Miss America.

I turned my head to my father and watched him. Mom and I held hands. My brother sat to my right. Beyond the stained-glass windows that featured biblical scenes, Westerly quieted. The rich were coming back to Watch Hill. Lesbian seagulls swirled around the belfry and cawed contrapuntally with the church-bell tolls. My parents were more at ease that Sunday: their social security checks had arrived to cover their grocery bill and gas bill. We argued earlier in the day over whether they should ask for food stamps. Mom said she'd rather starve than ask for food stamps. Some weeks they went without meals.

108.

After the baptism, I boarded the Metro-North headed into Manhattan. Joyful, I felt the enormous clang of industry and bustle of hope that place is. The train drew closer and closer to the projects and the tall buildings—I began to taste the gray dusty rush of the subways, feel the jolt of pedestrians: my heart jumped with the upsurge of drafts and hammer of advancements that define that city. I pushed through the turnstiles, got on the 4 train at Grand Central, connected to the 1 train, and emerged on Christopher Street. I hurried up the steps. I wended my way to services. Past the Three Lives bookstore with its fire-engine-red trim I went, each pane of glass displaying a beautiful book. I lingered there for a moment, the way one does in churches looking at the statuary.

A handsome gay man waved behind the counter inside. He'd mentioned to me last time I was there *he* was writing a novel, that he needed an agent, his dream beginning. Was he waving at me? Could there be love for me in the world? Could I accept it? What had Elizabeth Bishop said in a wishful way in her diary as she traveled on that steamer ship down to Brazil the first time? "Love will unexpectedly appear over & again." I acknowledged the handsome gay man and for once did not lower my eyes. I moved closer to the Hudson.

I glimpsed myself in the reflection of the window of a gay-male sex shop with leather swings and strawberry slick sex liquids. There I was—balding, glasses, wearing my black shirt and black pants and plastic priest collar smeared with my neck grime, my cassock tucked under my arm, flapping in the wind, practical shoes with arch supports, drab pilgrim, reserved, last Reece, almost extinct, my expanding eyebrows and ear hair all superimposed upon a large vibrating hot-pink dildo. A customer swung blithely in the sex swing, back and forth. John, my cousin, came into that glass. I saw us laughing next to the crazy aunt from the nuthouse on her day pass—how strange time was, doubling back. To the air I said, "Look, John! Look where we are now." The customer decided against the sex swing and instead bought a plunger.

My cell phone rang. In the basement massage parlors young Chinese men mashed their fists into the oiled buttocks of the older men while wind chimes played. Happy endings went off all over the Village like popped champagne corks. A Boston lawyer had called to tell me I'd won the Amy Lowell grant—the poetry grant that allowed you to live abroad for a year. I called my bishop in Miami.

"What should I do?" I said.

"I think you should go to Madrid," he said. This statement was based on the fact that I had spent a summer working in a Trauma 1 emergency room in downtown Hartford, where there was gang violence and much Spanish spoken. I'd kept telling him I needed to learn Spanish, more and better, that two months in Honduras wasn't enough. He'd listened.

"Wait where you are, I have a friend there and I'll call you right back." His friend was the Episcopal bishop of Spain. My Miami bishop was on a phone in his car, I could hear palms swooshing as if he was in a car wash. Madrid. I liked the sound of it. I'd never been to Madrid.

Five minutes later I had been invited to live in Madrid for the year, take Spanish grammar classes all day long with my Amy Lowell money, and be ordained there. I squinted in the light, through the film of my dirty glasses. Planes in the blue sky circled JFK or LaGuardia. I heard church bells. I turned towards Saint Luke's, towards my murdered man. I slipped into my parish, Saint Luke's, where I worked, the world's most famous gay church, ground zero for the AIDS epidemic.

I thought about Hopkins's "terrible" sonnet that finishes:

> *I am gall, I am heartburn. God's most deep decree*
> *Bitter would have me taste: my taste was me;*
> *Bones built in me, flesh filled, blood brimmed the curse.*
> *Selfyeast of spirit a dull dough sours. I see*
> *The lost are like this, and their scourge to be*
> *As I am mine, their sweating selves; but worse.*

These strings of sharp monosyllables! Who will ever or has ever written this way? No one. When you read Hopkins you feel he's making up his own language.

The speaker here is not illuminated by the light of day but destroyed by it. I well remember that from trudging the halls of the mental hospital. In a late letter to his friend Robert Bridges he wrote at this time of not having "inducements and inspirations" to write. He felt, like Herbert, that love was to be the "great moving power and spring" of poetry and the person he was in love with, according to this poem, Christ, felt cut off from him.

He closes this poem in these two triplets that are some kind of Eucharist. The bones of the speaker are wrapped in flesh, the *f*s harken back to the poem's opening with "feel" and "fell." His bones, flesh, and skin are a chalice brimming with sin. "Selfyeast of spirit a dull dough sours," dense self-hate pushes out any hope for Christ to attend. His idiosyncrasy is his sound today, pushing against the orthodoxy that pulled him in. With the strange charge of the words, the poem skitters off the page. Hopkins begs to be unleashed. The words are alive and lovable despite the despair they catalogue.

This grim poem ends with the speaker's heart going the way of the lost, in the company of the "sweating selves": As I imagine him in the chiaroscuro of that last room, with death near, I wish I could touch him on the shoulder and tell him of the wonders and freedoms that were to come, that one day a lesbian named Elizabeth Bishop, who persevered despite great challenges with alcoholism, would write her last poem and it would end with the word gay and an exclamation point.

Hopkins swirls with complexity. I leave the page unsure if I know what he means. It doesn't matter much to me. He wrote in defense of his poems to Bridges: "I was not over-desirous that the meaning of all should be quite clear, at least unmistakable . . . lines and stanzas should be left in the memory and superficial impressions deepened . . . I am sure I have read and enjoyed pages of poetry that way." I don't mind his impregnability. I know the ceiling of gay silence. His baroque ceiling is pleasurable to me.

Hopkins sang of his joy in God's creation, and once that abandoned him, he sang, when capable, of his despair. Sadly, Hopkins was far from enjoying the freedoms I've seen and known. Plath missed the Women's Movement. Hopkins missed Gay Liberation. Knowing that makes me think you never know what hope might come: what seems fixed and insurmountable, one day, is not—is not, is not, is not!

"I am gall, I am heartburn," Hopkins writes. Unlike Whitman, Hopkins cannot celebrate himself. I'd felt that. The poem ends in a hellish basement. Bad as life might be, Hopkins seems to be saying, it is not as bad as those lives damned without salvation. I've wondered if he truly believed this. He'd moved far away from how he had started out in his early poetic career writing lines such as "The world is charged with the grandeur of God." He ends this poem with two monosyllables: "but worse." Two monosyllables that double bolt our celibate into his sonnet. This is different from Herbert's "I did sit and eat." The effect here is of flailing rather than reclining.

I've felt closed down, shut up, silenced, politely not invited to speak, but I'd found my ways to manage in the world, and in the church that awaited me. I could manage. I'd find a way. I kept turning back to Hopkins and repeating his words, lines that leave him gorgeously crucified.

Like Dickinson, as Hopkins grew in his art he ceased to hope for publication and sometimes discouraged any effort to publish. He felt when he was stirred by the poetic passions it was sacrilegious to "make capital" from them. Priesthood trumped poethood for him. The collected edition of the Hopkins poems would not be published until forty years after he died. Then Bridges, his friend, would say at last "the war within" Hopkins had ceased.

I walked towards Saint Luke's that day in New York City. I was about to enter a congregation where my difference made *no* difference: the woman who swung the incense had been a man and the choir soloist belted out the doxology like Freddie Mercury. If Sylvia Plath had lived and then turned into Julie Andrews and spun around the Swiss Alps, singing, that gets close to what had happened to me. I thought of Hopkins and his sonnet "God's Grandeur," written early, when he was full of hope and faith and less disappointment:

The world is charged with the grandeur of God.
It will flame out, like shining from shook foil;
It gathers to a greatness, like the ooze of oil
Crushed. Why do men then now not reck his rod?
Generations have trod, have trod, have trod;
And all is seared with trade; bleared, smeared with toil;
And wears man's smudge and shares man's smell: the soil
Is bare now, nor can foot feel, being shod.
And for all this, nature is never spent;
There lives the dearest freshness deep down things;
And though the last lights off the black West went
Oh, morning, at the brown brink eastward, springs—
Because the Holy Ghost over the bent
World broods with warm breast and with ah! bright wings.

Bright wings I had. Bright wings to carry me all the way to Madrid. The Holy Ghost was in the air. My brothers and sisters from Oscar Wilde to Stonewall had trod and trod to get to where I was now. That war within quieted. A large debt of sorrow had been paid for my sweet life. Memories of my father came into my brain—how he had wanted to write and be a writer and somewhere along the way much of that was sacrificed for us as a family. He loved reading and writing but gave his life over to a job I wasn't sure he liked. His job had paid for my education. I was following in his example as I was following in Gentle Hop's example. Much had been done on my behalf. There had been sacrificing on my behalf. I'd been cavalier. To the busy New York air I said, "Thank you, Dad." Then I said, "Thank you, Gentle Hop."

Follow Me

109.

Love, because I had love I gave love to a life I now loved. I clutched hands and flowers and phones and pens and a Bible insistently. I started blurting out "I love you" randomly. I said it to strangers now. I could never say it enough. It would never be a mistake.

I immediately loved that tattered humble cathedral with buckling windows in Madrid, cracked window glass, chipping paint and sewage that backed up under the office. I felt the walls loved me. That tiny twig of the church founded for Spanish Anglicans, closed during the Franco dictatorship. The place smelled like an old book. More accurately, the place smelled like an old book that had been stuck in a box in a basement for forty years.

Several minutes past ten. Madrid was waking up that Sunday of my ordination. My parents and my brother and my father's gay godparents had flown over for the event. It would be my parents' last plane trip. No children in the tiny street lined with four-story nineteenth-century brick buildings with balconies. A silence of yearning entered my new small living room where I put down my new cup of Spanish coffee. The ceilings were high with large white molding. Eight suitcases were lined up on the shiny old pinewood floors.

Where was it all going? Time seemed mysterious. Seconds and hours and years circled rather than went in a straight line. I could measure it from year to year: a long sentence at the end of which was my death, smaller than the period at the end of this sentence. Yet there was a time that was not linear. God's time. I thought about that more.

I dressed in a black faded shirt and black dress pants left over from my Brooks Brothers days. My plastic white collar rested in my hand, I shook it like a soldier with a bandage ready to attend to the wounded. Around my neck swung a huge set of keys the bishop gave to me. I jangled sounding like the coins the homeless shook in their paper cups.

I came down the four flights of burnished wooden steps with the iron railings. I strode through the courtyard, past cracked walls, as neighbors readied their espresso machines, swore and grumbled. In a high tiny rooftop apartment, someone topped out an impressive sustained sexual climax, a long monkey yowl. I entered the sacristy. I donned my full-length cassock. I fastened the black buttons at the top. I cinched the black fabric belt around my waist with the fringe ends. I looked quickly in the spotted mirror next to a cheap broken plastic clock where time stopped. I pulled on my giant white surplice that billowed like a parachute, then a colorful stole my mother had made for me, I kissed in the center as I was taught to do before it went around my neck. A uniform appealed to me. A uniform for a profession that Herbert said was characterized by love: he wrote in *The Country Parson* that "love was the business and the aim" for parsons. The uniform advertised that. What a magical thing to have a uniform that signaled love.

In my hand I held a tattered program, the white paper browned by the dirty fingers of the poor who I would learn had fingered these pages for years waiting for their bags of food on Saturday evenings. Finally, I snapped my white plastic collar in place behind my head, a circle that, once snapped, put me all together again in one piece for the world to see me different—a choice weighted with a history of trying mightily to hide what was different in me. I turned the latch of the thick old door that went into the cathedral. The cathedral was three stories high and largely plain: red stained glass with cracks, cream walls with stains, biblical commands stenciled onto wood, plain pews, red cushions, a black-and-white marble floor, and a cross without Jesus on it. John Calvin would be pleased. The severity of the architecture was reinforced by parishioners and clergy who did not genuflect or bow or do anything that might resemble the Catholics. Saint Luke in the Fields this was not. The bishop stood for my entrance. He began to speak in beautiful Madrid Spanish, elegant and rich. "Id en paz" was lisped: I-*th* en pa-*th*.

Less than twenty people that day. The crowd looked like one you might find for an early movie matinee. I stood before the bishop and the Bible, ready for love. Jesus said: "Follow me." I couldn't see him. But then I couldn't see most of my poets either.

My mother, my father, my brother, Roger, Dan, and I stood. It would be the last time my parents would ever stand up in that way for me. My brother had struggled to get my mother across the street. Her walking had grown more unsteady. The jet lag had deeply affected her blood pressure medication. She stood in her pew wearing a feathered hat with a veil. She sweat and looked as if she might cry out of confusion. My father looked at the ceiling. My brother held them up. One on either side. My brother probably had been in a church only one or two times in his life and all those times were on account of me. "Adoption" is a recurrent word in my Christianity. Adoption comes up in the Westminster Confession of Faith where it says we are "partakers of the grace of adoption . . . and enjoy the liberties and privileges of the children of God." The irony did not escape me that morning that my brother had behaved like a more loyal son. I'd been the prodigal. I'd been estranged from my parents. He'd gone back quickly to them. He'd adopted us. Not the other way around.

My brother glowed more handsome than ever that morning in Spain. He was tall and trim, his striking features were full of all the ambiguity of Jesus as painted by Leonardo da Vinci in *The Last Supper*. Even if he'd been hurt and betrayed he was still standing at the table and breaking bread. My brother took in the full measure of our odd family and loved it in the subtlest way. He'd behaved like a priest.

I'd left him alone. I'd let him be he, be free. Spanish filled the cathedral. We understood not one word.

110.

I took Spanish classes four hours every day. Then I came home and fell asleep. The school and classroom were in a basement. My brain was crammed full of the subjunctive. Young Spaniards lovingly spent their time shoving grammar down my throat. Declensions poured out of my ears. All my Amy Lowell money went down that basement staircase. Having the classes in the basement felt symbolic as it underscored the humility slash humiliation I felt every day I opened my mouth. The root of humility was the Latin *humus*, meaning of the earth, and acquiring all this language and constantly getting my accents wrong was pounding my ego into the ground with a mallet. Everyone in the class was a young girl and a nanny and advancing past me class by class. I kept at it. Not being someone that gives up. It would be years before the benefits showed on my tongue. I began to get a sense that if I was after any fluency I'd need to drop perfectionism. Speaking perfectly was the death knell to language acquisition. That also applied to being a new priest. Perfect priests were boring. When I tripped, or mixed up a reading, or did something imperfectly, the Spanish congregation moved to the edge of their pew and wanted in, wanted me.

Richard Blanco came to visit me that golden Amy Lowell year on Calle de la Beneficencia 18. We sat in my living room, the Spanish sun illuminating the bright wood floors to a coppery color. I had a large apartment that year and all over the blank walls were taped flashcards with Spanish words. As we walked past, the walls would flutter with language, the flashcards like wings, as if Richard and I were huddled together inside a butterfly hatchery.

"Adrienne Rich just died," I said. "Did you see?"

Richard and I shared instantaneously how much we both loved her twenty-one love poems. Saying the same thing simultaneously happened to us. Then we dismayed over poetry's fragile, tiny readership, a common enough pastime for poets.

Neither one of us could have predicted that President Barack Obama would be inviting him to the White House to read for his second inauguration in 2013.

"Why are we doing this?" Richard's forlorn look seemed to say to me that morning regarding poetry. His brooding midnight-colored eyes encased in a face that had drawn in hundreds of gay men and probably many women too, maybe even gay ones for that matter. I'd elected to pursue friendship with handsome Richard, discerning that friendship might last longer and be more rewarding than pining.

Richard's handsomeness was legendary: tall, muscular, with pouting lips that sucked in desire like a vacuum cleaner, a voice so deep it made men and women shake in their loins. He exuded sex from every pore. He was impressive as a carved marble statue of a naked Greek athlete. We were both invited to Books & Books in Miami, not knowing each other, and were asked to take a favorite poem to the reading. We took *the same poem*. Elizabeth Bishop's "One Art." That did it. Friends for decades.

I said to Richard, "Let's have a reading!" My tone displayed all my Midwestern gee-whiz enthusiasm, an innocent guffawing tone that caused me to say "yuppers" in the same sentence. Like that, we did it. My fellow Cuban priest swung a light over the avocado tree in the patio, the bishop made tapas, ten people came and Richard read his poem, "Looking for the Gulf Motel," which went:

There should be nothing here I don't remember . . .

The Gulf Motel with mermaid lampposts
and ship's wheel in the lobby should still be
rising out of the sand like a cake decoration.
My brother and I should still be pretending
we don't know our parents, embarrassing us
as they roll the luggage cart past the front desk
loaded with our scruffy suitcases, two-dozen
loaves of Cuban bread, brown bags bulging
with enough mangos to last the entire week,
our espresso pot, the pressure cooker—and
a pork roast reeking garlic through the lobby.
All because we can't afford to eat out, not even
on vacation, only two hours from our home
in Miami, but far enough away to be thrilled
by whiter sands on the west coast of Florida,
where I should still be for the first time watching
the sun set instead of rise over the ocean.

There should be nothing here I don't remember . . .

My mother should still be in the kitchenette
of The Gulf Motel, her daisy sandals from Kmart
squeaking across the linoleum, still gorgeous
in her teal swimsuit and amber earrings

stirring a pot of arroz-con-pollo, adding sprinkles
of onion powder and dollops of tomato sauce.
My father should still be in a terrycloth jacket
smoking, clinking a glass of amber whiskey
in the sunset at The Gulf Motel, watching us
dive into the pool, two boys he'll never see
grow into men who will be proud of him.

There should be nothing here I don't remember . . .

Blanco's rhapsody about his Cuban family in exile felt close now. His words surprised me there on the patio in an unconscious way. Ironic. Now I was the one with the broken language, adjusting to customs not my own. There was no denying that. Every time I opened my mouth in Spain I wavered between gullible and stupid.

For all the poem's longing, with its repetition of "should still be," as he read it that Madrid night, the poem reclaimed what Richard had lost in a new and different way. Poems stanched loss. Poems repaired things. The poem's restorative chant reminded me time was going forward and my own parents were going backward. The poem encouraged me to appreciate every little thing.

The poem refreshed my awareness of immigrants: Wasn't I harkened back to those cocktail parties with my mother, who had held immigrants close to her? The poem made me more tender towards my own mother that night. Poetry glued places to people. Poetry reconciled things.

Poetry flattened the world with its honesty, removing the obstructions to delusion—the poem hinted at my white luck. I couldn't change history or what had been given to me because of who I was, American, white, male, raised in a Midwestern suburb, sent to a private school, invited into any country club without question. But I could change how I saw the world. I could spread luck. I could elect to be vulnerable and awkward and open. My friendship with Richard brought this to me. Poetry placed our names together in the estate of the spirit. We were brothers.

Richard was bilingual from birth—born to Cuban exiles in Madrid, then raised in the United States. I represented a reverse trajectory. Not once did he make fun of my entering his language of Spanish. With every single word I mispronounced, he corrected or gently encouraged me. Never once did he say, as a cranky old Episcopal priest had once said to me, "You're too old to learn Spanish." He welcomed me.

Richard left. His poem rooted in me as the delicate isolated apprehensive world of the immigrant he described grafted onto my nerves. I leaned into Madrid. All the elegant facades and doorways big as elephants pressed into me. On the Madrid street were the *carnerias*, the ham hocks, lined up, hanging and hooked from the ceiling with their little black hooves pointed down—a proud display of butchery, the elegant brute spirit of Spain: how the present cut the past into little pieces.

Then something accidental happened. Other writers who were friends of mine came. Poets circled the cathedral with poems. A series began to form when I wasn't working in my office with the blue tiles. The poetry kept opening me. Maybe because I was speaking Spanish all day. My English took on a new meaning. If there'd been a drawbridge to my art, the cables snapped and the walls toppled. I needed poetry and I wanted to celebrate others. Above my head a Spanish crucifix, Christ's corpse shriveled like a raisin. I soon had the poets reading in a little bookstore. As each poet finished their poems, the audience clustered around their knees, they would inhale and the sound resembled the sound after a sermon in church—a throat cleared, a body shifted, perceptions rearranged. There at the Desperate Literature bookshop, named after a line from Roberto Bolaño, on Calle de Campomanes 13, near Metro stop Opera, up a windy cobblestoned street, where tourists mixed with gregarious prostitutes, I invited poets to share their work: I built a shrine.

111.

Bishop wound up in Brazil on a lark and then stayed. Plath settled in England. Merrill ended up in Greece. I came to Madrid as a guest, and then the Spaniards adopted me and asked me to return to help the cathedral. I said yes.

Between the first visit and my return, I received a Fulbright and spent a year working as a chaplain and a teacher in an orphanage called Our Little Roses in San Pedro Sula, Honduras. San Pedro was dubbed "murder capital of the world." Three people were killed every day outside the ten-foot wall where I lived surrounded by armed guards. Behind those walls were palm trees whose fronds waved like hands, electric blue mountains close to the color of a Dürer painting, and the world's best mangos and coffee. The beauty jarred against the poverty: the injustices rubbed against my heart like sandpaper.

I worked with a group of seventy-two abandoned and abused girls, teaching them poetry. As a priest, poetry was my trump card, because I felt more confident with the material than with catechism books. Teaching Honduran girls poetry altered me, awakened me, their stories of lost mothers stayed with me, how those mothers had escaped across borders with the help of opportunistic "coyotes," to become cleaning ladies who never saw their children again.

Those girls. Those girls. Those girls formed the foundation of who I became as a priest. One girl wrote in her poem:

> *Life needs love,*
> *love needs life.*

They believed Christ had saved them and had no problem telling me so. Jesus or the Church or nuns or priests were rarely the jokes they are in America or Europe. "Religious people are the ones who come here and help us" is all they would say to me. I was one of them. They were listeners more than evangelizers, circumspect observers, they were like my grandmother in that way: I was ambushed by seventy-two versions of my grandmother.

Or these girls mirrored my brother, adopted and left with the mystery of who his birth mother was. I'd wronged and over-fathered my brother and that was behind me now, here with the girls, might I love better? Jesus said:

> Let the little children come to me, and do not hinder them, for the kingdom of heaven belongs to such as these.

They had a confidence that is hard to describe. The treasure of family that I'd blithely tossed out for ten years was the deep loss they knew in their bones. Because they'd lost their mothers, it made them stronger than most people. Like my brother in that way.

They were exquisite theologians teaching me what I needed to know: gratitude, humility, generosity. In addition, they unabashedly loved me. Not at first, but gradually and fully. After all I was a tall white man who as such represented every imperial force that had smashed their country. And yet, they adopted *me*. Why?

The fact that I was gay was both not said to my face and

talked about incessantly behind my back. This speaking of what was odd about me was not gossip, it was a mass intervention to undo the shame in me. How could I know that? Who would have expected it? Much went unspoken in their pasts, as did in mine, and that was the kismet that was between us: they recognized me. If shame is a cancer, they'd survived it and they, for reasons I never will understand, wanted me to survive it too. Over my year there, they cut that shame out of me like seventy-two expert surgeons. What they were saying to me was what I'd needed to hear all my life: "It doesn't matter that you are gay, God loves you. Now, get busy. No time to dawdle." They said this without saying it. I don't know if that makes sense, but it is the truth.

A lady whom I met during my Brooks Brothers days had a son who was a director, and she suggested we make a documentary of the project. Crazy? Maybe. But my life's course has been suggested to me in offhand ways. I called him up and asked, and he said yes. Before I knew it, we were moving in a pack of six as the crew tried to track poetry being taught. We bumbled and sweat and tried to capture what we couldn't see, as the disciples in the Book of Acts must have in their search for the Holy Spirit.

I became the fundraiser for the film. By default, I might add. The original New York fundraiser lost interest. Films, unlike poems, need money. I knew the girls now and I knew the place, and they'd loved me *into myself*, and that, it turns out, is what you need to evangelize.

After my time there in Honduras, I spent time in the States, raising money in churches, all the way from Martha's Vineyard to a small island off the coast of Seattle, from a rich church in Miami to a nursing home in Northfield, Minnesota. In addition,

I put together an anthology of the girls' poems for publication and went from publishing house to publishing house in New York trying to get someone to take it. The amount of rejection I faced with their book humbled me to new levels. But then I once had been ignorant of Honduras like the people I showed the book to. The river of children and mothers streamed into the States during my sleep. The girls stayed in touch on Facebook and kept encouraging me: *¿Cómo estás? Te quiero. Hay que continuar.*

In between I spent time with my frail parents. I wondered when my parents would die. How would I bear it? Think of the girls.

112.

I have been an alien in a strange land.

—EXODUS 18:3

I traveled to Wyoming, to a twenty-thousand-acre ranch called Ucross, not far from Laramie. I was at a writers' residency at the same place and in the same room where Annie Proulx had worked on *Brokeback Mountain*. The room was a converted waiting room for the train station, as if writing and waiting were synonymous. I worked on pages—my makeshift nest.

On Sunday a farm couple collected me at the ranch and drove me in their pickup truck into the town, population twenty-five, to church. The husband drove without speaking, the wife had the Bible in her lap, the cover worn. We sat, three across. They were fundamentalists. They did not ask me personal questions. I asked them questions. How long had they been married? How many children did they have? What were their children doing now? We chuckled about progeny.

The foothills in Eastern Wyoming rose golden and purple and amber. Deer stalled among the hayfields. Some deer pressed their wet noses into the grass.

The church was in an Elks Club with faux-paneling, an accordion room divider the color of Band-Aids, metal folding chairs, a drop-down ceiling with bright fluorescent lights, and a dusty plastic fern stuck in an ice bucket.

A young blond cowboy bore his testimonial. Christ was his savior he said. His hands rough and chapped, his muscles bulged under his checked shirt, his blond hair stuck out. I wanted him. The twenty or so people gathered supported him with soft sighs. He grew vulnerable speaking of his faith. Validation filled the room under that ghastly light.

"We enjoyed the boy's testimonial," said the wife afterwards. I had too. What would happen if I had stood up under the light and spoke?

113.

"I have cancer," Mark Strand said right away. His tone sounded as if he was talking about an ugly vacation spot he was going to visit. He did not look sick. He was in his seventies but he looked a decade younger.

He had an unbelievably handsome face: the forehead, eyebrows, nose, cheeks, and chin were defined and cool as if carved by marble. I'd seen such faces on Victorian furniture or cornices of the tops of buildings. The whole thing wrought with confident grandeur. Many must have fallen in love with that face.

Sylvia Plath's son was in the news. I'd waited for some news of him. The obituary stated that he never mentioned the story of his mother or her poetry in public. He kept it to himself. He was living in Alaska and had become one of the world's leading experts on the behaviors of salmon. While his girlfriend was in the house, he went into the garage one fine morning and hanged himself. He was forty-six years old. I thought of Arthur Miller's penetrating line in *After the Fall* about his life with Marilyn Monroe: "a suicide kills two people . . . that's what it's for." Plath's anger marked Ted Hughes: "If I've killed one man, I've killed two," meaning her father and her husband. She exacted revenge on Hughes: her death haunted him. But did her despair unwittingly land on her son too? Perhaps. Could feelings be inherited? Perhaps. If that was true, did my grandmother's uncomplicated faith skip my mother and land on me? Perhaps.

Plath crossed out references to her children in "Lady Lazarus." In draft after draft she wrote of her children in the poem and it kept falling out. Of her children she wrote: "Are they proud / Of their mum's profession? / Yes!" The poem was then to continue with her famous line: "Dying / is an art, like everything else." In her final version she edited out references to her children. My mother cooed over me in the early sixties. Outside, protests, assassinations, tenements. Whatever her despair, she had stayed in the world for me. I was proud of her.

Nicholas's end made me want to grab on to life. There I was with Mark Strand in New York City. Waiters always called me "sir" now. My mother clunked about in a walker in Old Lyme, Connecticut. Her walker's clank, thud, and drag sounded like Frankenstein's monster approaching. My father sounded more Southern, and I wondered if a part of him no longer felt the need to cover up his origins. I was there in the French Roast with Mark, who was talking to me about poetry, on the corner of Sixth and Twelfth in the Village. Poetry was the source. Middle-aged, about to be ordained, I saw myself reflected in the glass of the French Roast, my face superimposed upon New York, schools of humanity surged and passed across my face. Plath: *O love, how did you get here?* My heart was a salmon determined to spawn. I wanted to write, live, pray, minister, travel, act, risk, laugh, be.

Mark bore my unused name: two Marks mirroring each other. Marks making marks. I was drinking a cup of coffee with Mark. Behind him, the large plate-glass window across which was moving swathes of humanity: a throng of Eastern European women in babushkas, then students with backpacks, then the poet Sharon Olds, her hand shaking with a cup of coffee, then a muscular Asian man in a tank top with biceps large and gleaming and undulating. I stared.

"When do you leave for Madrid?" Mark asked.

I had been back and forth between Spain and the US, presenting papers with gold seals and wax seals. Behind inch-thick bulletproof glass, clerks were stamping my paperwork, their staplers moving flamenco-dancer fast.

"Soon, I just have to wait for the visa to come through now," I said.

"I love that city," Mark responded. "The light . . . just before it gets dark." His voice carried the timbre of someone who had spent time in museums.

"Did you know Elizabeth Bishop?" I asked suddenly. It was a jump, but Mark wasn't surprised. Who loves a jump in thought more than two poets in a coffee shop in New York City? I have a theory that poets better understand their connectedness through story swapping, we make up a secret incidental class based on the art. I have converged with people I wouldn't otherwise have met—a circle that makes a lineage, like AA, a camaraderie of the guild.

"Yes . . . well, I met her a couple of times . . . I wouldn't say we were friends, really, the first time in Brazil, I don't think, frankly, she cared for me that much, or my poems . . ." he said. Another puzzle piece about Bishop clicked into place.

"Tell me about her . . ." I asked, like a child beseeching a parent for a bedtime story.

"She asked me a lot of questions about Lowell. About who had won which prize. She was keenly aware of the prize winners." The waitress came near, her breasts jacked up and pushed forward, with tombstones tattooed on each one. Mark admired this unique presentation.

"Elizabeth was so proud of her lover's physique," he said.

"Lota?" I asked.

"No, this was later with Alice," he said. I'd only recently had the nerve to mention to friends how attractive I'd found a man's physique.

"Oh," I paused, factoring this into my portrait of Bishop—the reticent alcoholic lesbian who lived in Brazil for seventeen years, writing poems that eschewed her humiliating drinking and her difficult orphaned childhood.

114.

"Do you want me to place your name on the list of those wanting healing when I get to the cathedral?" I said to Mark the second time we met. We were on the Upper West Side. Weeks had passed. I was my young six-year-old self, standing next to my father. Mark felt distant. With distant men I thrived. I moved like a hummingbird.

"I'm not religious," Mark said, bemusedly. He wore a black Calvin Klein turtleneck. Fall tumbled down the canyons of New York.

"My father was Jewish," he said. He said this to put me off. I assured him I was not meeting him to evangelize. Priests whispered behind my back; I wouldn't be surprised if they thought of me as the worst evangelist.

"My mother is half-Jewish, just like you then . . ." I added, revealing the part of my mother that moved in her unconscious, never resting, like a shark.

Mark left his cupcake uneaten. He looked sad. The grit of New York glittered on our cheeks. Mark and me—one poet about to die, the other about to be ordained. Mortality must have been with him at every moment. I didn't know what that felt like. Being tested for HIV gave a hint. After testing negative I wanted to push death away, as if it could *never* touch me, but it will. The smell of coffee and trash and baked bread coated us.

In the news two things repeated. First, John Hinckley Jr. had been released from Saint Elizabeth's and was going home to live with his mother. He was sixty years old. Second, Jodie Foster, who was in her fifties and had given birth to two children born through an anonymous sperm donor, accepting the Cecil B. DeMille award, said publicly for the first time she was lesbian. Her delivery was ethereal, brilliant, obfuscating—it required one almost to take notes. I'd been in college circling the graveyard and plotting my suicide when Reagan had been shot. Now Hinckley was coming home to his mother. Now Jodie Foster, who'd been terrorized by Hinckley's love letters, was coming out of the closet in a brainy elliptical acceptance speech in Hollywood, merging her forked life. Release and forgiveness and freedom wafted in the air. Those emotions, a recipe for mercy.

115.

Snow sheeted Saratoga Springs. A writer escorted me to my writing studio in a wooden structure called West House, part of Yaddo, the Trask estate left to artists in perpetuity: Plath, Bishop, and Strand had been there. The studio had been Plath's. I paused. Look for the signs, the Gospel of John insists. The studio was in the attic, up thirteen white steps that turned in the middle. Hughes had been there with Plath. They were planning to return to England to start a family.

Blizzards came. I'd been sent my proof pages for my second book of poems, which had been accepted by Jonathan Galassi at Farrar, Straus and Giroux. When I met him in New York and signed the book contract, we did so on Bishop's writing table from Brazil, which was in his office. It was small. The size of a suitcase. Another sign.

He'd given me my last edits after eleven years of going over those poems. The title of the book was *The Road to Emmaus*. The title referenced my favorite Bible story in the Gospel of Luke. Like that of the prodigal son or the one grateful leper, the story of Emmaus occurs only once. It concerns two disciples who do not believe Christ is real. One is named Cleopas and the other remains unnamed. They are full of doubts as they walk to Emmaus, seven miles out from Jerusalem, when a stranger falls among them. The stranger is Christ come back to encourage them. But they don't see him at first. Only when they break bread in Emmaus do they realize Christ *is* Christ, and then their hearts go off like rockets. Then the two disciples run back to Jerusalem and can't shut up.

Caravaggio renders this scene with brown-black bittersweet shadows, illuminating the human experience that we don't realize what is in front of us until it is gone. This story echoed my experience with Durell and others in my life—Nana, my parents, my brother, Ms. Young, Nick Thorndike, Merrill, P. Much I'd taken for granted. Delay marked my appreciation of humanity. Emmaus scenes crowded my book.

I had followed Louise's advice, I sought a new sound. I'd tried prose poems, longer poems, and metrical verse as well, all distinct from the lyric in my first book. I'd pushed poems to their limits until they sounded like prose but weren't quite. I broke my own poetry sound barrier. The book was quieter than the first, for I had grown quieter. The sound sang to me from the white pages before me at Yaddo. The sound was forgiveness and compassion and reconciliation, which is quieter than damage. Different from the first. I couldn't look anymore at these poems. I'd given them everything. I was empty.

Most artists at Yaddo that February were lesbian. They told me they preferred their artist residency bare bones without cocktail parties. Women came in on trucks with sporting gear. I liked the practicality they brought to the dinner table: all napkins were reused, all coffee grounds were recycled, conversations were undramatic. We met in an enormous dining hall—handed-down cracked oil portraits of New England benefactors, their jowls the color of old butter, their closed mouths full of money, their eyes like bank locks, stared out from the walls.

I was the only artist asking how to get to church on Sunday. I thought about Flannery O'Connor, who had been to Yaddo and sent her manuscripts from there to Farrar, Straus and Giroux.

Her rigid Catholic vision on which she hung those amazing stories of Southern grotesques. I'd read her many times over before I knew I'd become a religious person. She needed convention for her unconventional self. As did I. There were different ways at Jesus. O'Connor talked about how Catholics had to submit and Protestants could have more fun with things. She wrote: "Please let Christian principles permeate my writing and please let there be enough of my writing (published) for Christian principles to permeate. I dread, Oh Lord, losing my faith." I wanted Christian principles in my work, and I did not want to lose my faith either. I saw things grayer than she. O'Connor wrote: "I write the way I do because (not though) I am a Catholic." I wrote as I wrote because I was an Episcopal fabulist to her Catholic literalist. The poems in their snazzy font gleamed under the February Yaddo light: my treasure map to Emmaus.

I worked through the proof pages and Galassi's careful edits. Always opportunities to rearrange! The page is a collage of guesses. I thought of Bishop's line from her elegy to Lowell: "Repeat, repeat, repeat; revise, revise, revise." Snow came down and down, tapping on the mullioned windows.

Above the giant library desk I worked on there was a skylight that was like a glass chicken coop with a set of pulleys attached to it. I stuck my head up into it, surfacing, and looked out at the white world. Pine trees glistened. A beautiful strong limber woman cross-country skied. She was the unnamed disciple in the Emmaus story. We don't know anything about that disciple. The disciple could have been a woman. This woman was called by her art and followed her call. All of us were going somewhere to spread good news. Her snowsuit swished between her thighs. I sealed the envelope. Sent the book to New York City.

116.

The third time Mark and I met, we went back to the French Roast in the Village. Months had passed. We'd both had books of poetry come out, his collected and my second. I uncrossed my legs. Too feminine. To my relief, Mark did not ask me about my sexuality. Mark had about him a politeness of someone from his generation that is largely gone now, perhaps these old manners still exist in Europe. His gentlemanly avoidance made a space for me to be unaddressed.

In my fifties, a scarf circling my neck, an American about to abandon America, I chilled. The sky above us the color of a weathered wood shingle. Mark's famous stanza came to my mind:

> *We all have reasons*
> *for moving.*
> *I move*
> *to keep things whole.*

I had reasons for moving, as Plath had hers, as Bishop had hers, as Herbert had his, as Merrill had his, as Dickinson did *not* have hers, as Hopkins had his, as Strand had his—the small quick brushstroke look of his stanza emphasized the nervous nature of my reasons to move. Why my intermittent, urgent need to open the suitcase? Should it have surprised me in my fifties that I'd moved much? Mom, Dad, my brother, and I did not stay put in the Midwest. Minneapolis commands commitment. It'd given us much. We'd betrayed it, left it, rarely gone back, rejected the Midwestern convention that charms many. We were changed—Mom changing who she was, Dad changing who he was, my brother changing who he was, me changing: all changed by our changes. Maybe that was why we had moved much. To keep things whole.

Mark and I were cut from the long list for the National Book Award. Mark said, "Don't worry about this." We needed, I sensed from him, to keep moving. When Tennessee Williams lost the Oscar for *A Streetcar Named Desire*, he wrote: "One part of me despises such prizes and the vulgar standards they represent, but another part of me wants to be 'The Winner' no matter what. When and how can we ever get over that, and have a dignified humility about us and a true sense of what matters?" Half of me wanted to follow Emily Dickinson into her beloved isolation, the other half wanted to be the winner. Mark listened with the expression of someone who had been waiting in a post office line for several hours. Mark was after larger subjects. His dismissal of winning and losing as important was offering me a blessing before our peppermint herbal tea.

"This is good, you moving to Madrid. This is good," Mark said. As he said it, it became real. Would Madrid make me whole? Perhaps.

"I think I will continue this little author series in Madrid," I said to him. "Would you like to read for it?"

"Yes, of course," he said although he made it sound unlikely.

Mark had more questions for me about why I was becoming a priest—it fascinated him. How inarticulate I was on the subject of my passions. A part of me didn't understand how or why

I had become a poet any more than how or why I was becoming a priest: the more people asked the less I knew. I knew I wanted both things very much. My answers seemed uninspired or verged on the bromides you find in the literature of twelve-step meetings or in Christian bookstores with their tchotchkes. My response needed more time. More time than Mark and I had.

117.

Goldfinches pecked at the thistle feeder. My mother fell down once more. Mark emailed:

Dear Spencer,

Well, we'll have lunch again. The reduced dosage has meant a lessening of those onerous side effects. I am feeling quite a bit better. Regarding our conversation, I'd like to have a soul, and perhaps I do, but I can never find it. I never write about it myself because I can't find it. Or, if I find something I take for it, it seems remote, embedded elsewhere, in a fable perhaps, or a joke, or some fictive concoction.

Yours, Mark

The note, written on the screen, ephemeral, was like the messages airplanes write across the blue sky. Much was going fast. Mark had cancer. He had a passing curiosity in searching for his soul. I was no expert on soul-finding, and what I thought I knew I wasn't comfortable disclosing, such things felt private. I wanted to linger over such subjects with Mark. The clock was at our backs. The date for my plane ticket to Madrid approached.

I did not know him well. I didn't know his poems well. I'm

aware of not attaching more meaning than there was to the man I knew. I've wondered if the relations I have with others are given meaning by my needs, wholly separate from the person.

Mark was a fan of Edward Hopper, and at times, those colorful fugitives in their hotel rooms were mirroring my life, and now Mark's. He wrote once about Hopper, "To have no future, no past, would mean suspension, not resolution—the unpleasant erasure of narrative." I had a loose grasp of the past and future in those days, and I wasn't ready to have my narrative erased. Mark sat in that Hopper hotel room, cancer erasing him.

The fourth meeting between us happened before I got on the plane and moved to Madrid. I'd known Mark for over a year by then, half my days spent opening and closing suitcases. His cancer had advanced. No more talk of cures in Germany.

"I've been doing collages lately. I am done with writing poems. I don't have anything more to say," Mark said to me, his head in profile. We were standing on West Tenth Street before the Emma Lazarus House. The trees had lost their leaves, they were etchings of their former glory. I wanted to fix Mark's statement, remove the negative. I had to bite my tongue not to say anything. I had a terrible time with patience, not wanting to fix Mark, or my mother sliding down the wall when I was six. I wanted to say, "No, no, you will write more, Mark." But I didn't. It was a major achievement for me. Fresh silence sluiced around us. Taxis trundled past. A homeless man came near. We lowered our eyes to avert his gaze. The air grew cold. The little battleships of snow at the curb were about to grow into icebergs.

"I don't think I am going back to Madrid," Mark said. Resignation moved across his face. "This is good you are going to live there," he said. The wind picked up like the current of time, picking clean the skins of the apartment buildings. Mark and I went to Jack's on West Tenth. No sooner had we sat down than Mark looked pained. "Time to go, kid," Mark said.

"Yes, but . . ." I stuttered.

"No, I really must go. I am tired, very tired."

"Yes," I said. "Yes." I hated endings.

I wanted to say *something* more to Mark, but what more was there to say to someone I wanted to know better but did not know that well? We weren't close. Or were we? Wasn't there that alchemical spark between us that fellow poets have with one another? New York was a brute. People were poised to take our table the minute Mark indicated he was done.

"Give my love to Madrid. Remember me on Hortaleza Street," Mark said. When he stepped out of the restaurant the bells in the door of Jack's jingle-jingled like the bells the acolyte shakes before the Eucharist. He walked away from me. He stepped off the curb and crossed the street, becoming part of the vast human stream of New York City. He stepped down into the subway on Sixth. His body submerged—tall, stately, Lincolnesque—his gray kind head gone without a trace.

118.

Yo lo vi.

—GOYA

We drove past the mental institution on the way into Oak Ridge with its lawn of red oaks. Uncle George and Aunt Pattie lived in a small house, one of the smaller old cemesto houses built when Oak Ridge went from three thousand people to seventy-five thousand people almost overnight. At the time the atomic bomb was built, my grandfather collected the uranium. The house models started with "A" and went up to "F." The houses became known as "alphabet houses." Cemesto was a panel made of cement and asbestos. Every thirty minutes, a house was completed. The houses were not expected to last more than seven years.

Dad and I walked in the door of their "A" house and Pattie started crying. Dad and George looked out the window. The small pecan trees in Tennessee watched us. John had been dead twenty-five years. "I see him every day," Pattie said, her Tennessee hillbilly sound italicizing her words "Saw him at the *Walmart* on *Wednesday*," Pattie said. George quieted her. But she wouldn't be quieted. George was good at taming wild things, as a youth he'd tamed a crow and a squirrel and they'd become his pets and had loved him. Now Pattie turned her head to George the way I imagine that crow and squirrel once had. Trusting him. His strong masculine certainty. She was shorter than us men, but the Tennessee room jerry-built to get its citizens through the war pivoted around her. The floorboards creaked. Our heads were close to the ceiling. There was a couch and two end tables from the sixties. Not much room to move around. Outside a child wobbled on a bicycle.

Their "A" house had three windows in the living room. The interior filled with dust motes. The light was a mustard-yellowy late-afternoon light. Out the window ash and black oak and hackberry and hickory and sassafras trees grew in their yard. Maybe there was a chain link fence. Dad and I stood in the doorway, tall and nervous the way our people stand in doorways, ready to leave at a moment's notice. I looked outside. Rock pigeons and yellow-bellied sapsuckers perched in the sassafras tree.

"I think about John *all the time,*" Pattie said. Behind her head, on a shelf, was a row of golden trophies. George and Pattie had taken up running after John died. They ran and ran and ran and ran and ran. They won several marathons. When Kathy died they doubled their efforts and won more trophies. John's sister Kathy had died of a subdural brain bleed in the intervening years, nine years after John. One story concerned her being drunk and falling down a set of stairs. She was thirty-six. While she lived, I'd talked to her several times about John. She couldn't make sense of his death. "Why'd he have to *die like that, Spencer*?" Kathy had said. John's murder killed her. George died in 2019 with dementia, John's name on his tongue. The obituary stated Uncle George and Aunt Pattie had run over 1,500 races in fifteen years. They ran until their knees gave out. Then they ran with broken knees. They were Cleopas and the unnamed disciple, on the road to Emmaus.

"Why did that have to happen to him, *Spencer*? I swear to you, I keep *seeing* him, I keep *thinking* I've seen him, clear as day, why I was in the grocery store just the other day and I looked up and I thought for sure it was John . . ."

Dishes moved over a sink in the "A" house next door. Pattie went on. I was relieved to be moving to another country to escape this sadness that was a deep part of me. But there is no escaping our loss. Pattie was Mrs. Rochester in *Jane Eyre*. No wonder Dad and I hadn't visited in thirty years.

"Somehow I keep thinking about John. *Spencer*, the other day I saw a bird and I swear that bird was John come to talk to me. John is *speaking* to me through the birds. I swear to you now that was a sign, he keeps *callin' me*, it is like he's not finished, he's not at rest, or *something*."

An old Ford truck moved down the street with a bad muffler. A TV blared. Uncle George, rough, dominant, quiet, bristle-headed, watched over Pattie as if she was his crow. Pattie's eyes looked for exits. We men formed a circle around her. Pattie had not watched her children get older but instead had cremated them. Pattie broke through our circle. She went to the window. She was distracted. Trapped and unaware of us in the moment. The room crowded with the screams of John as the men held him under. Pattie was at Jesus's tomb.

"Why *Spencer*, you look just like your Daddy, just like him," Pattie said.

"I had a cousin, named John," I will say time and again when it would come my turn to share in the AA circle. The Gospel of Mark: *to give His life a ransom for many* . . . John died. I lived. Or John died *so* I could live. Took me thirty years to see that.

That day in Oak Ridge, I vowed to keep *naming* John. I could let anonymous rooms all over the world know that John mattered. His life had meaning. I could repeat it like a gospel.

Jesus said:

The first shall be last and the last first.

We were last. I was last. The name died in me. Would we be first to see Christ? We Reece men waited that day. There was no stanching Pattie's weeping. Her children's ashes had blown over the Smoky Mountains—flakes alighting ever so gently on the red oaks, on the lawn of the mental institution now closed, on the bowling alley, on the roof of George and Pattie's house—the world, for one brief second, a blizzard of my kin.

119.

It is strange how people seem to belong to places—
especially to places where they were not born.
—CHRISTOPHER ISHERWOOD

I began work in the church office with blue tiles in Madrid.
Gay Pride went by outside the window with men in bikinis and
high heels. I touched the miniature bachelor around my neck,
yoked to urgency, emaciated as the AIDS patients. I thought of
the message he wanted everyone to hear. Few listened. Few.
People ignored him, the way people ignore poets. He tired. He
longed. He hungered. He knew loneliness and disappointment
until he was uncaged.

I was preparing things for our ordinations the following day,
a fresh set of new priests, men following my man. Women were
sometimes following my man with a desire to become priests
in man-driven Spain, but it wasn't an easy sell. My gay brethren
swelled out the window, beautiful bare-chested brown men
strutting, with their swollen pectoral muscles, their nipples
pointed out like light switches. Isn't there that story that Hopkins wrote his most electrifying verses, jammed with their
bulging sprung rhythm, while outside his rectory strapping
Welsh construction workers grunted and huffed? So with me. I
worked and wrote in a formal conservative church where being
out was shoved under the carpet: a polite silence accompanied

my personal life. I didn't complain. We were a poor church. We had pressing concerns—getting people shelter and finding them a bag of food. Working alongside conservative fundamentalist missionaries, always from the Southern states, I felt unwelcome in my faith. But I was not relinquishing my seat on that altar. I was done apologizing for myself. I chose the place as Hopkins chose the Catholics.

Spaniards groaned. Spaniards climaxed. In the bullfights the muscled bull was gored. I was alone as Jesus in his boat: *Again Jesus began to teach by the lake. The crowd that gathered around him was so large that he got into a boat and sat in it out on the lake, while all the people were along the shore at the water's edge.* Surely he must have wobbled? As I have. He needed distance to speak. Me too.

Christ hung on my chest. His spine torqued, a bent boomerang. It was late. The silver of the back of the cross stuck to the sweat on my chest. July, and Madrid was electrified with love, love rolled from the dark streets, the alleyways, kisses of beautiful men and beautiful women making a sound like something switched on, dark eyes focused—an impetuous black stampede of Spanish love I loved perhaps because it differed from my reserve—I wanted to belong. The Spanish current of untroubled touch often had eluded me, laces and zippers being undone dexterously out my church office window, things unsnapped with ease: a display of the talents of the flesh.

I had stapled the programs for the ordinations for a few hours. I was nearly done. My bishop and his wife had gone upstairs. Two Spaniards, my age exactly and long married—they had no children, which we didn't speak about. The bishop was bald, broad-chested, and blind in one eye. His wife was pretty—the face perfectly set, each cheek and lip defined by dabs of ruby and gold, the skin translucent—her beauty made us nervous. We were not a pretty bunch—scrappy, unshaven, with holes in our trousers, rank-smelling, breath to keep people at a distance—yet fusty joy came from us. A Protestant Spanish couple in Catholic Spain with me in tow. Rare as blue-footed boobies.

They said I could staple and collate in the morning, but something pushed me on that trembling night, there in Madrid, the city chosen by a king, who placed his thumb in the middle of the map of the dry peninsula and said, "Here is where I want my city," and thus under his imperious will the city was built, and some of that will vibrated in the gravelly voices of these people that use the imperative in their grammar constantly. Rarely have I been so direct as Spaniards or their king. But direct I have yearned to be.

One a.m. Madrid came into its voice. The printer worked. It took a while to understand all the instructions in Spanish, knowing which button to press when the machine dinged.

Christ hung around my neck. Single, childless, he gulped. His lungs filled with fluid. He was penetrable. He whose strength was effeminate. Nothing worse in my life than to be effeminate, every time someone referenced that in me my heart sank, as if I'd failed everyone. But there in Madrid, Christ cuddled me. As I had been mocked so had Christ. Although fundamentalists camouflaged any whiff of Jesus's submissiveness, I saw a mirror. I saw a way in: the Velazquez Christ, six feet tall, cast in ghastly green in the Prado with his head down-turned as Mark's had been, could be a portal. His ridiculous acceptance welcomed me.

My cassock, red stole, and alb on the hook, I tidied papers for the ordinations. Ponderous and deliberate I moved about the office. The computer screen's lunar glow lit up the stack of church newsletters, the broken stapler, the pencil sharpeners, the filing cabinets, the piles and piles of paper, me.

120.

I spoke Spanish more than English. I spoke it well. I spoke it poorly. Our little Blanco-inspired author series grew at the cathedral, poets came over from the States and England and Ireland. Then poets came from France, then Italy, then Greece, then Croatia. Suddenly, I had a staff of six volunteers. Then I had seven. Then ten. All young. All smart. All beautiful women. This aspect was accidental. The Holy Spirit kept sending me gorgeous volunteers. I encouraged them. A tattoo of millennials! I delegated. We made beautiful posters. We popped up in the internet. We Instagrammed. Facebooked. Twittered. If I'd scoffed at social media in the past, or was afraid of its unbridled cultivated happiness and trumpeting of exhibitionism, I embraced it now. We visited schools. Spanish children went wild for the poets. That moved me. I recalled how poetry had reached me and saved me and I wondered as I stared at class after class of boys and girls in blue uniforms if poetry might save *one* of them. If it saved one of those kids I felt we'd done something right. I hoped it might. We interviewed the poets at the Instituto Internacional, where Federico García Lorca had once read. We got the poets on the radio.

Around then, news of Mark's death reached me via the *New York Times*. I was dressed as a priest that day. I sat at a small café not far from the cathedral. No doubt that created space around me. In the small café called Pomme Sucre on Calle Barquillo, in a wired chair too small for my large frame, I took in a world

I was adopting as much as it was adopting me. Mark's death announcement gleamed through my phone.

Around me, display cases of fanciful pastel-colored pastries. Beautiful Spanish women held their heads regally as queens. Their giant wedding rings sparkled. A brown cultivated didgeridoo-hum surrounded me. I was part of the Spanish harmony even though alone. The world kept going. Mark was dead. I ordered another café con leche. I thought of that line from an unfinished Bishop poem, "No coffee can wake you . . . No coffee can wake you . . ." I felt *unwakeable*. Or I did not want to be awoken to life's cruel rule: we die. I felt myself circling. I tried to think linearly as if to comfort myself from the unsettling thought of how rapidly the earth was spinning around, casting off souls left and right; time to get on with what I must try to write, I thought, or time to arrange for the next poet to come.

We branded ourselves the Unamuno Author Series referencing a famous exchange of friendship during the Spanish Civil War, between Miguel de Unamuno and one of our priests Reverendo Atilano Coco. Although both died at the time of the civil war, Unamuno of a heart attack under house arrest and Coco shot by firing squad, for a moment a camaraderie sparked and held them together. Somehow through me, and our team, emanating from this unlikely cathedral, we were recreating this priest and writer silhouette again, where church and verse sparked love. We planned a first-ever international anglophone festival. I raised twenty-six thousand dollars in three months. We published a bilingual anthology, Hogarth Press-style, with a collage by Mark Strand gracing the cover. The *Paris Review* and the *American Poetry Review* ran ads for free.

Greg Pardlo came. I hosted him to celebrate his Pulitzer

for poetry in 2015. Knock, knock. I opened the giant wooden door, and there in the noisy Madrid street alive with dusty loud Spanish life Greg stood with his large suitcase. He had arrived from America. Greg was a handsome tawny-colored man, with an athletic build and an army-like posture. A wide mischievous grin, a delightful space between his two front teeth: all accompanied his eyes playful as a rabbit's.

Within minutes, an Englishman collected us to take us to the event. He opened the tall cathedral door and said to Greg, "You look so much darker than in your pictures." The remark was a razor slice. I said nothing. I was trying to read Greg's mind to determine what he thought. I couldn't read his reaction. The time was not right. Or was it? Uncomfortable.

Once we arrived at the reading at the famous Instituto Internacional, I ushered Greg in. The ceiling was light blue, the stage was raised with a dark polished wood. As I was getting him a glass of water and the reading was about to start another man, white and middle-aged, this time an American expat, said in front of us, "You look just like a German tourist with your shorts on, except for your skin color." I winced.

I had tried to pretend as if it didn't matter what someone's skin color was. I believed this once "progressive" attitude made me a better white person. I had intended *not to mention* Greg's skin for his Pulitzer visit and celebration. I assumed that living in Europe would allow me to forget race. But no. Race ran after me in Madrid.

The two men felt at liberty to comment on Greg's skin. If Greg was in a wheelchair would they have commented on that in the same way? If Greg was wearing a tiara what would they have said? If Greg was a woman what would they have said? Each of these marginalities (one of which I fell into) evolved out of completely different historical constructions. Yet I thought because I was gay that gave me equal footing in the marginalized department. I need think no more on this subject. Race was not a disability, gender, sexuality, or religion. I twitched. I stewed. These white men lived in a world that hardly ever questioned their skin color. These men were me. I was that world. My skin color had never been questioned, been commented upon, or singled me out for anything unless it was used to get me into worlds. I'd been unaware of my advantage. My first impulse was not to write about this.

The two men were threatened by Greg. They had both come to the reading, with their sentiments built up from their lives, and perhaps Greg's reading might push them to untangling their pathologies. But what about my inertia? My participation in it? I was astute at not saying anything, but when these stupid comments were directed at my guest, whose poetry we were honoring, I still stayed quiet.

Greg closed by reading his poem, influenced by and appropriating slave narratives, called "Written by Himself":

> I was born in minutes in a roadside kitchen a skillet
> whispering my name. I was born to rainwater and lye;
> I was born across the river where I
> was borrowed with clothespins, a harrow tooth,
> broadsides sewn in my shoes. I returned, though
> it please you, through no fault of my own,
> pockets filled with coffee grounds and eggshells.
> I was born still and superstitious; I bore an unexpected burden.
> I gave birth, I gave blessing, I gave rise to suspicion.
> I was born abandoned outdoors in the heat-shaped air,
> air drifting like spirits and old windows.
> I was born a fraction and a cipher and a ledger entry;

I was an index of first lines when I was born.
I was born waist-deep stubborn in the water crying
                    ain't I a woman and a brother I was born
to this hall of mirrors, this horror story I was
born with a prologue of references, pursued
by mosquitoes and thieves, I was born passing
off the problem of the twentieth century: I was born.
I read minds before I could read fishes and loaves;
I walked a piece of the way alone before I was born.

I loved this found poem where the speaker found himself. What bright music. The title taken from the subtitle of the abolitionist slave narrative of Frederick Douglass from 1845. I wanted to hear it again. I loved that it was referring back to something from another time and place and making it new. The poem smashed up against the non sequiturs of the white men. In the middle of the hot Madrid night, Lorca's ghost near, the priest merged with the poet in me, brought on by this poem.

Jonathan Daniels, the agnostic white Harvard student, in the early 1960s had a conversion experience at Church of the Advent and joined the Freedom Riders. He was shot while throwing his body in front of a fourteen-year-old Ruby Sales, a Black girl who had a rifle pointed at her by a Southern redneck. Daniels died. Sales grew up and went to the seminary Daniels attended and became a priest herself. I didn't have the guts to speak to the men at Greg's reading. I, who had wanted to correct my grandmother on her word choice of "colored" but had remained mute.

Paul, in his letters to the Galatians and the Philippians and all the others, emphasizes that everyone is one. The world does everything to reject this idea. Why? If I was a Christian priest then this was my business: unite people.

In *We Were Eight Years in Power*, Ta-Nehisi Coates writes: "White people are, in some profound way, trapped; it took generations to make them white, and it will take more to unmake them." Could a poem unmake me? The poem *opened* me.

I invited Greg over for breakfast at my cathedral apartment the next morning, moved with the hope that he might want to be my friend. Over steaming Spanish coffee, as a bright blazing light came into the Madrid apartment, I said to Greg, "Did that bother you? When that guy said what he said?" I was saying something, *something*. The risk might be he would be sick of talking about race to some uninformed white writer. James Baldwin balked about white people needing to figure this shit out for themselves, I understood that. Yet I craved guidance if guidance could be had. I didn't want to "walk a piece of the way alone" anymore.

Greg looked at the quill pen I kept in an ink well on my coffee table. He said, "I'm so used to that. I didn't take it personally. Listen, Spencer, I was recently in Little Rock, Arkansas, for a reading to celebrate my work, and on my way home someone had shouted from a car: 'Go home you goddamn nigger.'" Sadness bled across his strong masculine face. That broke something in me with a hammer. He fingered some stationery I had out.

Greg looked at me in my Madrid apartment with a gentleness. I held my breath. He said how much he liked my hundred-year-old student desktop from Ireland. I'd carted it around the world with me, its tilted writing top from when people used to write letters. Inside I'd stored my wax seals and glitter and whimsical stamps. Delicateness was in the air like when I prayed. We talked more.

"Why are you doing this?" I asked him. The conversation went longer than an hour.

"Because," he said, "with you it's worth it for me." Was he speaking to the poet in me? The priest in me? Or both? Something opened. Was this the most generous statement anyone has ever said to me? What began in Honduras had opened me to injustices. I opened wider. My work was not done. It would not be easy.

My Madrid fourth-floor room with the high ceilings filled up with a sacred quietness. The screams of the young Spaniards softened. Greg trusted me over a divide. Greg was patient with me. That afternoon we grew closer as the sun warmed our middle-aged faces, each that had known the same country, which was for the moment far away in different ways. I'd never conversed in the church like that.

Bishop had said once: "I like black & white, yellow & red, young & old, rich and poor, and male & female, all mixed up." If she came to our series that's just what she'd get. In that little cluttered bookshop, started by booksellers that had worked at Shakespeare and Company in Paris, with the dirty Turkish rugs and hot tea with leaves floating around in the glass, magic stirred. Some faith and hope and love I felt there, among my poets in that bookshop the size of a bloodmobile: but the most important was love. We were a congregation. My work, Greg was telling me without telling me, would be to replicate it *in* church. My art crackled on the page and bound me to others, which was an unexpected bounty. Poetry gave me more than I'd given it.

121.

Mary Jo Salter came to read for our series. I told her she couldn't possibly remember me as a nervous twenty-something from thirty years ago in Key West. She'd been a close friend of Mark's. I mentioned that conversation I'd had with Mark in New York, how I was trying to answer the question of why I was a priest. I could feel him in the bookshop asking me. I told Mary Jo I had more questions than answers. I expressed my quandary about attempting to explain what felt beyond words.

She considered. She paused. With the genuine kindness we poets give to one another, she had a suggestion. We two looked like parishioners exchanging information about an uplifting Bible passage.

"Look at a poem Mark wrote called 'Seven Last Words,'" she said. That night I went home. I read the poem that opened:

> The story of the end, of the last word
> of the end, when told, is a story that never ends.
> We tell it and retell it—one word, then another
> until it seems that no last word is possible,
> that none would be bearable. Thus, when the hero
> of the story says to himself, as to someone far away,
> 'Forgive them, for they know not what they do,'
> we may feel that he is pleading for us, that we are
> the secret life of the story and, as long as his plea

is not answered, we shall be spared. So the story
continues. So we continue. And the end, once more,
becomes the next, and the next after that.

My story continued—my life strained through the filters of religion and poetry. Mark wrote that "as long as his plea / is not answered, we shall be spared. So the story / continues." Not having a specific answer to life made life wonderful. This is what pushed life along, the endless unanswerable quality to it, which Christ swallowed whole until it killed him. The precipice where Christ hung is where the bramble of poetry thrives.

The moment I picked up the Norton anthology in my high school AP English class I was welcomed. I venerated those tissue-thin Bible-like pages where Strand and Plath pressed against one another, and then the pages of more poets: each collection another door that I opened to more rooms—many mansions. Reading poems helped me when I could barely blunder on with shame that crippled me. My suffering, my poetry, my faith converged as I read this poem by Mark. "No last word is possible," wrote Mark. Poetry was an ever-rolling stream. After Mark, after Mary Jo, there would be another and another. Our author series told "the story that never ends." Poetry and Christianity, once close in the time of Herbert, then divided in the time of Plath, Bishop, and Merrill, might come together again. In me. Poets got me to Christ. Rhyme evangelized me.

122.

Madrid, Madrid, I was in the middle of it now. I sighed with gratitude and freedom every time I took in my three rooms in Madrid. I felt liberty. I'd worked for this luck—and I'd been lucky. I threw myself into the literary series. I settled into my office work in the room with the blue tiles. I spoke Spanish. My English shrank. I lived in the center of the city. Exquisite wrought-iron balconies dangled with ivy. Men in capes and swirling mustaches sported *boiñas*. Women with their jet-black hair and brilliant red lips screamed *coño*, the common swear word that means vagina.

The king ordered the creation of Madrid around 1606, close to the same time the word "devotional" came into existence. I hummed and stepped among what was old and forgotten. I lived on the top floor of the Spanish Episcopal Cathedral *in the center of the center*. Put your thumb on a Spanish map. Put it in the center of Madrid, I breathed *right* under that. I'd been there a few years—seven I believe—and my boss, the bishop of Spain, told me when I asked how long I was supposed to be there that I held a *contracto indefinito*.

No one was more surprised than I was that I worked and lived there for so long. Spaniards perhaps thought my exaggerated face resulted from my *r*-rolling and lisping to try to follow the conversation, but it was my wonder. The place suited me, although there probably was no place or people more different from me: perhaps that is why.

I was the national secretary for the Episcopal bishop. As the Anglican Church spread through empire in the nineteenth century, it mainly rooted in English-speaking places: former British colonies, including the United States, where, largely because of the revolution, it called itself Episcopal rather than Anglican. Eighty million people nominally call themselves Anglican; the closer you get to Europe the more nominal they become.

The Church tremulously grew here in Spain, embraced by the Spaniards, *in* Spanish. Unlikely. Missionaries attempted to spread the Anglican faith into Portugal and Italy too, but Spain was where it caught most. There never had been a Reformation in those Latinate countries, but why Spain embraced the whole thing more than the other two I'm not sure, perhaps it was the stubborn and forceful quality I saw in that country that delighted me and caused me to step back. We were so wee and curious there in Catholic Spain that Spaniards were always astonished at our existence, no matter how many times I explained it: five thousand believers in a country of forty-three million Catholics. "You can be a priest and be married?" was said weekly. "You can be a priest and be openly gay?" they would have asked but did not, Spaniards being formal. British and Americans equally remained curious about us, but rarely curious enough to learn about our existence.

I helped the bishop with every manner of thing in Spanish and in English: I answered the door, I did the church newsletter (frequently with errors), I answered the phone, I traveled with him, I conducted services, I preached, I emptied trash, I cleaned the toilet, I handed out bags of food on Saturday. In between all of that, I had time in the office to look at the map with tiny pins of where our few priests worked and preached.

123.

Two Irishmen came to me and asked to open an AA meeting in our spare room. The room was full of dusty catechism pamphlets from the 1950s and broken toys and plastic flowers. An old Spanish lady came with her fan and served tea to immigrants until no immigrants came. Then she sat by herself singing hymns. Then she left. Then the room was empty. The two Irishmen opened the meeting and within a month they, too, had disappeared. By then the recovery community referred to it as "Spencer's meeting." I insisted it was *not my meeting*. I was occupied with the bishop of Spain.

Suddenly, like the hungry who showed up for the food distribution ministry, the addicts wanted *more*—more meetings. After a year we had ten meetings, then fifteen, and before I knew it I was making a poster with thirty meetings for which I was the contact in Madrid. I began sponsoring in between my bishop duties. Every other time the bishop swung the door open there I was with a shivering alcoholic or someone affected by the disease of alcoholism. *But when he saw the multitudes, he was moved with compassion on them, because they fainted, and were scattered abroad, as sheep having no shepherd.*

We opened Al-Anon, which began with a difficult woman who argued vociferously with me, attacking my shares until I told Mary Jane I needed to shut it down. She smiled all the way from Florida. "You need to stay the course at least a year." Damn. The lady left of her own volition. I held meetings with a laptop for about a year and a half alone, finding chat rooms online, delving deep into the internet like some modern version of Saint Teresa of Ávila's interior spiritual castle. Then one day, people started calling and coming. *And great multitudes came unto him, having with them those that were lame, blind, dumb, maimed, and many others, and cast them down at Jesus's feet; and he healed them.* Something wild pushed through my mouth and out my eyeholes and earholes.

124.

The bishop was traveling to Salamanca. I sat alone in the office for the day. Children played in the school across the street. My church office quieted. I was surrounded by deep-blue and white tiles. The ceiling had wild cracks, like an egg about to hatch. I had hundreds of pieces of paper taped to the walls to remind me of God knows what. The more Spanish went into my brain the more forgetful I became. I was the most imperfect national secretary that ever lived. I lived in my garret with the shared bath and kitchen. No one asked about my personal life. A European atmosphere influenced me, where Puritans made no sense and sex was less vexed. In Spain sex is a need and not a dirty thing. Madrid gave me ease when I wasn't looking, quietly, subtly, elegantly, Spanishly. Just like Spain to do that. Spain, lovely, lovely Spain. Siesta at two. The space heater hummed. I was happy, that curious emotion that once named disappears—I was happier than I'd ever been.

125.

I boarded the plane from Madrid to London. I was scheduled to visit the archbishop of Canterbury, along with my Spanish bishop, at Lambeth Palace. My bishop needed to meet with him. I was brought in to translate.

I landed. I hailed a taxi from Victoria Station. I barely understood the taxi driver's Cockney accent: it was like trying to understand the Cubans in Madrid, half the words were missing. In the cab I ate a Cornish pasty, which covered my black priest clothes in a snowstorm of pastry flakes. It was July. Hot for London. That English night along the embankments wide-eyed tourists advanced, sighed, perhaps it was their only trip to London. London: that silvery city so wide and deep with history and the roots of my language. Young couples pointed at statues and buildings and opened guide books. My parents were that once—young Americans full of wonder.

London spread vast and ponderous and lonely and cheery— all the dwellings with gutters lined up the color of silverware, and the formality of table manners settled over everything. The taxi sped towards the archbishop of Canterbury. Rows and rows of Georgian porticoes passed me by. People living their lives without concern for me.

Then I was there. Lambeth Palace, made of limestone and ragstone, timber and brick, impressed me. A kind porter welcomed me. He called me "Father Spencer." I would stay the night at the invitation of His Grace, which is how we refer to the archbishop. Decorum and convention comforted me as I stood before this palace. Perhaps unconventional people need convention more than most?

The peace I had found in the poetry of Herbert snuck up on me at that palace. I opened the paperback of Herbert's poetry in York thirty years prior and that led to *this* door, which led me back to Herbert again.

"Somebody loves us all," Bishop wrote in her poem "Filling Station," about a dirty little gas station that was tended for and loved. As Bishop zeroed her famous eye in on the filling station in the poem, she saw a taboret, a small stool, a word I learned from this poem. Bishop choosing an elegant word rather than "stool" in a poem about a filling station amused me:

> *Why the taboret?*
> *Why, oh why, the doily?*
> *(Embroidered in daisy stitch*
> *with marguerites, I think,*
> *and heavy with gray crochet.)*
>
> *Somebody embroidered the doily.*
> *Somebody waters the plant,*
> *or oils it, maybe. Somebody*
> *arranges the rows of cans*
> *so that they softly say:*
> *ESSO—SO—SO—SO*
> *to high-strung automobiles.*
> *Somebody loves us all.*

Somebody, or *something*, had loved *my* life, attended to it with taborets and doilies. I had a place. The surname Bishop and my constant use of the word "bishop" in my work life cleaved.

I stood before the palace gate, a Tudor door in a building from the fifteenth century called Morton's Tower, made of red brick with a crenellated roof like my freshman college dorm. Through the entrance I noted an old fig tree, raspberry-colored hydrangeas, green lawns, pebbled walks. A private, well-tended world, where gardeners worked the bushes, coaxed the vines. The hint of night scratched at the edges of the day. Something wanted to be liberated.

I bowed my head down under the low door in the wall, in my hand I fingered the key the kind porter gave me. In Old Lyme, my parents lay down in their bed with the plastic mattress cover, holding hands. My brother entered his gay gym in New York, a circus of muscles that made a church. Maybe Mary Jane started the Al-Anon meeting. My plot in Valley Grove had new grass. Martha and Robert had taken their spots next to me there. Standing before Lambeth, Durell would love this. The porter held the heavy door open, smoothed by years of religious hands. Once again, with decorum, he called me, "Father Spencer." He beckoned. I followed. I had a place. I stepped through the little entrance.

The following morning, I met His Grace. He wore a huge cross. He chewed his buttered toast, consumed by his iPhone, his index finger swiping over the screen. He told the bishop and me things. He spoke to the air above our balding heads. The conversation lasted fifteen minutes. His Grace did not ask my name.

126.

Outside Spanish children laughed and ran on the gray street. My office with the blue tiles quieted. We had buried a parishioner the day before, Don Zoilo. He was ninety. He loved to dance flamenco and tell jokes. I stared at the yellowed corpse in the coffin at the wake. His spirit had fled. I wondered where he now wandered.

The late afternoon light was imbued with the golden tones Goya captured: a Spanish hour, time languishing, those out walking spoke with husky voices, their tone sharp and sweet, timbered by cigarettes and espressos and the near constant use of guttural throaty swear words—¡Joder! ¡Hijo de puta! ¡Me caigo en la leche! ¡Me caigo en la Maria Virgin! which translated as *Fuck! Son of a bitch! I shit in the milk! I shit on the Virgin Mary!* People swung loaves of bread ready for a duel. Ladies wore diaphanous tops that blew over their breasts like curtains, and the bracelets on their hands shook up and down like kitchen drawers opening.

The bishop had left for an important meeting and the way he said it I knew I was less important, which didn't bother me but nudged me to wonder if I'd be there forever, whatever forever meant. I had no exact answer which made that moment of pondering close to a poem. Maybe life was best when it got close to a poem. The bishop cared for me, witnessed by his attendance to me in my early days there when I found out my root canal was infected and my tooth needed to be pulled: the bishop, with all his business to attend to, stood right there, beside me. Never forgot that.

Yet in his tone that Goya Spanish day was a nuance carried down from Franco who thought of Americans as "childish." We are an immature country. The bishop was right to be dismissive of me. I was not important. I was replaceable. There would be more secretaries after me. The bishop threw his cape over his shoulder and disappeared into the dry dusty afternoon.

I suddenly missed my home. *And Jesus replied, "Foxes have dens and birds have nests, but the Son of Man has no place to lay his head."* So, too, with me. At least no place permanent.

Someone knocked on my office door with a bag of used clothes. Someone tapped on the window to get the keys to open the door for AA, then for OA, then for Al-Anon, then for ACOA. They spoke in Spanish. They spoke in English. They handed me money for the rent. Before long the rent from the twelve-step groups covered my salary.

The light plumed and reddened and darkened like meat being cooked. The sun set late over Madrid. Citizens arose from long siestas and plunged into the finer arts of eating and love-making. The largest gay gym was situated directly across from my priest office. Every day I took notes for the bishop, beautiful muscular men streamed past my window with large dusty black bars. I took notes for diplomatic letters while men that resembled bulls rearranged their giant crotches. Hour by hour, men with rounded strong buttocks that gleamed and rotated like the wheels of locomotives inside moistened shorts rolled past me. Just before I turned out the light on the empty office, I saw through the bars one last gorgeous insouciant young tattooed man with jet-black curls in a tank top. He did not look at me. I looked at him. He sallied from the gym looking into his iPhone as if it were a votive.

127.

When Lota de Macedo Soares lay dying of a drug overdose in a New York hospital, Bishop found herself returning to Herbert. She wrote, "I've been reading some of the poems . . . some even help a bit, I think." Poets helped me. I say that with the same gentle, hesitant quality Bishop ended that sentence, "I think." It seems radical to say I was born again through poetry. But why not be radical? Herbert made his manual for priests in his day. I have now made this in the time after Plath. Plath, whose *Bell Jar* was a memoir before we fell in love with that marketable word. The notes she strikes in *Ariel* will linger on long after me. But one of the gifts of my writing this at double her age is that age, if you're lucky, brings compassion and, at least for me, softens the need to judge: I never could have written this without being weathered by time. My head needed to bald, my skin needed to tag, one beautiful tooth needed to be pulled, my eyes needed to squint, my knees needed to ache. Time humbled. *He restoreth my soul.* My soul fluttered in the cage of my skeleton. It flaps now. Listen. Flap, flap, flap.

128.

And straightaway, going in where the youth was, he
stretched forth his hand and raised him, seizing his hand. But the
youth, looking upon him, loved him and began to beseech him that he
might be with him. And going out of the tomb, they came into the house
of the youth, for he was rich. And after six days Jesus told him what to
do, and in the evening the youth comes to him, wearing a linen cloth
over his naked body. And he remained with him that night, for
Jesus taught him the mystery of the Kingdom of God. And
thence, arising, he returned to the other
side of the Jordan.

—THE SECRET GOSPEL OF MARK

Madrid chilled, fall was everywhere, Spaniards double-knotted their scarves around their necks. My high-ceilinged garret, without central heat, grew cold. The ancient occluded panes of glass jittered in their insecure frames. All the beautiful fireplaces had been removed under the Franco years. My heated hot-water bottles lay in the bed and my impossibly small heater whirred. Because our electric was on a low voltage, if I plugged in another heater all the circuits blew.

When not reading books (always in English, because I was ambushed all day with Spanish), I observed a giant water stain bloom and mushroom across my entire apartment. It started innocently enough, a small spot, and then slowly began to look like the map of an aggressive despot conquering more and more territory. The stain bloomed a dark-brown rust color with yellow extensions followed by enormous cracks. Eventually it spread over my entire three rooms. Years passed. Early on the bishop promised it would be fixed. But the bishop had a passion for procrastination beyond the Spaniards' stereotypical love of delay. The bishop's art of procrastination rivaled that of the great Leonardo da Vinci, who exasperated patrons with his long delays, which often left commissions unfinished. Bits of the wall flaked down on my open books as if it was *actually* snowing *in* my apartment. During my entire stay in Spain the stain remained unfixed despite weekly promises to call workers in. I learned to entertain myself by marveling at the disastrous stain's expansion and discerning various patterns and shapes from it. I looked upon the stain like a poem I was trying to understand.

I woke early and shook in my two layers of long underwear in my Madrid apartment. I wore two sweaters. After all the years falling all around me like chrysanthemum petals, with a few moments before morning prayer was to start, I went to the bookcase and pulled out my own second book of poems. Professor Matt Bevis at Keble College, Oxford, had asked me to come to England and give a reading, so I dusted the book off and opened it. I went to a poem I wrote entitled "Gilgamesh." I rarely looked at that poem. It brought back P. strongly. Like Bishop I had a superstition about talking about my work, let alone rereading it. Yet that morning the poem called me. I'd tried to give words to my love story with P. Plath said—once you give your heart to someone you can't ask for it back. Reading the poem asked for my heart back.

Gilgamesh is the Babylonian myth embedded into Genesis. The homoerotic portion got dropped. My poem tried to fill in my invisible gay life, to undo two thousand years of silence. The Bible had almost killed me. Leviticus wanted me stoned. Romans wanted me out. I wanted in. For most of my life that seemed the key thing I needed to tell people. I told few. In the poem I'd wanted to pull in whatever I could find that was homoerotic and had been cut out of the Bible.

I referenced the Secret Gospel of Mark, a mystical, possibly counterfeit rendering that included a gay love story with Jesus that some Gnostic father apparently shoved in a hole in the desert. Forgery or fact, the possibility sang to me, and had, literally, my name on it. A story the world would rather forget. Unpleasant. Subsumed. An absence. I wrote:

> In the secret Gospel of Mark,
> a man called the beloved disciple
> flees the scene of a one-night stand with Christ,
> smelling of the Zeus-juice of love,
> and wanders the streets of his neighborhood.

I was the beloved disciple. I didn't know that when I wrote it. Now that I was a priest I saw I had fallen in love with Christ, my gay brother. Poems signaled what was ahead before I knew it. I was writing down a title I would later need. I sipped my strong coffee, warming my innards. I began my descent to the sacristy for morning prayer. Poems are strange contraptions that fly across the page with Ouija power.

129.

My Lord God, I have no idea where I am going.

—THOMAS MERTON

I belonged to Spanish life. I did not belong. I never would. Not really. Spaniards were not easy to know. They rarely invited you into their houses and preferred to meet on the street. They were more formal than the British. They were silent as their unexamined dead dictator, who said: "One is a master of what one does not say, and the slave of what one does." Spain was a country of gregarious poker faces.

The Spanish day flew with my various chores: answering the door, taking orders, receiving used clothes, listening to fundamentalists, taking rent for AA or Al-Anon meetings, rearranging the bishop's schedule, organizing the priests' preaching schedules for three months out, doing the church newsletter, which had many onerous moving parts and that came at me like the Furies weekly, ordering receipts, cleaning the desk seven times over.

In between, I typed onto the keyboard the title "The Secret Gospel of Mark." I added "a memoir" below that title. I futzed, I deleted and undeleted that word. I was averse to the word "memoir"—first, saying it with a French accent felt pompous, and second, the word was close to "me" and "mammary." Despite the democracy of the form, despite poets in recent years taking to this form like children taking to a second language, it was hard not to say it without a wink.

What to make of my making? Truman Capote called *In Cold Blood* reportage, a reinvention of journalism. Was my book a reinvention? What was it? A memoir-breviary? A poetry devotional? Was I hammering devotions? "Devotional" was a hardly used word, and caused my writer friends, who were mainly agnostic, to avert their gaze from my announcement: devotionals had disappeared along with rotary dials and seemed of little use to the modern world. The *Oxford English Dictionary* stated the word "devotional" was first seen in 1648 and described a book "characterized by religious devotion."

I'd printed the book countless times on the church printer when the bishop would leave the office. I printed it on both sides and as a "*folleto*" through a PDF to save paper. Once the bishop had cross-examined me about how much paper we went through, to which I put on my best clueless expat face. For years, I took the book to a *papelaria* where they would spiral-bind or "*encuardenar*" it. I'd done this so much that I began to feel an alcoholic's shame returning to the same off-license for a liquor supply. Within a year I was rotating between three to four *papelarias*. I was a well-known regular. "How do you know all these people?" the bishop would ask. Underneath the giant watercolor-like bleeding stain in the apartment an entire bookcase of past drafts stood sentinel.

Mary Jane had been recently talking to me about my inability to take a bow. How that could be detrimental, a faulty New England modesty. That night when I'd locked the door of the office with blue tiles and ascended the four flights of varnished wooden stairs, I caught my breath and then chatted to her on FaceTime and saw clouds of my own breath. She asked me to take *actual* bows by myself in my cold room. She looked on from the tiny portal of FaceTime as if she was Rapunzel with her blond locks beckoning me from a miniature castle tower. I bowed again. I felt self-conscious, but following Mary Jane's prompts had led to a universe expanding like an accordion. I bowed. And bowed. While she clapped from her tiny portal in America.

And thence, arising, he returned to the other side of the Jordan. I was the beloved disciple in Mark's secret gospel: alone, inspired, not repulsed by my sex or my sexuality, having experienced love's cry and crash, the electricity of union, deserving of a full life as I was. I bowed from the far shore of the Jordan.

130.

I stepped into the wild jazzy throng of Spaniards on the streets to wend my way to a poetry reading in a small bookstore. December and I couldn't get warm. I wore long underwear and three shirts. I walked past the throng of recovering alcoholics smoking on the other side of the cathedral. Into the city I went.

Luis Muñoz was a young Spanish poet living in the States and teaching in the Spanish creative writing department at the Iowa Writers' Workshop. I'd met him one night a year prior at La Sanabresa, a haunt of mine on Calle Amor de Dios where food was cheap, the lights bright, and the three waiters named Joaquin, Joaquin, and Carlitos. One of the Joaquins, the older one, had a huge handlebar mustache and was full of the gruff love that embodied Spain: I knew he would kiss me on both cheeks when he saw me but in a rage he might kick me. I'd met Luis there along with his partner the novelist Garth Greenwell and the niece of Federico García Lorca, Laura. We spoke of Spanish poetry. Where it had been at the time of the civil war. Where it might go.

That cold night Luis was celebrating the publication of his new book of poems *Vecindad* (or *Environs* in English). He'd invited me to come. He was the heir to Lorca and Machado and Cernuda. I came early, and the small room in the bookstore filled with Spanish faces and my foreign face. I was shy and held back, failing to immediately introduce myself, and receded into the Spanish audience. I'm even shier in Spanish.

After seven years I was fluent, but at times words and phrases became inexplicably tangled.

Handsome Luis, in his forties, a bright Spanish warmth and generosity emanating from his fine features and large Buddy Holly-like glasses. He read a poem that night dedicated to Maricruz Bilbao, the last love of Mark Strand, about Mark.

ELEGY MANY TIMES POSTPONED

You see,
I remember him beyond memory,
in front of me,
smiling at the sun
(white hair spiked,
his cheeks eroded
by invisible water)
his hand held up to shield the sun.
In a crowded spot
(fresh voices and a bottleneck
with the buzz of people)
like the one we were crossing.
With that signature mix of his,
self-assured and savvy.

Poetry brought the dead back in this elliptical poem, which was "*beyond* memory." Was that why I was always clicking on my poems rather than attending to the voluminous church emails? Were poems a clearer portal than the cross to step into the eternal? To see beyond? Poets, from our small gleaming watchtowers, peer into blue screens, trying to fix something. It felt more than coincidental that I would sit in a bookshop to hear this poem about Mark read in Spanish. Maricruz, who had encouraged me with the author series, was there too. Mark was with us. We were at Emmaus.

"So long as men can breathe or eyes can see" wrote William Shakespeare in Sonnet 18, "So long lives this, and this gives life to thee." Muñoz's poem gave life to Mark. Mark *was* "self-assured and savvy," or in Spanish, *"confianza y calle."* Spanish expanded my brain: poetry expanded my world. I was determined to try my hand at translating this poem. Knowing full well the options for words were endless and all of them never perfectly correct, which largely mirrored my life as a priest, where translating the Holy Spirit through my being would be imperfect.

Mark had wanted to return to Madrid that last time I saw him. He did.

131.

In Durell's sister's obituary in the *New York Times* no mention was made of Durell. I hadn't heard from Durell's sister in years.

The Bishop scold to Lowell came back to me: "Art just isn't worth that much." More of that letter went:

> I'm sure my point is only too plain . . . Lizzie is not dead, etc.—but there is a "mixture of fact & fiction," and you have changed her letters. That is "infinite mischief," I think . . . One can use one's life as material—one does, anyway—but these letters—aren't you violating a trust? IF you were given permission—IF you hadn't changed them . . . etc. But art just isn't worth that much. I keep remembering Hopkins' marvelous letter to Bridges about the idea of a "gentleman" being the highest thing ever conceived—higher than a "Christian" even, certainly than a poet. It is not being "gentle" to use personal, tragic, anguished letters that way—its cruel.

Her scold had guided me: I didn't want to be cruel or violate trusts. I'd hidden the rape that split Durell in half and dug him down deeper into oblivion in the poem "The Road to Emmaus," and the sister had been pleased with the poem, long and accrued over time, cured by time, about her brother. She was content with the matter being handled opaquely in the poem. She and her brother were the two disciples leaving Emmaus. Opacity suited the poem. Opacity suited much.

132.

Christmas in Madrid. Very few Christmas trees. Spaniards prefer *beléns*, or manger scenes, and the holiday of the Three Kings, where they have parades and throw candies.

"You had a charmed childhood," my mother screamed into the phone. My parents had inadvertently found and read a section of this prose that I ran in a London magazine. I couldn't blame her for blanching at a less pleasant version of herself. She could not look back with any form of accuracy or circumspection. Or, perhaps, she had her version and I had mine, and both were true. God knows being the mother of me wasn't the easiest job.

"You'll never get a job in the church if you write this stuff," she said.

Eighty years of fear drove my mother. She was full of fear. What would happen to me? To her? She'd been domineering and strong. As a child she scared me.

"This is the worst Christmas of my life," she said. What was the opposite of her fear?

I said to Mary Jane, in a despairing tone: "This has gone on for fifty years—this tug of war." I wrote my brother who told me to wait it out. Madrid helped. My priest duties helped. For a week Facebook messenger ceased with its merciless doorbell.

Years ago with the high school bullies I couldn't see the point in loving them, but now I understood more. I wanted to try to love a bully where and when I could because it brought *me* peace. Arguing for the wrongness of the bully did not get me to peace. If indeed I thought of myself as complicated in my reactions to the world wasn't that true for the bully? I could justify my mother's wrongness all day long, but where would it get me?

Jesus's tough bargain: Love your enemies. No one else in history ever said such a thing. At times my mother had been my enemy. In the same breath she was on my side. Both things were true. I picked up the phone in my priest office. I held my breath. "I love you, Mom," I said. There was a great sigh, and was she weeping then? I didn't ask. I wept. The rope we both had pulled for decades dropped. We went on. I didn't mention the work named after the child who was me. We went on.

Something stirred between my mother and me in the ether where my words had landed and where we now staked our claims, a mother Bishop never had to confront. A mother Plath never became. A mother Dickinson never was. My mother would have appreciated opacity or simply silence. I kept my mischief finite. I went ahead for years and wrote this book without her knowing, for I did not know if I'd outlive my mother. When she did learn of it the world went on. This was a place I did not know before. That we could go on together.

Acceptance of her was not approval. The same could be true for her, her acceptance of me did not mean approval. For decades I'd confused them. Hopkins wrote in his journal in 1871: "What you look hard at seems to look hard at you." Had she been looking at me with more love than I'd understood? For a time I missed the love—like Cleopas. I ran towards Jerusalem.

133.

If you bring forth what is within you, what you bring forth
will save you. If you do not bring forth what is within you,
what you do not bring forth will destroy you.
—THE GOSPEL OF THOMAS

Herbert hoped *The Country Parson* would help other priests.
Who might be helped here? I've been a priest in a world where
religion is a tough sell and the more I do the less I know. Was
the author series ass-backwards evangelism? Had the twelve-
step groups erupted into a vineyard that church people could
barely understand, just as the Pharisees could barely understand Christ? Such things were Blakean chariots of fire that
built a Jerusalem. A priest is a person whose job it is to let the
Holy Spirit overtake them. It's a mess at best.

I see myself refracted through others. I can't paint the scene
of life without others in the painting. Doesn't feel accurate and
accuracy is most important to me. I've been a poet longer than
I've been a priest and I hardly know how to explain that either!
Why my unconscious pursuit of centering poetry portraits on
older male figures? Ralph followed by Durell. If I tell you my
father was distant and that was why I had followed fathers, the
answer no longer sufficed because it all seemed more mysterious than that. Autobiography played a part, but like religion,
poetry had to soar beyond the personal.

Young male poets were coming into my life, accidentally, and I turned to them—Tomás, Ruben, Joseph, Jeremy, Christian, and Richie—as Merrill once turned to me. As, indeed, I had once turned to my brother, but time and forgiveness had made me kinder. I had my brother to thank for my other brothers. Love was passing through me, I couldn't hog it, I had to let it go and spread it. Occult, penetrable, permeable, strange occupations they are—writing poems and preaching and praying. Why were sonnets the keyholes through which the divine poured in? I don't know.

My hands are covered in paint. My back hurts. I am standing back from a giant scene with a throng of characters—a whole mess of poets, enough to fill a Dostoevsky novel. The light in this studio diminishes, subtracting what I can see. Darkness bleeds into all the cracks and corners. There is an ineffable sense that something is coming to a rapid end. If I am to add myself after all this layering and texturing, let me, in the end, be smudged, like Mary Jo Salter's ballerina. Sfumato layered and fingered around the edges of my forehead and fingertips. Can you see me? Ah, yes. There I am. There, in the background. See, my head turned up—joyful, unfinished, without too many sharp lines.

134.

Could a lie have truth at its base?
—HENRI COLE

At eighty-six, my mother declared she wanted her DNA results. After a life of innuendo and speculation about her Jewish father, she wanted to *know*. My brother and I arranged for the procedure and sent the swab in. The results came into my iPhone that morning I was visiting from Spain. The pie with percentages indicated she was 98 percent Lithuanian and 2 percent Finnish and 0 percent Ashkenazi Jewish. I double-checked. Then triple-checked. She blinked when I told her, then watered a plant.

She said, "There's so much we don't know about my father. It's just one test." Data for these genetic tests drilled down generations. I did not counter her. What do genes prove? People say my brother and I bear an uncanny familial resemblance. What we know: it flowed more than congealed. Bishop got that right. In "At the Fishhouses," she concluded:

> *forever, flowing and drawn, and since*
> *our knowledge is historical, flowing, and flown.*

What we know is mercurial. How much have I hung on supposition the way my mother hung much on her imagined Jewish father?

That July day there was peace between us. They had recently moved since I'd last visited. Debts and foreclosures drove them from Old Saybrook. Old Lyme was old white people in tennis whites playing tennis and never seeming to work. Mom and Dad passed tenuously there in terms of their finances, and had managed to find a small cheerful duplex with two bedrooms and thin walls. They sat, getting thinner, without a car or TV. Neighbors checked up on them and drove them to doctors. They got meals delivered. Their ankles swelled, their shoulders shrank, their teeth browned. I loved them more than I could say. The sun set and turned New England copper. We did not mention the memoir or their defaulted mortgages or the intervention from years ago that freed me and not them. I was aware things might have gone differently.

Then it was time for bed. I patted my mother's hand, all roped up with veins. My father had gone to bed earlier and snored. The little apartment creaked from the wind and it felt as if we were on board a ship that had floated slowly across time.

It took me a good twenty minutes to pull my mother's shoes off her swollen feet. I tucked her in. The old yellow fans creaked in the Old Lyme heat. She had gotten much smaller. Where had that carefree girl in the polka-dot dress and white pumps laughing under a palm tree gone?

The hot July evening fell down around us. A few Yankee neighbors chatted and called their dogs in. A lone car went down the road. The sea kept going in the far distance. I kissed my mother good night on both cheeks as we do in Madrid.

I thought of Anne Sexton who struggled mightily with doubt and faith. One of her last poems "Rowing" ends:

As the African says:
This is my tale which I have told,
if it be sweet, if it be not sweet,
take somewhere else and let some return to me.

Then I did something odd. I slipped off my shoes beside the bed and climbed over my mom's body and lay down between Mom and Dad. I lay down as I had done when I was five in the apartment, while Walter Cronkite kept telling us everything was going to be okay. I lay down. There we were, three old grown adults, each of our faces now like note pads that had been scribbled on, wrinkled with joy and grief. Mother and son, my arm around her shoulders. Under her watchful eye I'd been loved—by a Christian who wasn't a Christian, by a Jew who wasn't a Jew, or a Jew who was a Christian, or a Christian who was a Jew, or—what?

135.

Today you will be with me in Paradise.

—LUKE 23:43

October 27, 2019, was my parents' fifty-seventh wedding anniversary. My father eighty-six, my mother eighty-seven, which meant I, their love-child, was exactly fifty-six. I tried to reach them through Facebook messenger. No answer. Then I tried to call through the church office phone. The phone rang and rang. I stared at the blue tiles.

My mother walked into the kitchen that morning for coffee. She swayed and became lightheaded. Then came seizures. She bit her tongue in two. She fell. The ambulance came. By midnight the ER nurse reached me in Madrid. Four days later I flew home to be at her side. She hallucinated. My father moved beside her like a distressed elephant. He had only a few hairs left on his head and he was missing more teeth. The blood clot went into the front of her brain, the occipital lobe, where all the organizational thinking happens. She was unable to get out of the bed, her motor skills compromised. Dad held her hand. My brother came in from Manhattan. We three stood beside her. There was peace between us. We waited to see what might come back from the dead. She repeated, "Help me! Help me!"

My mother drooled. I fidgeted next to her. Daydreaming or writing poetry had always saved me. Thinking of poems had been a way of praying. But I needed to be there, now, in that hospital room with my mother, I needed to be present, I needed to think of that hospital room and my mother *as a poem.*

The Connecticut streets went blue-black, much darker than in Madrid. The nurses said we needed to go. But Dad wouldn't leave. He held Mom's hand.

"Dad, we have to go now, the nurses need us to go," I said.

"Just ten more minutes," Dad pleaded.

136.

"Mrs. Reece, this is a memory test. The words are blue, sock, silverware, and moon. Repeat them back to me please," the well-meaning social worker said, her clipboard jutting out from her chest. My mother looked as if she was watching a foreign film without subtitles. She squinted. She smiled. She looked away.

Every night Dad and I left in the rental car and drove into the dark. Carter came back and forth from Manhattan. On one dark night, traveling down our cold New England corridor of a highway and passing stone fences, Dad volunteered that the intervention I'd tried to pull off had not been a mistake. I kept driving. Then, one night, as I squinted over the dash, the windshield fogging up, I asked Dad about their early marriage to pass the time. Strange. The two of us talking. Always my mother did all the talking.

"Well we didn't have much money then so we rented a cheap motel room in the Poconos." He paused then, and said, "And we had so much sex. We had sex with our socks on. Sex in every position you can think. Sex on the ceiling if we could have. God, we had a lot of sex." Then another pause, enough to give Puritan ghosts the shivers, "You came exactly ten months after that." I kept driving. Old Lyme so dark, hardly a street lamp, people snug behind fences and gates.

During the day, I asked around for rector jobs in dioceses. Rhode Island had a spot, as did Florida. Or what? Indiana? Where did I belong and to whom? I felt unsettled in America, the country had changed irrevocably while I wasn't looking— or no, was that not right?—had *I* changed when *America* wasn't looking?

Jesus said:

Come, follow me, and I will send you out to fish for people.

Both my mother and Dad liked the idea of Florida, not that they would ever visit. They firmly encouraged me to not move *too* close.

When I wasn't dealing with nurses and doctors and Medicare and Medicaid or a heating rebate or a renter's rebate, a landlady appeared in my in-box and threatened to evict if the rent was not paid.

The landlady wrote, "Your parents' rent is in arrears. I will give you ten days to pay it back. Until then I won't fix the toilet."

"What a bitch," Mary Jane said from Florida. "I understand her point, but she's not your friend," she scolded.

For a split second I was irate with my mother and her long attitude of living-beyond-her-means, her robbing-Peter-to-pay-Paul fiscal unconsciousness. I let that go. I sold paintings on the wall and searched through the silverware drawers, sweeping away mice droppings, hunting down maxed-out life insurance policies.

During the day my mother would look out the sealed

window like Mary about to be visited by Gabriel for the annunciation. Mary is often featured with a book, reading. I like that about Mary. She was a reader, a thinker, an introvert.

137.

Dad looked at me one day in the too quiet apartment, waiting to get to the nursing home: "Loretta fucked up," referring to the financial bind. Then he said, with his hands at his side, "I'm a failure."

"No, Dad," I said. "You are *not* a failure. Your worth to me is not connected to your money. I love you for who you are. You were a good provider. You gave your life to your work, you had integrity in your work. You loved your wife so much, all you wanted was to make her happy." It might have been the best sermon I ever gave.

Weeks passed. We had spats. We wept. We laughed, at times so hard Dad had more bathroom accidents than normal. My brother agreed to take over all the checkbooks. In his spare time, he sold a statue out of the living room. Before I knew it we had the $5,400 in back rent. Thanksgiving bled into Christmas. Plastic trees went up in the nursing home. Orderlies wore elf caps. Snow came. Dad leaked through his blue diapers.

138.

One December day, waiting in the faux-living-room lounge of the nursing home, which smelled like lavender cleaning fluid and shit, word came into my iPhone: after seventeen years of work, one solid year of thirty-five rejections from publishing houses, big and small, Jeffrey Posternak from the Wylie Agency wrote that with two hours left in the working year, Dan Simon from Seven Stories Press in New York City wished to accept the book you hold now. He wrote: "I think we are the perfect publisher for *The Secret Gospel of Mark*."

The doctor knocked on my mother's door. She was half-asleep in her wheelchair. Bach's preludes crackled into the small handheld radio by my mother's bed. Dad was reading the *New York Times*, turning the pages, the pages were wings and Dad was a rare gray prehistoric bird. My brother would arrive on the six-thirty train from New York. We three had worked without ceasing since the stroke. I'd never felt closer to my father or my brother.

I spoke to the doctor in the hallway. He said, "It's unlikely your mother will ever read again."

In her room, Mom said, "Come, Spencer, read me some poetry." We'd lived our lives for books. She'd given me that love. The smell of books had driven us to distraction.

Sharp jabs of Connecticut light pierced the broken blinds. A nurse was paged. A red light went off. Someone needed help.

I thought about my religion, which was a part of my life and not part of my mother's life. I thought about Mary and Christ. Who really knows what Christ was like with his mother? He needed to pull away from her. As I had done. And Mary? She was more indomitable than perhaps we give her credit for. Like many women, including my mom, we know little about her, she got written out of the record. I think when Mary received news from Gabriel that she would give birth, she knew what was coming—the pain, the suffering—and she did it anyway. My mother the same. There's unacknowledged courage in that sacrifice. Mary and Christ, they must have been complex with one another, a give and take, a power struggle, a reconciling, faded now under all the patinas of all the altars in the world.

Socked in her brain to the edge of death by a massive stroke, my mother's face rose in the blue twilight like a New England half-moon, and then she picked up silverware that wasn't there.

139.

It is finished.

—JOHN 19:30

Mom came home for Christmas. We'd been practicing trans-
ferring her from the bed to the commode to the shower with
questionable success. Dad cleaned her up and wiped her
behind every morning and afternoon and night. Sometimes
my brother and I lifted her. Sometimes we wiped her behind.
Diapers were stacked around the bed and plastic sheets were
on the mattress. Often now she said, "I'm sorry. I'm so sorry."
We shushed her.

The Old Lyme apartment piled with countless books was
a snow globe turned upside down, all of us shaken and the
world blurry. Some light inside my mother dimmed. She was
there mostly, but a part of her had gone. Where had it gone?
Was it in heaven?

Christ said it was harder for a rich man to get into heaven
than for a camel to pass through the eye of a needle. One of the
gates into Jerusalem was referred to as "the eye of the needle."
But it doesn't matter, every reader thinks of the improbable
visual of a camel trying to slip through a tiny hole like thread.
This phrase of Jesus's! How will we get to heaven? Who will get
there? Does heaven exist? Herbert wasn't overly concerned
about it in his poems. Dickinson wrote: "instead of getting to

Heaven, at last — / I'm going, all along." Was heaven there with me and my father and brother in that bleak Connecticut winter, as we drew near to our mother? Before I sent the landlady her money, she wrote and suggested I take out a loan to pay the back rent. She did not ask about my mother. Mary Jane said from Florida: "Don't worry, she'll get her money." Dickinson again: "'Tis not that Dying hurts us so — / 'Tis Living — hurts us more." The world had hurt us, the world would hurt us, but we had one another.

The term "little entrance" in the Greek Orthodox Church describes when the priest comes forward to read the Gospel— with such an entrance we spy some chink of eternity, words spoken break open the world. Many little entrances exist.

A poet reading his or her poems is a little entrance. The circles of AA and Al-Anon in church basements. Those meetings had little entrances. Someone opened their mouth and everything changed. Those little entrances led me back to the church.

Nowadays a sermon or a liturgy, incense, a soprano soloist, or a needle-pointed kneeler assures me that I am loved, that the world is watched. Not always, but often. Dickinson:

> *I never spoke with God*
> *Nor visited in Heaven —*
> *Yet certain am I of the spot*

The spot of God with my mom was small. Yet bright. I held her veiny hand, which was cold. My devotions were closing. I'd come full circle. I finished where I started. Stars were nailed in that cold New England sky. We'd come to our little entrance.

"I love you, Mom," I said.

"I love you too, darling," my mother said, the words garbled as she wept. Her mouth hanging down where once it had gone up at the sight of me. Mom had changed but there was hope. Mom looked smaller in the wheelchair we'd found at a thrift store, delicate as a baby in a crèche.

We were tired that Christmas—Dad, my brother, me. I'd bought a Christmas tree, the needle-and-sap smell filled the house, but not one of us had the energy for decorations or lights. The great green dead tree filled the house with life. We were night watchmen after long shifts, or three kings who'd taken a long journey to see a savior.

ACKNOWLEDGMENTS

Ucross, MacDowell, Yaddo & Civitella Ranieri, thank you, each place granted me a residency where I worked on this book over the past seventeen years.

Portions of this book appeared in *Granta, American Poetry Review, Book Post, The Bennington Review, Commonweal, Salmagundi, Little Star,* and *At Length.* One section appeared in *The Poem's Country: Place & Poetic Practice* & another in *Sunday Morning: Reflections on Episcopal Worship.*

Peter Hawkins, Matthew Marland, David Wallace, Jonathan Farmer, Ralph Hamilton, Anna Huddert & Luke Neima: without your encouragement, no book. Lawrence Schimel for encouragement with translating Luis Muñoz. Gratitude to Ann Young, Jeremy Voigt & Reverend Travis Helms for support, friendship & reading the text close to the end. Gratitude to Kathleen Flenniken, who read the book time & again, as the years passed, & helped me title it. Javier O'Donnell & Maricruz Bilbao for friendships that mean more than you know. The Unamuno Author Series team for creating something beyond our wildest dreams. And that room, 18b, to the left of the cathedral, where the electric shorted, all the faces, all of us searching, you know who you are, you helped support this work without knowing it.

Cody Upton & the American Academy of Arts and Letters

who provided unexpected financial support in a difficult time close to the end of working on this book.

Jeffrey Posternak at the Wylie Agency for believing in the book for so long, & Lauren Hooker who acquired the book, & Dan Simon who championed it. Thank you Seven Stories Press for believing in this book.

PERMISSIONS

Grateful acknowledgment is made to the following for permission to reprint previously published material. Best efforts were made to secure permission with authors, estates, and publishers to reprint quotes and poems.

Sylvia Plath, "Ariel," "Daddy," "Lady Lazarus," "Nick and the Candlestick," and "Fever 103°." Copyright the Estate of Sylvia Plath. Reprinted with the permission of Faber & Faber with world rights, and Harper Collins with US rights.

Elizabeth Bishop, "Over 2,000 Illustrations and a Complete Concordance," "Crusoe in England," "Sestina," "In the Waiting Room," "Little Exercise," "One Art," and "Sonnet." In addition to portions of two extracts from her letters. Copyright the Estate of Elizabeth Bishop. Reprinted with the permission of Farrar, Straus and Giroux.

Robert Lowell, "Skunk Hour." Copyright the Estate of Robert Lowell. Reprinted with the permission of Farrar, Straus and Giroux.

George Herbert, "The Altar," "Prayer (I)," and "Love (III)." In addition to extracts from one of his letters. Grateful akcnowledgment is made to Nicholas Ferrar, who published the poems after Herbert died.

James Merrill, "The Broken Home," "Clearing the Title," "Christmas Tree." Extract reprinted from letter is in author's possession. Copyright the Estate of James Merrill. Reprinted with the permission of Penguin Random House, Knopf.

Emily Dickinson, "In the name of the bee," "The Meadows—mine," "I'm Nobody! Who are you?" "The brain—is wider than the sky—" "Success is counted sweetest," "This is my letter to the World," "Pain—has an Element of Blank," "Wild Nights—Wild Nights," "I Dwell in Possibility," "This is the Hour of Lead," and "To fail within a Chance," in addition to two letter extracts. Reprinted with permission from Harvard University Press.

Gerard Manley Hopkins, "I wake and feel the fell of dark, not day," "Binsey Poplars," "I am gall, I am heartburn. God's most deep decree," and "God's Grandeur." In addition to an extract from one of his letters. Grateful acknowledgment is made to Robert Bridges, who published Hopkins after he died.

Roberto Sosa, "The Poor." Copyright the Estate of Roberto Sosa. Reprinted with permission from Curbstone Press.

Richard Blanco, "Looking for the Gulf Motel." Reprinted with permission from The University of Pittsburgh Press.

Greg Pardlo, "Written by Himself." Reprinted with permission from Four Way Books.

PHOTO BY PETE DUVAL

Spencer Reece's first published book of poetry, *The Clerk's Tale*, was selected from the slush pile by Louise Glück as the winner of the Bread Loaf Writers' Conference Bakeless Prize and published by Houghton Mifflin in 2004. The titular poem was adapted into a short film by James Franco in 2010. Reece is also the author of the poetry collection *The Road to Emmaus*, published by Farrar, Straus & Giroux in 2014, a finalist for the Griffin Prize and longlisted for the National Book Award. He is the recipient of a Whiting Award, a Guggenheim Fellowship, and a National Endowment for the Arts fellowship. For several years he lived in Madrid, where he was the national secretary to the Episcopal bishop of Spain. After returning to the US he joined a parish following the death of the parish priest from Covid-19. He lives in Queens, New York.